23 TYPES OF GUYS YOU *MIGHT* MEET ON SOCIAL MEDIA

How to Be Wise as Serpents and Harmless as Doves In Dating

JANICE HYLTON-THOMPSON

{Please note that scriptures are highlighted for effect}

23 TYPES OF GUYS YOU *MIGHT* MEET ON SOCIAL MEDIA
How to Be Wise as Serpents and Harmless as Doves In
Dating

ISBN: 978-1-946242-08-2
P.O. BOX 422
BELLEVILLE NJ 07109

Thank you

My Parents in The Faith

To my parents in the faith, my daddy, my Abba, the Bishop-Elect, Marvin Bradshaw Sr., and First Lady Edna Bradshaw. Words cannot express how thankful I am for you. You have saved me from so many counterfeits and wolves in sheep's clothing, thereby saving my life, ministry, and destiny.

You taught me how to glean between gold and counterfeits. You taught me how to sift between tares and wheat, how to differentiate between a shepherd and a wolf in sheep's clothing. You taught me how to learn and know God's word for myself and how to tune into the spirit, lay my head on the breast of God, and hear him for myself.

You taught me how to serve, from sweeping the sidewalk in front of our beautiful little church to cleaning the bathroom, to serving you both water to quench your thirst as you proclaim the words of the Lord. I love you both and am forever grateful. I AM WHAT I AM BECAUSE OF YOU!

My Hubiliciousness

My wonderful husband, Michael, you are the best thing that has ever happened to me next to the Lord Jesus Christ. Truly you are an expression of the love of Christ to me and our beautiful children. Thank you for your kindness, gentleness, your grace to bless and encourage me to take as much time as I needed to write and study. I am so grateful to and for you.

May the grace of the Lord Jesus Christ continue to overshadow you. May the blessings of the Lord overtake you. May all your hopes, prayers, dreams, and desires come true. Thank you for, and I appreciate you for being a continual covering of protection and for your unyielding love for me and our babies. Your profession of love, provision, and protection is a gift and blessing.

Have I told you lately that you make the best cup of coffee on this side of heaven? Thank you, and I love you.

Dedication

23 Types of Guys You Might Meet on Social Media is dedicated to all my beautiful princess sisters who desire to get married. This book is for you who are tired of not getting your desired result and are ready to take your dating to another level so that you can meet your Boaz. I pray that the Lord will grant you the desires of your hearts.

I pray this book will help you to renew your mind, thoughts, ideas of dating. I declare and decree that this is your season and that your Boaz and Psalm 23 Husband will find you. I love you, and I'm praying for you always.

Did you know that if you are in Christ, then you are the King's Daughter? Yap that means you are a princess, the daughter of the King of kings. So, as you read, I want you to keep in mind that you are a daughter of the God of heaven and earth. Here are a few scriptures to help you renew your mind about your new identity in Christ. Also, the following scriptures present a blueprint of how you are to set your mind as you read *23 Types of Guys You Might Meet on Social Media.*

Your Royal Highness – Princess

Hello Princess, as you begin to read *23 Types of Guys, You Might Meet on Social Media,* at this moment I humbly ask that you shift your mindset. You are no longer "that girl" but you are now a part of the royal priesthood. From the moment you accepted Christ, your title became Princess.

Therefore, I pray that you renew your mind to the blessings and promises of the Lord of your high calling of the title Princess. You are now seated in Christ in heavenly places on the right hand of God the father. Thus, you have delegating authority and power. Here are few scriptures to help you to shift your mindset.

Romans 12: 1 beseech you therefore, brethren, by the mercies of God, that you present your bodies a living sacrifice, holy, acceptable to God, *which is* your reasonable service. ² And do not be conformed to this world, but be transformed by the renewing of your mind, that you may prove what *is* that good and acceptable and perfect will of God.

1 Peter 2 ⁹ But you *are* a chosen generation, a royal priesthood, a holy nation, His own special people, that you may proclaim the praises of Him who called you out of darkness into His marvelous light; ¹⁰ who once *were* not a people but *are* now the people of God, who had not obtained mercy but now have obtained mercy.

Ephesians 2: ⁴ But God, who is rich in mercy, because of His great love with which He loved us, ⁵ even when we were dead in trespasses, made us alive together with Christ (by grace you have been saved), ⁶ and raised *us* up together, and made *us* sit together in the heavenly *places* in Christ Jesus.

What Is Your Name?

Genesis 32: ²⁷ So He said to him, "What *is* your name?"

He said, "Jacob." ²⁸ And He said, "Your name shall no longer be called Jacob, but Israel; for you have struggled with God and with men, and have prevailed."

Ephesians 2: ¹And you *He made alive,* who were dead in trespasses and sins, ² in which you once walked according to the course of this world, according to the prince of the power of the air, the spirit who now works in the sons of disobedience; ...

John 1: ¹²But as many as received Him, to them He gave the right (KJV uses the word "power.") to become children of God, to those who believe in His name: ¹³ who were born, not of blood, nor of the will of the flesh, nor of the will of man, but of God.

2 Corinthians 5: ¹⁷Therefore, if anyone *is* in Christ, *he is* a new creation; old things have passed away; behold, all things have become new.

Galatians 3: ²⁶ For you are all sons of God through faith in Christ Jesus. ²⁷ For as many of you as were baptized into Christ have put on Christ.

Watch Your Eyes, Ears, Heart & Mouth

Proverbs 4: 23 Guard your heart above all else, for it determines the course of your life. 24 Avoid all perverse talk; stay away from corrupt speech. 25 Look straight ahead and fix your eyes on what lies before you. 26 Mark out a straight path for your feet; stay on the safe path 27 Don't get sidetracked; keep your feet from following evil. (NLT)

Proverbs 7: My son, keep my words, and treasure my commands within you. 2 Keep my commands and live, And my law as the apple of your eye. 3 Bind them on your fingers; Write them on the tablet of your heart. 4 Say to wisdom, "You are my sister," And call understanding your nearest kin, 5 That they may keep you from the immoral woman, From the seductress who flatters with her words.

Deuteronomy 11: [18] "Therefore you shall lay up these words of mine in your heart and in your soul, and bind them as a sign on your hand, and they shall be as frontlets between your eyes. [19] You shall teach them to your children, speaking of them when you sit in your house, when you walk by the way, when you lie down, and when you rise up. [20] And you shall write them on the doorposts of your house and on your gates,

1 John 2: 16 For all that is in the world—the lust of the flesh, the lust of the eyes, and the pride of life—is not of the Father but is of the world.

Habakkuk 2:² Then the LORD answered me and said: "Write the vision
And make *it* plain on tablets, That he may run who reads it. ³ For the vision *is* yet for an appointed time; But at the end it will speak, and it will not lie. Though it tarries, wait for it; Because it will surely come,
It will not tarry.

Table of Contents

Do You Want to Get Married?

23 *Types of Guys You Might Meet on Social Media* is a book for marriage-minded women-princesses only. If you don't want to get married, please don't read this book because it will irritate your soul! However, *23 Types of Guys You Might Meet on Social Media* is for women who are tired of the games and the insanity of doing the same thing repeatedly while expecting a different result. This book is very dear to my heart because I lived it.

Furthermore, I know what it's like to desire to meet my Boaz and my Psalm 23 Prepared husband. Filled with a lot of my personal stories and experiences, *23 Types of Guys You Might Meet on Social Media* will take your dating—aka data gathering skills—to deeper depths and higher heights so that you can meet and choose your Prepared Husband. So, c'mon lovelies, sit back, relax, and sip on this most delicious and hot *23 Types of Guys You Might Meet on Social Media* tea!

Princesses, this is a laid back, kick your shoes off, lazy on the couch, hanging out with your girlfriends' type of book. It's a grab your favorite drink, tea, a cup of chocolate or dunkacinno, lay your head back, and hollar kind of book. Please, relax, have a girl's night, and laugh while gathering the low-down data on the guys you meet.

With a dash of slang, Ebonics, and text language, *23 Types of Guys You Might Meet on Social Media* will have you laughing to life. You will be falling off the couch, spitting out your drink, and grabbing your stomach as it gently tugs on your heartstrings because it will bear witness to your spirit. *23 Types of Guys You Might Meet on Social Media* will serve you several glasses of sparkling truths! It will cause light bulbs and twinkling stars to go off all around you as you wish that you had this book years before.

Furthermore, as you read *23 Types of Guys You Might Meet on Social Media,* you will come face to face with some of the guys you've already dated. You will realize that they were using you, but you will praise Jesus that it didn't work out. Filled with lots of godly wisdom and spicy truths, this book will have your mouth watering for more knowledge to quench the thirst of your data gathering skills. So, fear not my beloved, skillfully gathering data is an art. Trust and believe that after you read these words, you will be wise as serpents and harmless as doves in dating.

Countless women who have read my book *The Naked Wife* have told me they met a Mr. Nurse or Purse or Mamma's Boy. I love that because, as you read *23 Types of Guys You Might Meet on Social Media* and in your life, you will be able to identify who you're communicating with. Broken down in types, these men will have some things in common, but they are different. Additionally, while many of the guys might sound similar, it's important to note that it's the specific language that's used. Let's sharpen our data collecting skills with wisdom, grace, and vision. Remember to be wise as serpents and harmless as doves in dating.

Introduction

At the publication of *23 Types of Guys You Might Meet on Social Media*, it is 2019, and we are living during the technology age. We spend a lot of time on social media vs. being out being social with people. I am amazed at the difference in the way we communicate today versus twenty years ago, even with our children; I have two, born twenty years apart. My oldest is special needs, and I wish we had the technology my three-year-old has now. The advantages I have now could have done so much to help my daughter learn. How we meet new people today is so different from how we did when I was younger.

Today, we can meet many people online while we're sitting at home in our PJs, drinking a cup of hot chocolate, with our uncombed hair, unbrushed teeth, and no makeup. We don't have to wait to meet new people at events, churches, or even face to face because of Skype and other software. With several social media platforms available, we're presented with multiple opportunities to meet someone without leaving the comfort of our homes. Facebook, Twitter, Pinterest, and Instagram, and others are powerful tools.

Additionally, there are several online dating sites that you can join to meet a potential mate. However, this book is not about "online dating" but about how to vet the men you meet on social media. You can be in a group of ten or twenty thousand people, comment on someone's post, and suddenly, you've made a new "friend." Because it's so easy to connect with men you've never met, it is crucial for you to learn to navigate social media dating with wisdom. You can learn about wisdom by reading **Proverbs 8** and the book of **Proverbs** as a whole.

Furthermore, I like to think of some of my favorite women and wives in the Bible. Rachel met Jacob at the well, and he fell in love with her. Rachel was beautiful and had a lovely figure. Abigail was a woman of great wisdom. Unfortunately, she was married to a foolish man, Nabal. However, Abigail saved her household from being annihilated by King David.

Ruth was full of grace and was chosen by one of the richest and wisest men in Bethlehem, Boaz. Ruth and Boaz are the most exemplary couple in the Bible, and many women refer to their future husbands as "Boaz." Finally, Esther was wise, beautiful, and feminine and was chosen by the King to be his new Queen. Also, please read **Proverbs 7** to see the story of a "simple young man." You will learn how to avoid the foolish decisions that put you at risk of being taken advantage of.

Again, please note that I am not speaking about online dating specifically but social media in general. Because we have multiple avenues of meeting men online, it is crucial to date or gather data on more than one guy at once. Reading and applying *23 Types of Guys You Might Meet on Social Media* will equip you with a great deal of information about the different types of guys you might meet. Remember, "social media" doesn't necessarily mean "online dating" but meeting guys online in general. This includes all social media platforms.

In *23 Types of Guys, You Might Meet on Social Media;* you will learn how to identify dating games and not waste your time on foolishness. You can gather data just by paying attention to how men behave online. Now, princesses, this does not mean you should stay home and be online 24/7. Dress up, go out, live your life, enjoy this beautiful world. Attend various activities, enjoy the sceneries, attend events in your community and abroad. I still prefer meeting people the good old-fashioned way. I met my hubby at a networking event while I was marketing my first book, *Praying for Our Children.*

Sisters, before we jump into this most informative book about *23 Types of Guys, You Might Meet on Social Media*, allow me to plant a seed in your heart, mind, spirit, and desire. If you want to be married, it is essential to know what type of man you desire. Allow me to share with you about The Psalm 23 Husband. Because as you read, I want you to remember the goal in mind as you date to choose a husband who will love you like Christ loves the Church. Finally, please remember to only date men who want to get married and most importantly, men who want to marry you.

The Psalm 23 Husband

While this is only a sample of The Psalm 23 Husband aka Mr. Shepard, as you read *23 Types of Guys You Might Meet on Social Media*, on dating, aka gathering data, please keep The Psalm 23 Husband, all the way in the front of your beautiful mind, thoughts, dreams, hopes, and desires. To read more about The Psalm 23 Husband, check back with me periodically. It's coming soon.

In the meantime, if you have been in the church any length of time, I am 99% sure you have memorized, read, or heard of Psalm 23. I believe it is the most popular and known Psalm there is. What is a Psalm? A Psalm is a song. There is a book of Psalms in the Bible comprised of 150 Psalms or songs. Additionally, there are several other Psalms throughout the Bible. So, what is a Psalm again?

Let's look at Psalm 23 from the King James Version. If you are not familiar, the bold is the Psalm itself, and the regular type is my translation. Again, please remember that this is only a sample of what I have written. A more extensive version is coming soon.

The Lord is my shepherd; I shall not want.

Your husband is a choice, so choose wisely because he is to be your lord (covering), leader, provider, protector, and professor of love. Therefore, you shall not lack any good thing. Your husband is to be like the shepherd who gently loves, directs, and leads his sheep. As a shepherd loves his sheep, provides for their every need, and protects them, so will your husband.

He maketh me to lie down in green pastures;
he leadeth me beside the still waters.

Your husband is to provide a comfortable home for you and your children. Your husband is to lead a life of peace; thus, he will lead you to a life of peace, also. In this way, your husband will set the tone and atmosphere of your home.

He restoreth my soul; he leadeth me in the path of righteousness
for his name's sake.

Choosing the right husband is vital because he will restore your soul, which consists of your will, intellect, and your emotions. Your husband will lead you into the ways of the Lord: righteousness and right standing. Because God has anointed and blessed him with you as a gift, he must answer to the Lord about you.

Yea, though I walk through the valley of the shadow of death, I
will fear no evil, for thou art with me; thy rod and thy staff they
comfort me.

Yes, you'll walk through some tough times. Life will happen, but you ain't got nothing to worry about because your husband got ya! Your husband is with you, and his name, strong arms, and his bank account will comfort you.

Thou preparest a table before me in the presence of mine enemies; thou anointest my head with oil; my cup runneth over.

Some guys often ask what we bring to the table as women. Well, they are wrong, wrong, wrong! Your husband is to provide a table before you. Your husband is to provide all your needs, and his favor runs from your sparkling crown all the way down to your pretty li'l toes. Your husband is to provide so well for you that you'll be running over with all blessings.

Surely goodness and mercy shall follow me all the days of my life, and I will dwell in the house of the Lord forever.

You see, ladies, your husband is to be a good man. Your husband is like goodness and mercy; therefore, he will cover you like a momma bear does her cubs. Your husband's love will overshadow you for the rest of your days, and he will have you living in the house he bought you and not his mamma's basement or a shelter! Your husband won't shack up with you because he values you and will marry you.

Ok princesses, I just wanted to share that little snack with you before we jump into *23 Types of Guys You Might Meet on Social Media*. Please keep The Psalm 23 Husband, aka Mr. Shepard in mind as you read. I have a whole lot more on Mr. Psalm 23 Husband, aka Mr. Shepherd, in another book coming soon. Now are you ready to dive about *23 Types of Guys You Might Meet on Social Media*?

What to Do After A "Breakup"

Princesses, you probably picked up *23 Types of Guys You Might meet on Social Media* because you've realized that you have entangled yourself in a web of lies, deception, wasted time and broken and disappointed heart. Additionally, used and crumbled up cookie aka kitty kat aka vagina. Well, this realization and acceptance are good. Confession is good for the soul, and it's better late than never.

Have you experienced something like the following? You met this guy and you "THOUGHT" he was the one. So, you put all your marital dreams, hopes, and desires in his flimsy, full-of-holes basket. However, he screwed and dropped you like a hot potato. Then to make matters worse, he got himself a new girl quicker than a New York minute. Your deceived li'l heart is broken, and you're rubbing your disturbed head that holds your crooked crown. Wasting all your precious time asking yourself where you missed it, wandering in the wilderness of make-believe of your delusional mind that he was the one.

Looking over all his texts and messages, rewinding your conversations in your head. When you went out, he treated you like the queen you are. It seemed as if he was all the way in, and you ASSUMED, he was only seconds away from getting down on one knee and popping the big question. Having flashbacks of good times, but he dropped you and took your confidence, assurance, and your crumbled-up cookie with him.

Now you're emotionally wrecked, broken down, worn out, and disappointed. Hung down with shame, picking up your tender kitty bits, while trying to mend a broken and a shattered heart. Why? You just can't believe he didn't want YOU. Oh, he wanted your kitty kat, but he didn't want YOU! Accept it, dearie. You weren't his ONE.

Ok, wait a minute. Rewind and come again! First, why are you breaking up with or being dumped by men that you're supposed to be gathering data on? Why did you jump into a full-fledged "situationship" with a man that you didn't have any data on? Why are you having sex, making babies, and living with men who haven't married you? Why are you buying houses and cars, playing house with men who will not marry you?

As of today, I want you to drill in your brain that dating is ONLY about gathering data to see if the guy is a Psalm 23 Husband! And if he is a Psalm 23 Husband, does he want to be one to you? Additionally, it is crucial for you to understand that dating is also the process of elimination. As you gather data, if you learn that he is not adding up to your standards and what you want in a husband, please do not continue to waste time with him. Instead, drop him and move on.

Many women make the mistake of thinking because they like the guy, then that means he's going to like them, too. You see, men and women are different in our dating process. Most women meet a man and think to ourselves "he is the one." However, a man meets us and ask himself if "she is the one." I will discuss this further in an upcoming book, but can we agree that there is a difference between a statement and a question?

Princesses, please try your very best to understand the following: Just because a man is husband material does not mean he wants to be your husband. Unless he has begun the process to be your husband, don't claim him or treat him as your husband. Oh, and please continue to date, aka gather data on other guys.

Do not for God's sake; get into any "situationship" with any man! Do not allow your emotions to run rampant! Do not get your marital hopes and dreams up because he "seems" like a nice guy or he's the one. You don't know that! Do not make assumptions because he texts and calls you and takes you out. Remember that ALL MEN WANT TO HAVE SEX! Not every man you meet will want to profess his love, provide a comfortable life for you, and protect you. Until he begins the process and follows through, it doesn't mean anything.

If you think it's getting serious, ask him to meet your father! This will cut the fakes considerably. If he doesn't want to meet your father or father figure, he shouldn't be in the running. So, princesses, get up, brush yourselves off, hold your heads high, straighten your crooked crowns and backs, and say, "HE WAS ONLY A TRICYCLE!" In your anointed little hands, you have *23 Types of Guys You Might Meet on Social Media.* Included you have a whole lot of information about how to be wise as serpents and harmless as doves as you date, aka gather data.

Yap! Think of all your mistakes—foolish, desperate, and thirsty ways of trying to get a husband as you learning to ride a tricycle. You didn't know any better, so you did the best you could do. Now you have *23 Types of Guys You Might Meet on Social Media*, which will equip you to know better. And because you know better you have been enabled to do better. And NEVER, EVER, as long as you live, act, behave, and be thirsty like you were before.

What is Dating?

*D*ating is all about getting information or vetting a person. In other words, you meet a guy or several guys, and you gather information or data about them so that you can make an informed decision about them. Twenty years ago, we only had home phones and beepers. Today, we have smartphones, social media, and various other ways to communicate with others. Many churches were against "dating" when I was younger. People would often say, "Christians don't date." As a young woman who always wanted to get married, I was confused by this.

I never understood how we were to meet a potential mate, get to know them, and decide if we want to marry them without getting information on them through dating. Could that be why the divorce rate is now over 50% in the church? In the past, people were getting married only because they were saved. However, they didn't have things in common, and sometimes, they didn't even like each other. Saints make the mistake of thinking that if two people are saved, then they can get married and make it work! That is not true!

In some churches, the belief is that God is going to send us the perfect mate, so we should marry them. There was no need to get to know one another because God sent them, meaning they must be just right for us. That didn't sit well with me either. I am incredibly picky, and I had a good idea of the type of husband I desired. I wasn't going to up and marry some man just because we were both saved.

My problem was I wasn't meeting the type of man that I would want to marry. Since the teaching in many churches was that being saved was all that was needed for a couple to get married—and the sooner, the better. The church's way of meeting a man and going straight to the altar was going to leave me single forever. Many brothers expressed interest in me, but I refused even to go out with most of them. I needed a man to be more than saved because I wanted to have things in common with my husband. Additionally, financial security was a must because I hate lack and debt, and I am allergic to struggling through life.

However, as I got older and studied for myself, I have learned that "dating" means merely gathering data or information about a person. When done correctly, dating has nothing to do with sex, shacking up, having babies out of wedlock, taking care of a man, or anything that is against the Word of the Lord. Dating is for the simple purpose of gathering information about a potential partner.

Some churches teach us that God will send your husband to the church, and then you two will get married. This has confused many Christian women and has resulted in many remaining single, waiting for their Boaz to come and find them at the church. (I write extensively on Boaz in future chapters.) Some young women feel that when they meet a man, they are to be loyal to him automatically. As a result, they refuse to date aka gather data on anyone else because they believe they are in a relationship and need to be faithful to this man they just met. That doesn't make any sense, does it? If you meet a young man that you are getting to know, why would you be committed to him when you just met?

Would You "Date" Three Guys at One Time?

Here's a question I post to many of my Christian sisters: "If you meet three guys in one week who want to take you out, who would you go with?" They all said they would go out with the first guy and forget about the other two because to do otherwise would be cheating. But how is that cheating?

You are not courting, engaged, or married to the guy you just met yesterday. How is going out for coffee with guys #2 and #3 cheating? How can you assume that guy #1 is your "Boaz"? How do you automatically decide that this guy you just met and know absolutely nothing about is to be your husband?

The crazy thing that I see many women do is automatically commit to being in a relationship with guy #1 without getting to know him first or getting any information about him. The problem comes when he's not the man she needs. What if he doesn't attend church or believe in giving tithes and offering? Maybe he doesn't believe that a husband is to provide for his wife and family. Sadly, instead of walking away, many women try to turn guy #1 into the man they need.

Committing to men without having the proper information to make an informed decision has resulted in many divorces, not only in our churches but our nation, in my opinion. This, my dear, is the dilemma that many sisters are in. I will be writing more extensively about dating soon. But for now, please be informed that it is okay to DATE and GATHER DATA on guys who show interest in you. So, if you meet three brothers in Christ in a week that all want to take you out, you at least need to talk with all of them so you can gather data about them to see if you have things in common.

You shouldn't meet a guy and automatically jump into a relationship with him and begin to plan a wedding with this man you don't know. Now, there are a few instances when people have met, and both knew they were meant for each other. However, that's not the norm. Therefore, it is essential to gather data on potential mates, so you can get to know your "ONE."

What if you refused to go out with or at least talk to guy #2 and #3 for guy #1, and come to find out, he doesn't even want to get married? Now the other two are gone because you automatically thought guy #1 was your Boaz. Or what if you fell head over heels in love with guy #1, and he doesn't feel the same way about you? But guy #1 strings you along for five years because he needs to live off you, saying he's gonna marry you. Some men will also go as far as giving you a "shut up ring." Ladies, you don't want to force a man to marry you. You are a gift and a prized possession. You should be treated as a special gift to your husband.

Why Waste Time?

Over the years, I have seen many women, and sadly, some of my sisters in the Lord, wasting years while waiting for a man to marry them. They become trapped in a "situationship" with four kids, a mortgage, three car payments, and a whole lot of debt, only for their "Boaz" to leave them and marry another woman they've known for three months.

If you are stuck in a "situationship," it's time for you to decide your position. Do you want to waste more time, or do you want to decide today that you're worth more than shacking up with a man while he dangles the promises of marriage to you? There are four steps to saying, "I DO." (More to come on that.) In the meantime, be open, use wisdom, and welcome opportunities to DATE and gather DATA on possible prospects who want to marry you.

Be mindful though that, sometimes, gathering DATA could only take a conversation. I got very skilled in gathering data with one conversation. If you are proficient in collecting or gathering data, you might decide, *"Nah, don't want to talk to or go out with this guy."* The critical factor is to be open to meeting new people and finding new opportunities.

What Is Dating Like?

Here's a memorable thought I have had about dating for years that has saved me from lots of drama and wasted time. Date many but court one. Therefore, dating is like trying to find the right job: most likely, you will go on multiple interviews. However, in dating, the difference is that you don't do the hunting. You make yourself available to be found by the hunter. Please don't be like me. When I graduated college, I was so scared that I didn't have a job lined up that I took the first one I found. It paid me less than $18k per year. LOL!

Many women are like me with my first job. They take the first man who shows an interest only to have regrets later and questions about how they ended up with him. So dating is like job hunting, but you allow the men to hunt you. Or let's flip it. Here's an example: You have a job opening, and there are twenty prospects. How do you get to the best candidate since there's only one job position available?

Do You Want to Know a Secret?

Ladies, here's a secret that we don't seem to think about. The same way you are gathering data on a guy you might be interested in, it's possible that various guys are collecting information about you also. I've had many guys inbox me to say how they loved my pictures, posts, or comments. Some offered to take me out, attend church with me, and so on. And yes, others were fishing for a free meal or an invitation to come over and "hang out."

How do you, like the saints of old used to sing, "wade through the water, children"? How do you sort out who's who, who's serious, and who's just trying to get some "cookie"? Who is trying to see if they can shack up with you or who is looking for a come up on your dime? Most importantly, if you meet a prospect, how do you get your questions answered and collect the data you need to make an informed decision about him?

How to be Wise as Serpents and Harmless as Doves in Dating

One of my favorite Bible verses, while I was dating, was **Matthew 10:16.** I will use a few different versions for understanding purposes. **Matthew 10:16** in the New King James Version says, **"Behold, I send you out as sheep in the midst of wolves. Therefore, be wise as serpents and harmless as doves."** The Complete Jewish Bible states, **"Pay attention! I am sending you out like sheep among wolves, so be as prudent as snakes and as harmless as doves."**

Also, the Message Version reads, **"Stay alert. This is hazardous work I'm assigning you. You're going to be like sheep running through a wolf pack, so don't call attention to yourselves. Be as cunning as a snake, inoffensive as a dove."** Finally, the Good News translation states, **Listen! I am sending you out just like sheep to a pack of wolves. You must be as cautious as snakes and as gentle as doves."**

Notice the persuasive and descriptive words that these various translations use to get our attention. Can you feel the intensity of "Behold, pay attention, stay alert and listen"? Here, Christ wants to get our undivided attention, so that we can focus and take to heart what he has to say. One of the descriptions of a dove is that it is innocent. In other words, act as if you don't know. You need to combine the wisdom of a serpent and the innocence of a dove in dating.

Please, be mindful that Jesus was using this verse to encourage the apostles as they were going out to evangelize the world. However, what I love about the Bible is that we can use verses to apply to our current situation.

And so, as Christ encouraged his disciples before they went forth into the world, I want to help you before you begin your journey of gathering data on the guys you might meet on social media. It takes work to be wise as serpents and harmless, soft, and innocent as doves. Remember, you need to have two qualities at the same time, ladies. This verse tells you that you need to be *both* wise *and* harmless and gentle while dating and gathering data on the guys you meet.

You also need to be wise about the information you post on social media, especially if you hope to catch the eye of a possible prepared suitor. For example, we know that some guys love boobs and butts. So we have pictures of our booties and boobs showing in many of our photographs, hoping to catch the eyes of a suitor. Do I need to tell you that many women who lead with their bodies get used for sex, abused, and left?

However, what I find is that men who prepared themselves to be husbands in every definition of the word often prefer modest and chaste women. I'm all for being sexy, sensual, and shake what ya mama gave you—but in moderate and discreet doses. So ladies, please delete the excessive advertising pictures. Have a little mystery about yourself. Guys like to hunt and discover treasures.

Thou Shalt Not Judge?

The scripture phrase "don't judge" must be the most misused portion of scripture in the entire Bible. People love to quote this phrase but not the verse in its entirety. Even folks who don't believe in Jesus or the whole Bible in context are quick to cite this partial verse. Well, as you read on and study about judging, the Bible also states in **John 7:24 that we are not to judge based on outward appearance and that we are to judge righteously.** In other words, decide based on all the information you can get.

Here's the truth! People do judge: decide about us based on our outward appearance. I don't necessarily think that Jesus was talking about choosing a mate in this context. Unfortunately, we use scripture out of context all the time to fit our circumstances and often to make people feel guilty. When God speaks about women and men in the Bible, he often tells us how pretty and handsome they are.

King Saul was tall and good looking. David was good looking and had red hair. Rachel was beautiful, and Leah was tender eyed. Rebecca moved with grace, and Ruth was diligent in picking the grains. So when it comes to men choosing us, they do look at our outward appearance. Our outward appearance is what attracts most men to women.

Even the great and anointed Prophet Samuel judged David's brothers based on their outward appearance. God, however, looked at the heart and not the outward appearance because he wanted a King after his own heart. You can read more in the Book of Samuel. Our outward appearance is what people see first. And let's not forget, ladies, that men must be physically attracted to us. Men don't marry us because we are sweet and have a sweet spirit only! They marry us because they are physically attracted to us and being sweet is the icing on the cake.

So, you can't possibly have all your ass'sets and boobs showing on social media and then say, "Oh don't judge me based on that 'cause that's not who I am." I want you to see my heart. Well, here's a little wisdom. Show the world who you are. Show possible suitors something about you other than your ass'sets and boobs to create a conversation starter.

Who Are You?

We want men to look beyond our ass'sets, boobs, and naked pictures, and we get mad when they don't. Or we say, "I'm more than my ass'sets and boobs." But men don't know that. Many pictures that men see say "sex." It doesn't say "wifey." So if you want men to look beyond the naked pictures, then show them something beyond the nude images. What are your gifts and talents? What do we do for fun? What book have you read lately? How will you be a blessing to your future husband's life? Do you play any instruments? Are you an expert cook or baker? Be mindful, though, that some man will want to invite themselves over.

Be creative, discreet, and mysterious. This way, you will create a conversation starter online with men who are curious about the real you. Why not be authentic, fun, and graceful? Post beautiful, friendly, modest pictures of yourself. Share posts that show the cute, funny, and serious sides of you. Think about your future and that of your husband. Don't post anything that will haunt you later or embarrass you both.

As I mentioned earlier, I met my husband at a networking event while selling my first published book, *Praying for our Children*. When we met, he said he was going to call and take me out. I said okay, but it took him about a month to contact me. And no, I didn't call him first. I figured if he wanted to take me out, he would contact me. Ladies, I had on a little black dress right above my knee, with knee-high boots and fishnet stockings. My knee-high dress and boots left just enough leg showing, and guess what he complimented me on? My legs! His exact words were, "You must have your mother's legs." Lol! You see ladies; you don't have to show it all, just enough to be mysterious! Read all about in a new book coming soon.

About a month later, I posted a few pictures of myself in my favorite suit at another event, where I happened to be on a date. I mentioned something about my waistline, and he commented about it being just fine. Not only did he like those pictures, but Guy #3 (that I will share about later) and several other brothers in the Lord loved them. See, the whole idea is to live and enjoy your life, and during that, your Boaz will find you.

Well, Mr. Thompson stepped up, messaged me right away, called me, and took me out about four days later. I did not accept same day dates or the next day. I prefer men who put some thought and planning into dates. Interestingly though, I wasn't even thinking about Mr. Thompson, since we hadn't spoken since we met a month before. However, we did exchange contact info and added each other on Facebook as part of the networking event. (Note: I do not recommend this with the guys you meet.)

So you see, those few pictures I posted helped to get me a phone call, a date, an engagement ring about nine months later, and finally marriage. LOL! His excuse for not contacting me earlier was his end of year reports that he needed to complete, so he was swamped with work. Over the years, I have noticed that around the end of the year he is busy, so he wasn't lying about it.

What's Your Type?

I know many of my deep church sisters like to say, "Oh, it doesn't matter. As long as he is saved and loves the Lord, he's good."

Please stop lying, ladies! Have you ever wondered that perhaps you haven't met your "Boaz" yet because you have not declared what you like and want? **Proverbs 18:21** tells us that **death and life are in the power of the tongue, and those who love it will reap its fruit.** So what are you saying about your husband to be?

What type of man do you like? Do you hope for the Barack Obama type, the thug on the street, the average Joe, or the in-between type? Do you want a husband who will provide completely for you or someone who needs your income to help with bills? Do you need an established man, a man that's struggling to make ends meet, or someone who's waiting for a miracle?

Do you want a husband who is born again, or can he be spiritual? Do you want a man who is a Bible scholar or average? Do you want to marry a preacher, teacher, or the man in the shelter? You must know all these things as you gather data. Once you know for sure what you want, you will not waste time on someone who doesn't fall in line with your expectations.

How about a minimum wage man who can only contribute while you work two and three jobs so that you can carry the household? Some men want to be kept. Are you ok with marrying a kept man? Some might think you are shallow, but all these things matter in your marriage. And the funny thing is all the ladies that think I'm shallow often post about struggling, can't pay their rent or feed their kids. I think that's the craziest thing ever. At the publication of this book, my husband and I have been married for almost six years. We have never fought about money. I have never had to worry or wonder how we're going to make ends meet. He provides well, and that makes me feel safe and secure. How many couples do you know who fight daily about money? Isn't money trouble one of the top reasons for divorce?

When I was praying for my husband and dating, I was specific about what I desired. I wanted a husband who could provide for my daughter and me. My father always said that the least a man/husband could do was to put a roof over his wife's head and food on her table. That stuck in my head!

I wanted a husband who did not need my income to provide for us. I wanted to work because I wanted to and not because I had to help him to put a roof over my head. So if I met a man and while gathering data, I learned that he needed my income to provide for me, I wouldn't proceed with him. I didn't care how sweet or kind or loving he was. If he needed my help to provide for me, I was no longer interested.

Live, Love, and Laugh

Princesses, live your lives, have fun, and show the real you. If you wear makeup, do you have any pictures of yourself not wearing makeup? I have pictures with and without makeup, my hair stacked on top of my head, making silly faces, and more. Remember, potential suitors, are also collecting data on you. What are your gifts and talents? How are you preparing yourself to meet your Boaz? As I mentioned earlier, I took some time from dating to write my first book, *Praying for Our Children*. However, I met my Boaz while I was marketing it. Do you have a sense of humor? The picture that got Guy #3 in my inbox was a silly one I posted of me with bulging eyes, and he loved it!

Every picture of you shouldn't be in a fancy dress. One of my tips for navigating online is to "beware of those who paint a perfect picture all the time." Show some imperfections, mistakes, and mess ups. Even though my now-husband didn't call right away, I did notice he that liked my posts on Facebook daily. Hmm? Perhaps he was collecting data on me and watching for that month? I, however, wasn't collecting data on him because I had other suitors pursuing me, and I was busy dating. As far as I was concerned, he was just lovely a guy I met who said he was going to contact me but didn't.

I didn't have any time to waste on a guy who didn't follow through. Since he hadn't contacted me or asked me out yet, I had somewhat forgotten about him. I thought he was nice, he seemed intriguing, and I wanted to talk to him again. But unless he made the first move, I wasn't going to contact him. Let me share this little tidbit. There were two other sisters I invited to attend the networking event with me, and they both declined. Why? One had choir rehearsal, and the other was at church for a meeting.

Eight years later, as of the publication of this book, they are both still single and spend every waking moment at the church. When will it click for Christian women that we need to participate and enjoy events outside the church? Sad to say, we aren't even "friends" anymore. Our friendships changed when I got engaged. I invited both of those sisters to my wedding.

One was to be my maid of honor but didn't follow through with the events leading up to my wedding, so in the end, I took the dress back, and we haven't talked since. (I bought all of my bridesmaid's dresses and accessories.) The other sister and I are not in touch as we once were. We chat here and there on a few Facebook posts but nothing else. So you see, ladies, it is vital to have a life outside the church.

Incidentally, many of the sisters who I came up with in the church are still single today. And many have passed childbearing years, but you know—Sarah had a baby at ninety. At least that's what church folks like to say. That cliché is another misunderstanding of scriptures that is keeping Christian women single! God had a set time for Sarah and Abraham to have Isaac. Sarah was ninety, and Abraham was one hundred. That does not mean we need to have children at ninety years old.

As Christian women, we need to have a balanced life inside and outside the church. Sadly, I was one of those sisters who spent every waking moment at the church while at the same time, crying about why God hadn't sent my husband. Except for the activities I did with my daughter, my life was church, work, and school. I wasn't living and enjoying my life, attending events, and meeting new people.

How to Navigate Social Media Dating

When you hear the word "navigate," what comes to mind? The first thing that comes to my mind is GPS. When I'm going to a place that I don't know how to get to, I type my destination on my phone and Boom! The directions, along with a very soft and kind voice, direct my every turn. The first part to navigating social media dating or data gathering is to know who you are.

Ladies, answer these questions honestly:

- Who are you?
- Are you whole?
- Have you dealt with the pain of your past?
- Do you have low self-esteem?
- Where are you going?
- Are you willing to settle for less than your heart's desire?
- What is your purpose in dating?
- Do you want to get married, or are you looking for a "good time"?
- Do you know what you want?
- Are you ready to be a wife?

- Do you know what it means to be a wife?

- What is your definition of a helpmate?

- What is your understanding of submission?

Do You Know Your Identity in Christ?

Do you know who you are? Do you know your identity in Christ? A few years ago, I wrote a book for my daughter called *In Christ I Am....* I have suggested it to many women who I talk to, and they often say, "I don't want to read that. I'm not a child." I go on to explain that, though I wrote it for my daughter and teens, anyone can read it because we all need to know our new identity in Christ. Often, some still refuse until I ask, "Can you tell me seven things that God said about you in the scriptures?" When they end up stunned and stammering, I suggest they download a free sample.

So I pose the same question to you, my dear sister. Do you know seven things the Lord has said about you? Do you know who you are in Christ? Do you know your rights as a daughter of the King? Do you know that you have power and authority through Jesus Christ? Do you know that you have delegated authority?

Proverbs 18:22 declares that **death and life are in the power of the tongue...** In other words, you will have what you say. Like Jesus, who spoke to the sea and commanded it to be still, you also have delegated authority. Jesus commanded the deaf, mute, blind, and the sick to be healed. You have that same authority.

You can read more @ www.janicehyltonblog.com for a sample of seven things God said about you from my book *In Christ I Am....* I encourage you to study and meditate on one per day until it gets down in your spirit and heart.

The Naked Wife

My book, *The Naked Wife*, revolutionized my life and my view of marriage. There are many naked wives in our churches.

What is The Naked Wife? The naked wife is a wife who is not being covered by her husband. Be it his profession of love, provision, or protection. I found with several of the ladies I interviewed that many of them ignored red flags. As women, we need to stop ignoring red flags when we date. Red flags are signs that God is showing us to help us walk away in hopes of keeping us from going into a covenant marriage with men we are not equally yoked with.

For example, when I was single, I had negotiables and non-negotiables of what I wanted in a husband. My number one non-negotiable was that my husband had to be born again. Therefore, I wouldn't date a guy who was not born again because I am rooted and grounded in my faith. I knew what the Lord said about being born again and the importance of not marrying a non-believer. And no, I did not want to "help" him become born again so that he could be a husband for me.

Many women end up being The Naked Wife because they ignored red flags and turn a blind eye to the man in front of them. Instead, ladies, I encourage you to marry the man in front of you. If he's abusive while dating, it will only get worse if you marry him. If he can't keep a job or love to work and provide for himself, then he won't want to work to take care of you and your children.

The King's Daughters

id you know that you are the King's Daughter? God Almighty of heaven and earth is your heavenly father. Your identity as the King's daughter is in the king. Yes, this is a book I wrote as a follow up to *The Naked Wife*, coming soon. If you were The Naked Wife, and you are ready to try again at dating, it is my heart's desire that you will realize you are no longer Naked. However, you are now covered by your heavenly father with his love, compassion, and grace, making you a Daughter of the King.

Perhaps you have never been *The Naked Wife* but just a woman who desires to meet your special someone and have found it challenging. Regardless of your circumstances or past experiences, you are The King's Daughter, and you need to live as such. Remember that you have delegated authority, and as a Princess, you need to stand out and be different. Here are a few things to keep in mind as you navigate social media.

1. Have standards: What do you want in a husband?
2. Don't be thirsty: Don't throw yourself at men in their inboxes or send explicit pictures and messages.
3. Be a Lady: Allow men to pursue you. Be subtle, yet intriguing and mysterious.

4. Be pursuable—for the right man: If he wants you, he will pursue you. If he wants you for cookie or wifey, men will pursue. It is up to you to entertain or pass.

5. Be available—appropriately: While I believe in making ourselves available, don't be like a ho'tel. Don't be on the phone, texting and messaging a prospect 24/7. Men quickly get bored, especially when they haven't put in the work to take you out and get to know you on a deeper level.

6. Know your worth: Jesus paid the price for you. You are a purchased possession; therefore, don't put yourself on clearance.

7. Have fun: Remember that you are to live and enjoy your life as you wait for the manifestation of your Boaz.

Woman with an Issue

One of my favorite stories in the Bible is about the Woman with the Issue of Blood. I love that story because it speaks to many women. The fascinating thing about this story is that, after twelve years of suffering and not being able to find a cure, she was healed when she stepped out of her comfort zone.

God moved for her. Jesus said it was her faith that made her whole. She already had the foundation of what she needed to be healed. This has touched me to the core of my soul. Jesus didn't just heal her issue, but he made her "whole" in every area: body, soul, and spirit. I wrote about this extensively in both *The Naked Wife* and *Daughters of the King*, but I will mention it briefly here.

The Makeup of Mankind

We are created in the image of God. God is tri-part, and so are we. The Godhead is made up of the Father, Son, and the Holy Spirit. Likewise, we are spirit, soul, and body. Our body is our earth suit and authority to be in the earth realm. Our soul houses our intellect, will, and emotions. So when we talk about our minds, we are talking about our "souls." And have you heard of soul ties?

Finally, our spirit is the part of us that is most like God because God is a spirit. When we accept Jesus Christ as Lord, it is our spirit that comes alive, according to **Ephesians 2:1: God quickens us or**

makes us alive. When God placed Adam and Eve in the Garden of Eden, he warned them not to eat of the fruit of the tree of the knowledge of good and evil. God warned that, if they ate, they would surely die. However, God was not talking about physical death at that time, but He was talking about spiritual death. Therefore, it took Adam's body almost one thousand years to die. Sadly, both Adam and Eve died spiritually when Adam partook of the fruit.

And that is why, in **Ephesians 2:4-6**, Apostle Paul states, "**4 But God, who is rich in mercy, because of His great love with which He loved us, 5 even when we were dead in trespasses, made us alive together with Christ (by grace you have been saved), 6 and raised** *us* **up together, and made** *us* **sit together in the heavenly** *places* **in Christ Jesus.**" Consequently, it is our spirits that are made alive or quickened when we make Jesus Christ Lord of our lives.

What Are His Intentions Towards You?

My spiritual father would ask guys who expressed interest in me what were their intentions towards my daughter and me.

I am so grateful that I had a father in my life to teach me how to navigate the dating world. Ladies, there are some great, gifted, and godly guys out there. However, there are also some gross, greedy, and gruesome guys, who are tools of the enemy. According to **John 10:10, "The thief does not come except to steal, and to kill, and to destroy. I have come that they may have life, and that they may have *it* more abundantly."** Some males are being used by the enemy to carry out his plan of destruction. And my father always told me that some men want to use me to get another notch on their belts or as a "toilet."

But fear not, ladies. Our big brother Jesus has overcome the world. Just because there are counterfeit, or pretend husbands, that doesn't mean there aren't excellent and great prepared husbands available. What you need before you open your legs, jump into a relationship, move him into your house with your kids, or turn your life over to a man is to know what his intentions are. If you want to be married, then you need to make better decisions. See, many women give up the "cookie," thinking he will marry them. However, these days, "cookies" are a dime a dozen. Yes, some men want to conquer as many women as possible, but that doesn't mean you have to be one of them.

In my book *The Naked Wife,* I wrote about taking the "cookie" off the table. The quickest way to see what a man is about is to take the cookie off the table. Sex is not up for discussion, especially with some strange man you just met. Unless you are both at a place in data gathering and heading in the direction of marriage, sex is still not up for discussion. You simply respond with, "I don't want to talk about that at this time." If he persists, then you know he's only after the cookie. Again, please stop discussing sex with every man you meet.

However, please be aware that this is a challenge to some men, and they will try to get you not only to talk about sex but to have sex. Stand your ground and refuse. Thankfully, not talking about sex might also decrease the guys that are interested in you because some might see it as a waste of their time. While many will stick around to test you, it is up to you to keep your celibacy. That will show you if he is really about marriage or about making another notch on his belt.

Sex and the Church

Let me be clear! I am not encouraging fornication, shacking up, or making babies out of wedlock. The Bible is clear about sex and marriage. God created sex for marriage, and that's final! However, let's address the big elephant in our churches. We have lots of babies born every day to single mothers and fathers in our churches. So, saved single people are having sex. I wonder what would happen if the women in our churches would close their legs to men who are not their husbands? P.S. I had my daughter when I was sixteen years old.

I got married at thirty-five and had my second baby at thirty-seven, currently working on baby number three at forty-one years old. So, please know that I understand the whole 'baby out of wedlock' thing. BUT what I did not do was have more babies I couldn't take care of without a husband. And this is not about sexual freedom. Please note that this book is not for you, beloved if you feel that I'm trying to dim your sexual lights. Neither is this about babies-out-of-wedlock bashing or anything like that. I can hear someone ask, "Well, what about the men?" The same goes for the men folks too. But you know what my father always says? "All men want to have sex!" But I didn't have to lay with any of them.

Therefore, my children are twenty years apart because I was determined not to have another child as a single parent. So, princesses, I know exactly what I am talking about. I closed my legs to many men who wanted my body but didn't want me. And that's including married men! Many men wanted my "cookie" but didn't want to profess their love, provide for my daughter and me, and protect us. They didn't want to go through the process required for me to turn my life over to them.

You see, ladies, if he loves you, then he will honor and cover you by taking you before the throne of the Lord so that you can both be blessed. If he loves you, then he will do right by you. That's why you can't be easy, like Sunday mornings. The truth is, ladies, while you desire a husband and want to settle down, have kids and a family, and do things God's way, not every man you meet wants the same. Or he might want those things, but he doesn't desire them with YOU but will pretend to fulfill his selfish needs. He might see you as prey. He might see you as desperate or an opportunity to add another notch to his belt. He might see you as "cookie," rent, food, clothes, a free meal, or a paycheck.

I desire that, as women, we will begin to think carefully about what we want. We need to love, honor, and value ourselves more. In doing so, we can stop allowing these men to use our bodies like toilets. As women, we need to stop entertaining men who don't love, honor and respect us enough to bring us before the pastor, our family, friends, and the Lord and make us their wives.

Do You Need to be Fathered?

Ladies, do you want to know how serious a man is about you? Tell him that your father or father figure wants to talk to him.

I am aware that many fathers are not present or have passed on. But if there's a man in your life who loves and adore you as his very own little girl, then ask him to be your father figure. A father figure must be a man of honor and respect. He needs to be a man who's not trying to get into your panties but a man who can teach you about other men. And no, your mom can't be your father figure. My dad always says that men know other men. A man can sweet talk your mother the way he can you. That is why you need a man's man to speak to these men who express interest in you.

One of my favorite verses is **Proverbs 22:6,** which states, **"Train up a child in the way he should go, and when he is old he will not depart from it."** This means that both the mother and father are needed in a child's life. Both parents need to have input in the child's life to help frame their outlook on the world. A crucial factor that I believe get many women in trouble is not understanding that men and women are different. Men and women think, see, and hear differently. Because of this, when we say something, many times, the meaning varies. Additionally, men view us differently.

So a man who you're interested in might say something like, "Well, I'm not ready to get married right now." You, however, hear, "IM NOT READY TO GET MARRIED RIGHT NOW BUT I NEED

YOU TO MAKE ME BE READY TO MARRY YOU RIGHT NOW."
Ladies, here's a little secret. The truth is, what he means is that he
doesn't want to marry YOU! Why? Many men who stated that they
were not ready to get married will meet a girl and marry her in six
months. Ladies, when a man speaks, you need to hear him. If he's
not ready to get married and you want to get married, the best
thing for you to do is move on.

As mentioned earlier, I had my baby girl Alexia when I was
sixteen years old. Bishop Bradshaw and First Lady Bradshaw became
my spiritual parents when I was about seventeen years old. I had
always wanted to get married from an early age. My father would
often say to me, "Baby, there are just some men who want to screw
you. Not every man you meet wants to marry you. You need to
wait for that man who wants to marry you. Only in the eyes of the
man who values you, wants to love you, protect you, and provide
for you, are you worth something. To every other man, you are just
"cookie," an opportunity, a paycheck, a shelter, a baby momma,
someone to play with, or a victim."

Additionally, my dad always told me, "Baby, you are not a wife
when you get married, but you need to be a wife when he finds
you." I was an avid reader, so I spent a lot of time reading about
marriage, singleness, sex, and studying the Bible. And I am happy I
did because the knowledge I gained saved me many heartaches,
pain, and disappointments. Your father or father figure should help
you to choose your husband. My father was a considerable influence
on the husband I wanted to choose. And my husband had to get
my father's blessings and approval for me to marry him. If my

father did not approve of my husband, I would not have married him.

I will be writing more about The Anointing of the Father soon.

Do You Want A Prepared Husband?

Christ & The Church

The relationship between Christ and the Church exemplifies the relationship between a husband and wife. And so, to learn about marriage and how a husband should treat his wife, our perfect example is our Lord Jesus Christ and how he cares for the church. Jesus said in **John 14:3, "And if I go and prepare a place for you, I will come again and will take you to myself, that where I am you may be also**." Ladies, you see, Jesus made plans and went to prepare a place for his bride the church.

Likewise, a man who desires to be married needs to prepare or develop himself. So that when he meets his wife, he needs to be a PREPARED MAN. I will be writing more about a Prepared Man in the future. But for now, when you pray for your husband, pray that God will send you a Prepared Man. Additionally, remember The Psalm 23 Husband, also known as the Shepard. A Shepherd is a man who is prepared and aware of his surroundings and what is needed to care for and tend to his sheep.

A Shepard already has plans in the springtime: where his sheep will graze in the winter. Why? Because the Shepard is fully aware that his flock is dependent on him. When the flock has eaten up a pasture of land, the shepherd doesn't ask the flock what they are going to do. The shepherd already knows where their next place of grazing is. More to come about the Psalm 23 Husband, also known as the Prepared Husband and the Shepard.

I will write more about what a husband should be in an upcoming book on marriage. And look out for *The Psalm 23 Husband*, coming soon also.

Do You Know That Your Husband Is A Choice?

Remember earlier I shared about the Psalm 23 Man/Husband? And how about praying for God to bless you with a PREPARED HUSBAND? Again, my father has always told me that I'm not a wife when a man marries me, but I should be a wife when he finds me. Did you get that? In other words, be a wife and have a wife mentality while you wait for your Boaz to find you. The wisdom that I should be a wife when my husband finds me revolutionized my thinking and dating style.

Finally, one day, something said DING, DING, DING, DING, "If I should already be a wife when my husband finds me, then that means he needs to be a husband already when he finds me." Not becoming one, not working on being one, he should already *be* a husband. To that end, princesses, you need to be mindful of The Psalm 23 Husband. Please understand that a prepared man who is looking for a wife is ready to take on the responsibility of a husband; he is about the business.

A prepared husband is not about wasting time, entertaining the wrong type of woman, or having just a girlfriend! He's not about shacking up or making babies out of wedlock. He's not sitting back with folded hands waiting for his wife to come and help him become a prepared man. He has taken upon himself to be prepared for his wife!

A man who has prepared himself to be a husband is ready to walk in his God-ordained role of a husband. You see, a prepared husband is a call and an anointing. While every man has it in him to be a husband, many do not walk in the anointing of a husband. Being a godly and anointed husband begins with having a heart like Christ. Being a Psalm 23 Prepared Husband requires sacrifices, selflessness, commitment, and discipline.

A prepared husband is a man who has sought the face of God for the vision for his life, his wife, and children. A prepared husband is a man who has prepared himself to profess his love to a woman, protect her and provide for her. A prepared husband is a man who is in submission to Christ because he understands that, for his wife to submit freely to him, he first needs to submit to Christ. A Psalm 23 Husband is one that has the heart of a Shepard and is a man who is an example of Christ and can be an example to his wife and children. A prepared husband is a leader and a visionary.

During my time of singleness, I met a variety of men. Meeting various types of guys helped me to sharpen my data collecting skills. I got to the point where I could meet a man, speak with him for a few minutes, and I would instantly know if I wanted to talk to him again. How, might you ask? Well, I knew exactly what I wanted in a husband. I had my questions in my head, so when I met guys, I knew exactly which questions to ask to see where they were. Once I got what I needed, if I felt that I didn't want to talk to them again, that would be it for me. I HATE TO WASTE TIME!!

I'm reminded of the story in **Matthew 9:37-38,** where Jesus said, **"The harvest is plenty, but the laborers are few."** Jesus's answer to the lack of laborers was that we pray for laborers. So, ladies, I submit to you that you pray for the Lord of the harvest that he will raise up prepared husbands for you. This is my daily prayer for all my sisters.

A Male Vs. a Man

The Apostle Paul said in **1 Corinthians 13:11, "When I was a child, I spoke as a child, I understood as a child, I thought as a child; but when I became a man, I put away childish things."** Princesses, I submit to you that just because a man has a penis, that doesn't mean he's a man or even husband material. A male must grow into being a man and prepare himself to be a husband. As Christian women, it's crucial for us to understand that many wolves are presenting themselves as humble lambs.

However, with a little wisdom, the eyes of the Holy Spirit, and prayer, you will be able to spot a pretender vs. your prince. It is essential to determine who is genuine or, like the saints of old used to say, "Who in the twinkle of an eye." With a bit of navigation skill, you will be able to spot a fake in seconds.

What Are the Three P's of a Good and Godly Husband?

There are three Ps of a good and godly husband. Now ladies, please keep in mind also The Psalm 23 Husband. He is our blueprint to what a good and prepared husband is, along with the example of Christ. If you look carefully at the relationship between Christ and the Church, you will see how Christ portrays the characteristics of how a husband ought to be. I will write more about this in an upcoming book, but I will share a teaser here.

From the New Living Translation, **Romans 10:9** states, "**⁹ If you openly declare that Jesus is Lord and believe in your heart that God raised him from the dead, you will be saved.**" Now let's apply that to the responsibility of a husband. Notice, like Christ, who showed his love by dying for us, so the husband is to show his love for his bride. The bride's only responsibility is to accept.

Profess-Openly Declare

While a profession of faith is the first step to being born again, it is the last step for a husband. But I'll list it first. A husband is to declare openly before witnesses that he loves you and wants you and only you. Be mindful though that any man can profess his love for you in secret. That is why we say love is an action word. Christ loves the world, so he died for us all. Therefore, it takes a prepared man who has prepared himself to be a husband to take it a step further.

A prepared husband will take you to your pastor, your family, your friends, and the Lord and marry you. By doing so, he is making a public declaration and profession of his love for you. That's the reason you allow a man to ask you to marry him, ladies!

Provide & Belief

Before a man marries you, he needs to show you that he can provide for you. This is why you don't get married before you know him and have all the facts. See, we can believe in our hearts that God raised Jesus from the dead because over five hundred witnesses saw him. The Bible declares that he is sitting on the right hand of the Father interceding for us.

Additionally, the Bible declares that we are seated in Christ on the right hand of the father. Therefore, a man is to show you how he will provide for you. Forget this talk about he got you, and ya need to trust him, and he'll do what he's supposed to do. No, ma'am. You need to see the proof yourself. I cannot tell you the countless number of women who were swayed by a man's words with no evidence. And once the stuff hits the fan, they end up homeless, living in a shelter with their children.

My spiritual dad taught me that a man is to provide for his wife and kids. So ladies, how can you marry a man who doesn't have a job, can't keep a job, or can't get a job? Some men have criminal records that are such a mess that they can't even shovel snow. Why would you marry a career criminal whose future is uncertain? Think carefully before you marry a man who is not marketable.

The Bible encourages us to count the cost, according to one of my favorite portions of scriptures, in Luke 14:28-30. It states, "**28 For which of you, intending to build a tower, does not sit down first and count the cost, whether he has *enough* to finish *it*— 29 lest, after he has laid the foundation, and is not able to finish, all who see *it* begin to mock him, 30 saying, 'This man began to build and was not able to finish'?**"

Beloveds, I live by this scripture. I can't marry a man based on his words that he "got me!" I need to see proof. I need to see the credit report, the W2, the blood test, the police report, and I need to talk to other people about him! Stop this foolishness about, "But he said..." Yeah, and three months later you find out that what he said wasn't true, but you were being controlled by your emotions and your kitty that you didn't take the time to RESEARCH WHAT HE SAID!

Many women marry men thinking they will take care of the men. But it will only be a matter of time before the woman gets tired of doing her husband's duty. It doesn't matter how much money a woman makes; we all want to be taken care of and provided for. But because of your emotions, you might foolishly say, "Oh, I have enough money for us both," or, "I don't need him for his money."

The thinking that you don't need his money is foolishness! By not choosing a husband who can provide for you, you're taking on the provider role, and you are taking away his manhood. I hate to say it, but a man who can have his manhood taken away is not a prepared man. And he is not the Psalm 23 Husband! Now in all fairness, some women don't mind taking care of men. I'm just not one of them, and I hope you're not either.

Here's another thought; what kind of man would get with a woman so that she can be the provider? Think about that, ladies! Also, I know some men who intentionally choose overly aggressive women because they know that they will take on their roles. Ladies, these males are not men! They are looking for what I call a mom-wife.

Protection & Peace

Romans 10:9: "If you confess with your mouth the Lord Jesus Christ and Believe in your heart that God raised him from the dead you shall be saved."

A husband who has professed his love must have shown that he can provide and protect his wife like Christ professed his love for the Church, providing for all her needs and protecting her. A husband who can't provide for his wife will not be able to protect her.

I am amazed by the number of women who cry about how they work two and three jobs while their little son-husbands stay home and play video games. He hasn't worked in two or three years. My mouth hits the floor; what information did they use to choose this man? What was it about him that made her lay with him, have his babies, and move him into her home with her kids that she was already struggling to provide for? What was it about this man that doesn't work that made her marry him?

When you get married, an exchange takes place. You are giving your husband all of you, and he is giving you all of him. Indeed, you are turning your life over to him, and it is a husband's responsibility to provide for and protect you. How can he fulfill a husband's obligation by playing video games all day and not making any income? When you choose The Psalm 23 Husband, you will have no fear or cares for your life.

If a man already has two or three kids that he's not taking care of, why would you open your legs for him? If he hasn't worked in ten years, why would you marry him and then cry three months later that he ain't even trying to find a job? Do you know why you'll be complaining a few months later? Because your emotions have died down, and now reality has set in! Therefore I beg of you princesses: please do not allow your feelings to lead you when you are choosing your husband. Do you want to have chemistry? Yes! Chemistry is crucial! But you need to command your emotions to be under the blood of Jesus and not rule you. Live in reality while you're dating. Pay attention to the red flags. Sweetie, the red flags will not go away. They will only get worse if you turn your life over to an unprepared man!

What is it about a male who is looking for a woman to take care of and provide for him that makes him sexy? What information did you use to decide to be with him? What was it about him? Was it his eyes, his charming smile? Was he friendly, kind? But he wasn't saved, and he doesn't love your God. He can't even take care of himself, so he won't be able to take care of you. He hasn't worked in years, ain't trying to get a job, can't keep a job. Or maybe he is abusive. Look at the whole picture, ladies!

See, if we don't want to be a part of the statistics that fifty percent of marriages fail, we must begin by choosing better husbands. I do, however, believe to some extent that there is a shortage of "good men." Look at the number of males who are in jail, those who don't like women, those who are on the streets, and those who aren't able to be good husbands, which affects the number of good men available. Also, look at the number of men vs. women in our colleges, churches, and the workforce.

I do believe that many of the issues that affect countless numbers of our men today are the attacks of the enemy. The enemy knows that if he can get the head, then the rest of the body will follow. By attacking our men, the enemy knows that women and children will be left unloved, unprovided for, and unprotected. In spite of this, it is still not a reason to marry a man to "help" him become the man he needs to be so that he can be all that you need him to be.

Therefore, as praying women, we ought to pray that the Lord will raise up good and godly husbands. Pray to the Lord of the harvest that he will send us Psalm 23 Husbands. We ought to pray that God will raise up men of standards and example to teach males how to become men and good husbands. Once an issue is identified, we need to do something about it because God created us to be problem solvers.

The Bible said **Isaiah 4:1 "In that day so few men will be left that seven women will fight for each man, saying, 'Let us all marry you! We will provide our own food and clothing. Only let us take your name so we won't be mocked as old maids.'"** So yes, I think there is a shortage of good men, especially for women of color. We need good men who can profess their love, provide a comfortable life, and protect us. Some women think any man is better than no man at all. That is a dangerous belief, in my opinion.

When men approach us, we don't have to get into a relationship, open our legs, or marry them because the choice lies with us. The man/husband you choose will determine the rest of your life. It will be either a life of peace, love, prosperity, and happiness, or one of struggle, stress, poverty, anger, and resentment.

You see, a husband is a choice. **Proverbs 18:21** says, **"The man who finds a wife finds a treasure, and he receives favor from the LORD."** But this is a two-way street, ladies, because **Psalm 65:4** says, **"Blessed *is the man* You choose, and cause to approach *You, that* he may dwell in Your courts. We shall be satisfied with the goodness of Your house, Of Your holy temple."**

So just because he finds you, that doesn't mean you have to choose him. My dad always told me that any man could find me because I am a wife, and many of them are looking for a wife, whether they are a husband or not. I will write on this more extensively in my upcoming book *He*.

Standards vs. Desperations

I will talk more about standards in my book for singles, but I'm going to touch on it here. To navigate the journey of meeting guys on social media, you need a destination. What is your purpose for wanting to meet someone? Remember I mentioned about the GPS earlier? When you hear the word standards, I want you to think of a GPS, which helps to guide us if we don't know where we are going. That way, your standards or directions allow you to know where you are going and what you want in a husband.

Now, I know many ladies say they don't care what kind of man they get. I can't say that because I believe that my husband determines the rest of my life. Think about that for a second. The man who will be your husband will be responsible for you. He will speak and make decisions for you. Again, the man you choose will determine the rest of your life. Your husband will be your power of attorney; you will have children with him and raise them together. He is to be your professor, protector, and provider.

Therefore, it is essential to vet men properly, so you don't end up with a "fool." Just any man will not do! You shouldn't marry a man just because he's tall or has a big dingaling. Choosing a husband is like putting a puzzle together. I am amazed when some women begin to have issues in their marriages. When I ask why they married their husbands, for some, it's "because he was good in bed." That's it? You married him ONLY because he was great in bed? Marrying a man because he has good hair is also not a good reason. You must think more extensively, deeper, and further than that. Now, I'm not saying to pass up on a man with good hair. What I am saying is, marrying him solely because he has "good hair" will cause you to be *The Naked Wife!*

Having some standards and knowing what you desire will save you a lifetime of stress, regrets, bitterness, and resentments. Because of your standards, you know what you want, where you're going, and how you're going to choose wisely. In Biblical times, women didn't have much choice in who they married. If a man came along and were able to pay her dowry, the family would allow it.

Even though I can't stand Laban, who is the father of Leah and Rachel, I respect him in this instance. When Jacob wanted to marry Rachel, Laban didn't just give her to him. Jacob couldn't pay her dowry or show he could provide for her because he had to run away from his homeland to save his life. As a result, Jacob agreed to work seven years, which ended up being fourteen years, for the woman he loved and wanted.

The same went for Rebecca, also. When Eleazar went to find Isaac a wife, the Bible says Abraham sent a lot of merchandise with him to show the family that Isaac would be able to provide for their daughter. You see, when a man asks a woman to marry him, what he is saying to her and her father is that he is ready to take on the responsibility for his daughter. If you have been taking care of yourself, this man is saying, "Let me take over taking care of you."

Ladies, when you marry, your husband needs to complement your life. He needs to provide a better experience for you than you were providing for yourself. I recently read where a woman commented on a post that at least her minimum wage boyfriend who just moved in with her is contributing to the household. Lol! I was so disgusted I didn't even say anything. My dear sisters, you deserve to be taken care of and provided for.

What Will You Do When Your Ticking Clock Strikes Midnight?

Don't just hurry to marry a man because your clock is ticking. Trust me; I understand the "ticking clock!" Remember, my children are twenty years apart. You need to ask, "Why should I marry him? Will he make my life better or bitter? Can he protect and provide for me?" I will be writing about the ticking clock soon. Having my first child at sixteen, getting married at 35, having my second child at 37, and currently trying for baby #3 at 41, trust me, I understand the ticking clock.

This is where that saying, "I can do bad by myself" came from. Why get married or be with a man to do the same as you were or worse? You were paying the mortgage all by yourself, and now he can't even pay the cable bill. He was living in his momma's basement, and now he's moving in with you. Instead of him taking care of you, you are providing shelter, clothes, and food for him and putting money in his pocket. That's not a husband, ladies! That's another child that you must take care of and feed.

That's why, once there's mutual interest, it's important not to let your emotions guide you when choosing a husband. Am I saying you shouldn't like him? No! Of course not! Your emotions will get you into trouble if you don't keep them in check. Don't get emotionally connected to any man or his dingaling. Some men only have a dingaling to offer! However, it takes more than that make a marriage work. Wives can't live by dingaling alone!

What's Your Price?

How much does it cost to have your body? Every woman has a price. **Proverbs 31** talks about the virtuous woman's price or worth being higher than rubies. So we all have price, ladies, for men to get between our legs. I want to scream every time I read where a woman says she met a guy, and he's so nice that she wants to give him "some." Are you kidding me? He is sweet and took you out, so his reward is your body? Do you know what I realized? We don't know and understand our worth. We don't value our vaginas and understand how precious our bodies are. I will be writing extensively about our vaginas soon. Oh, honey, its gonna knock your socks off!

So: What's your price? Is it that he's a nice guy? He comes to see you? He provides dinner and a movie? A plane ticket? A pocketbook or shoes? A few dollars? Empty promises and steaming lies? What is your price? Is it allowing him to move in with you and shack up while he stashes his cash in hopes of finding the right woman to marry? See, therefore you need to know what you want in a husband.

When I was dating, if I met a man who wasn't ready to get married, wanted to wait to get married, was trying to get himself together before he gets married, and so on, guess what? He wasn't a prepared man, so I would move on. You see, I wanted to get married, and my husband was a prepared man who was looking for me. Not a man who wanted to play house, use my body while he lives off me, eating up all my baby's food, and drinking her milk.

Do You Have a List of Things you Desire in Your Husband?

A husband is a choice, so choose wisely. I know we want perfection. But there is no perfect man, other than Jesus. The Psalm 23 Husband, who is a prepared man, does come close, though. I am a big fan of "The List." The list is your standard, GPS, navigation, banner, or guideline. Please note also that I use the word "things" because it could be characteristics, qualities, desires, etc.

Church folks used to say, "Throw out your list because when God sends you a husband, that's it." My question was, however, how do I know God sent him? People say, "Oh, you will just know." Yet divorce is still over 50% in the church! Many women married men they didn't vet properly and are living in hell on earth. Please, see my latest book, *The Naked Wife*. Recently in one of our sister churches, an elder shot and killed his wife in front of their children. Did God send him? Was it God's will for him to abuse her and kill her? I'm sure he was abusing her all those years.

I wonder what the church folks told her about her abusive husband. I know for a fact that church folks have told many wives of abusive and cheating husbands to stay with them and pray that God will change them! So basically, I had no trust in what church folks told me about the type of husband I wanted. The only person I listened to was my father in the faith.

For those folks who say for us to throw out our lists, do you know that God has many lists? He told Adam and Eve what not to do: don't eat from the tree. Before God gave Adam a wife, God gave him a job so that, when he got his wife, he would know exactly how to tend to her and her needs. Think about The Ten Commandments as a list. And what about Jesus's list of the seven "I Am's." In my yearly Bible Reading Plan, I am currently reading in Exodus about the instructions God gave for the tabernacle and its furnishings. It is one of the most beautiful portions of scriptures. God gave specific guidelines for the people to follow to achieve the greatness and beauty that the Lord wanted to share with his people.

So if God has many lists, what's wrong with us having a list of things we desire in our husbands? Likewise, I encourage you to write down what you want in your husband. **Proverbs 21:22** says, **"He that finds a wife, finds a treasure."** But verse 21 says, **"Death and life are in the power of the tongue and you will have what you say."** Here's a thought-provoking question: What are you saying about your future husband? What kind of husband do you want? Do you pray for your future husband? If you don't care what kind of husband "God sends you," what are you saying about your future husband?

Habakkuk 2:2 talks about writing the vision and making it plain. As a writer, I often scribble different thoughts and ideas down and hang them all over my house. When I see them, I will confess them, and they remind me of the promises of the Lord. Also, I have created book covers ahead of time to help me to envision and complete them. Let me share this tidbit with you. I love businessmen. Unfortunately, I wasted some time dating men I didn't like. But I always said, there must be at least one saved black man who works on Wall Street who's looking for a wife. Guess where my husband worked when we met?

When I was looking for a house to buy, I knew exactly what I wanted. My daughter was nineteen when I got married, so I wanted a house that had a third-floor inclusive apartment where she could have her own space. Because of this, I refused to look at any houses that didn't have a third-floor apartment. My first realtor tried to get me to look at homes that didn't have what I wanted, and I eventually dropped her once the contract was up. My new realtor, Felix, found me the home that we purchased. See ladies, if a man doesn't have what you need, don't waste your time with him. Drop him quicker than a New York Minute.

Even though we found the home, I had to compromise a little bit. While our new home has a third-floor apartment, it doesn't have a powder room on the first floor. That was not a necessity for me, so we went ahead and made the purchase. My husband didn't care what kind of house we bought as long as I was happy. He said he only needed a place to lay his head. But he wanted to make sure I was pleased with the house.

So, with prayer, fasting, counsel, and wisdom, write down what you desire in a husband. Read the stories of the Bible, where men wanted to marry women. My favorite story of all time is that of Ruth and Boaz, second being Rachel and Jacob, and finally Isaac and Rebecca. Ladies, these men were well able to profess their love, provide for, and protect their wives.

As mentioned earlier, when Jacob wanted to marry Rachel, Laban, Rachel's father, asked him how he would provide for and protect her because Jacob had nothing. Earlier, Jacob had to flee his home to keep his brother Esau from killing him. You see, Jacob and his mother Rebecca, tricked Isaac, who was Jacob and Esau's father, into giving Jacob the birthright. Biblically, the birthright belonged to the eldest son. But God had already made a promise that the younger son would rule over the eldest. Jacob and Rebecca only needed to trust the Lord.

So, when Jacob fled for his life, he had nothing with him. And he didn't have anything to pay for Rachel's dowry. Therefore, Jacob agreed to work seven years for Rachel. Laban tricked him and gave him Leah instead, but he agreed to another seven years for the woman Jacob loved. Thus, Jacob worked for fourteen years for Rachel. You see, ladies, stop giving yourself away for free.

A Tithe

Now, sisters, even though you might have your list, please be flexible. Allow me to use myself as an example. I suggest that you make a list of ten things, both negotiable and non-negotiable about your husband. NEVER, compromise your non-negotiables, but be flexible with your negotiables.

When you think of your list of ten, think about your ten fingers and write your list on them. I like to align ten with a tithe because tithe means ten. As in, give God what is His, and He will bring you the increase. Also, when it comes to writing your list on your fingers, think of **Proverbs 7:3: "Bind them on your fingers; write them on the tablet of your heart."**

Here are a few other verses that mention writing things down. **Deuteronomy 6:8 says, "Tie them to your hands and wear them on** your forehead as reminders. ⁹ Write them on the doorposts of your house and on your gates." Of course, these verses are referring to the Word of the Lord. However, I used those verses to help me to remember what I desire in a husband, thus my "write them on your fingers" analogy, and again, ten means a tithe.

Did someone ask, why just ten things? Well, think of each of the ten as branches. Each branch has fruit, or results, which we need to pay attention to. For example, a man who is born again has specific characteristics or fruits of a man that has a relationship with Christ. Let's take a quick look at some of the things I had on my list as a single woman.

What Did My List Look Like?

Non-Negotiables

My list comprised ten things, both negotiables, and non-negotiables. My non-negotiables are must-have, while my negotiables could go either way. The number one requirement on my list of ten for my Psalm 23 Prepared Husband, is a must-have. If he doesn't meet that, there's no need to go on to #2 on my list. Therefore, I wouldn't go any further if he didn't have my #1.

1. He Must be Born Again

At the top of my list was a man who was born again and loved Jesus. So, if a guy approached me and asked me out, but he was not born again, that ended it. We wouldn't have anything to talk about or pray about. I'm not gonna be the one to speak to him about Jesus; he can call my pastor about that. I don't believe in evangelistic marriages. You know, those are the ones where women get the men saved and then marry them only to find out they were only saved long enough to say, "I do." Then, after the reception, you find out that he is still a devil! NO, MA'AM! LOL!

But a lot of women say, "Well, he's not born again, but he is nice." NOPE! Stick to your list. Being born again is a non-negotiable for me. He must be born again! If he isn't, we are not going out. If he says he intends to get saved, that's a trick to get you to marry him! A man saying, he intends to get saved is like a man who doesn't have a job, can't keep a job, or who don't like to work saying, "I intend to get a job once we are married." Ladies, that's an old trap!

I have already gotten the information that he is not saved. Plus, I don't believe in wasting time! Don't allow a man to get in your spirit. If he is not a believer, shut it down! No need to stay on the phone for hours talking and dreaming when you know that man doesn't love your God. If he doesn't love your God, ladies, he cannot love you like Christ loves the church!

2. He Must be a Tither

The next requirement on my list was that he must be a tither. Ok, let's say you met a brother who is saved. However, during a conversation, you find out that he is not a tither. NOPE! I'm not going to try to convince him to pay tithes. That's a personal decision and should not be forced. I'm a giver, and I don't need anyone messing with my ability to give. I don't care what people say; I am a witness that tithing and giving to the Lord works. I want a man who brings his tithes and offering to the Lord.

I know so many women, both in and out of the church, who have struggled with husbands who don't tithe. In the husbands' minds, they think, "She's giving the money to the pastor so he can drive around in a big fancy car." See, I didn't want to have to go through that. That is why I vowed never to marry a man who doesn't understand the importance of tithing and who is willing to give freely!

And yes, some of these men are believers! I'm not sure how they are born again, but don't believe in giving, but okay. I noticed something important about my husband once we started talking. He travels for work sometimes, and on some Sundays, he had to fly out. Often, I heard him say that he must stop by the church and drop his tithes off before going to the airport. I was so impressed with that.

To this day, after five years of marriage, tithing is at the top of what we do with our finances. We have NEVER had a fight or argument about tithing or giving to God. We always agree to give to the Lord. Any amount of money that comes to our home, we always give to the Lord.

3. He Must Be a Gentleman

You might be thinking that this should be the first on my list. Wrong. Once you meet a guy via social media, chat group, etc. and you begin to talk, you can pick up in conversations or talk about church and your relationship with Christ. However, it's mostly in going out with him and being with him that you will find out if he is a real gentleman or a pretender. But what if in conversation you find out that he is not saved or doesn't believe in tithing? Why would I waste my time going out with him to find out if he is a gentleman? The two most essential things on my list he doesn't have, so there's no need to go on to number three on my list.

Now, with my husband, because we met at a networking event, the first thing I noticed about him was that he spoke well, was knowledgeable of various topics, and most of all, he was a gentleman. We also talked about church, and I learned that he attended the most prominent Baptist church in our community. In talking about church, when he asked me out later, I would find out if he was saved and a tither. Please be mindful that not because a person attends church means that they are saved. There are many unsaved folks in our churches. Princesses, use wisdom, be flexible and open, and have your list in your head and heart. Tweak when necessary to get the data you need.

I love a perfect gentleman. Oh, my spiritual father is a gentleman, a man's man, and I love him dearly. My guy must be a gentleman like my father when I meet him. If he needs me to teach him how to be a gentleman, I am not the one for him. I love a man who is caring and thoughtful, someone who will open doors, pull out chairs, send flowers, help me put my jacket on, and protect me as I walk.

Yes, Lawd! I love a man who is respectful and who can have a conversation that stimulates my mind. And that is one thing I love about my husband. We can discuss every topic. From the Bible, politics, world affairs, current events, you name it; we can sit and talk for hours. I got so good at this that, when I met some guys, I just needed to speak to them for a few minutes to determine if I would go out on a date with them.

Again, this was ONE thing I noticed about my husband when I met him. He was such a perfect gentleman; I was in awe. As mentioned earlier, we met at a networking event, where we sat across from each other. We talked most of the evening in between me trying to sell my first published book, *Praying for our Children*. I didn't even notice he was interested, but he kept talking to me until he got my attention.

Mr. Businessman was such a perfect gentleman that I felt compelled to hug him and say thank you when I was leaving. Of course, this was after he asked me for my number and said he would call to take me out. I remember him saying, "Wow, no woman has ever said thank you or given me a hug for being a gentleman." To this day, he says that was one of the things that set me apart from any other woman he has met. Plus, he thought that I was smart for selling my book at a networking event.

4. He Must Have a Good Job (Career)

Yes, I said it! Some women are so fake and phony it's sickening! They fight for the struggling men, where they must pray every month for the Lawd to put food on the table. They marry a man who can't provide for himself, much less a wife and family, and then they cry and moan two months after because they are struggling. "He ain't got no job!" Or they're about to be homeless, and they gotta move in with her momma! Girl, please!! Ain't nobody got time for that mess!

Deep down, every woman, no matter how much money she has, wants to be taken care of by the man she is lying down with, who is supposed to be her provider and protector. I wish women would stop trying to be politically correct and tell the truth! Struggling puts a strain on everyone. I made a decent income when I met my husband and still wanted a husband who could take care of me.

Neither would I marry a man who made less than me or someone I had to help put a roof over my head. Please allow me to clarify about the man who makes less. I wholeheartedly believe that wives should be able to live on their husband's income ALONE!

Only the foolish and simple-minded people will ask what a wife will do with her income if she has one. Please read Proverbs 31 several times and slowly! See ladies: therefore I couldn't marry a man who needs my income to pay the mortgage and put food on the table. As far as a man making less. The most crucial question is, "Can we live comfortably on his income ALONE?"

There's a well-known couple who recently got married. They are both millionaires, but she has more money than he does. Of course, the foolish and simple-minded men were all over social media talking about how she married a man who has less money than she does. If she's a millionaire and marries a man who has less money than she does, then what's wrong with those who are making $50K, who won't marry a man who is making $10K per year? Answer these two questions for me. Can a couple live comfortably on one million dollars per year? Can a couple live comfortably on $10K per year? I even saw one guy's pay stub that had four orders of Child Support Payments being taken out. His take-home pay was $46 per pay

God is a God of abundance and prosperity. I struggled enough as a teen and single mom. I refused to get married and continue to struggle. For this reason, I wanted a husband who was well able to provide an enjoyable and comfortable life for me, my daughter, and our family. Specifically, my guy had to have a great job with great pay, benefits, and dental. Good job equals a wonderful and stress-free life if the couple knows how to save and balance. I know way too many couples who are struggling. Wives stressing and asking for prayer every month 'cause they don't have enough money to pay their basic monthly expenses. Yet they will be all over social media defending the struggle life when women like me say, "We don't want no struggle man!" Please!

Some trifling women will say, "Oh, but those are the men who cheat on you and abuse you." Here's a question: Why is it that? Are you telling me that broke and struggling men don't cheat and abuse their wives? Divorces take place every day! Are the couples separating only because the men are well-off and able to provide? There are no poor, broke, busted, and disgusted men getting divorces? Stop making excuses for the struggle life, ladies!

Again, I believe a wife needs to be comfortable living on her husband's income ALONE! Now, some women don't care if a man works or not. Some women are even fine with taking care of a man just so that they can say they have one. Sorry, I am not one of those women! So ladies, if he is making $25K per year, will you be comfortable living on his income?

Not, "Yes, but add my income" or "He can always get another job." But can you be comfortable, at peace, and not nag him to get another job? If your answer is not an honest "yes," leave that man alone. Many women get married with unrealistic expectations, which births resentment, bitterness, and anger. If women are honest with this ONE question, divorce could be cut down drastically.

I am not a ride or die chick. I have too many questions: 1. Where are we riding to? 2. Why do I have to die, since Jesus already died for us? So, if I met a guy who didn't have his act together, living in his momma's basement, looking for a sponsor, I was out! Nothing else to talk about. I refuse to entertain the bull crap! Ladies, you want a PREPARED HUSBAND! Not an adult male child that you must feed, clothe, and put money in his pocket!

God intends that the husband provides for his wife and family. It breaks my heart when a wife says she must work two or three jobs to keep a roof over her head and food on her children's table. In the meantime, there is a grown man in the home, who doesn't work or doesn't want to work. It is vital for women to choose better husbands.

When you have some free time, please read the story of Adam and Eve. God prepared a place for Adam—the Garden of Eden. God gave Adam a job to keep the garden, name all the animals, plants, etc. The last thing God did for Adam was to give him a wife after he established himself in the Garden of Eden. Notice, when Eve was brought to Adam, she didn't have to work to eat or to put a roof over Adam's head. Adam was prepared to provide for all of Eve's needs.

Eve was to be Adam's helpmate. Contrary to popular belief, a helpmate has absolutely nothing to do with Eve washing, cooking, and cleaning. That is the first thing people think of when they hear the word helpmate. Many believe that a helpmate is to help her husband pay bills, wash, cook, and clean. But if you think about Adam, he was eating and sweeping the garden before Eve came along. Many men desire a helpmate but have no idea what the purpose of one is. I will write more extensively about being a "helpmate" in an upcoming book for singles.

And in all my favorite love stories in the Bible, Ruth, and Boaz, Rachel and Jacob, Rebecca and Isaac, and Esther and the King, not one of those women washed, cooked or cleaned for the men to marry them. I followed the examples of these ladies when I was dating. I never washed, cooked, or cleaned for my now husband, yet in less than a year, he got down on one knee and asked me to marry him. He proposed in October and wanted to get married that December. I said no to getting married in December, but we got married six months later. So being a helpmate must not be about helping him wash, cook, and clean.

At the same time, I know many women who shacked up with men and washed, cooked, cleaned, and sexed them until thy kingdom come oh Lord and the men still didn't marry them. Many times, these men will leave these women and marry women who can't even boil water. And this is how you know you think it's about "doing." You will say, "She can't even cook or sex him the way I can." More to come about this soon.

Princesses, please note that there's a difference between a job and a career. I used the word "job" because it got the message across clearer. But he needs to have a career, not hopping from job to job having a different one every six months. Be sure to ask his longevity on the job and where does he see himself five years down the road. My husband has been in a marketing career since he was in his 20s. He is known in the marketing field. Can I tell you how safe and secure that makes me feel?

Negotiables

Let's talk a little about my negotiables. Princesses, there are no 10s. Marriage takes both the husband and wife working at it for it to work. This is why you should not marry someone who you don't have things in common with. Do not marry a man you need to change to make you happy. If you can't love him the way he is with his faults and all, it's best to just walk away. You're not perfect, and the men you date won't be either. The man you marry will not be a perfect man, but he should be perfect for you.

Therefore, it's vital to have some negotiables as you date. Therefore those ten things, both non-negotiables, and negotiables are essential. Your negotiables are things that can go either way. You must weigh them to see if the negotiables will work for you. Again, honesty is essential here because the husband you choose will determine the rest of your life. Also, please don't be afraid to walk away if you realize that this situation will not work out in your favor. If he is a pig while you're dating and engaged, be assured that he will be a bigger pig when you're married.

Now, someone might say, "Wow, she didn't say anything about him being kind, thoughtful" and so on. Remember earlier that I said each of my desires is a branch with fruit? Well, a man who is born again has specific characteristics. That's why it's crucial to have your list and check it once, twice, and a third time, and again. If you don't understand the responsibilities of a husband, how can you choose wisely? If you don't know the characteristics of a believer, how will you be able to check his fruits? I can't tell you the number of wives who have said they regretted marrying their husbands!

1. A Man with Children

One of my negotiables for a husband was a man without children. As mentioned earlier, I was a teen mom, so when it came to the man, I would choose, my preference was for one who didn't have any children and was not married. However, if I met a great guy who was a good father, took care of his kids, and fit my other requirements, I could marry him.

However, I had a limit on the number of children he could have. I wouldn't marry a man with a lot of children because I would probably end up having to take care of them. For example, there was a father of five who was divorced, who asked my spiritual father about me; I refused to even meet him. Why? He was looking for a mother for his children since he had full custody and was in the military, which meant he was away from home often.

I am a believer in the statement, "To thine own self be true." I don't like too many people in my house. Plus, I already had a child with special needs. Additionally, I wanted to have about two more children. So, let's add that up. His five, plus my one, plus I wanted another two, then him, and myself. That is ten people I would have to take care of! Can you say, "No way!" Additionally, I didn't know if any of his children had special needs. I was never interested in a man who had a lot of kids.

Now, some women have the grace to take care of many children. I am not one of those women, and I know that about myself. I think many women aren't honest about what they can deal with. Someone might say, "Oh, just go ahead and marry him with his five children and trust God to see you through."

Seriously? While we need to trust the Lord daily for our marriage, trusting God to see you through a situation is like being in a wilderness. You know that you will receive eventually, but your marriage is not meant to be like a wilderness that you need to trust

God to see you through because you bit off more than you can chew.

Another question you need to ask yourself is: Do you want to? A desire to serve is a must. Marriage is a ministry. For me, no, I don't want to take care of 5 additional children. I don't want to deal with all the responsibility that those children come with. Currently, my baby is three years old, and, he brings me such joy. Oh, I love it when I clean up his playroom, and he is shocked to see it. But then he gets all his toys and pours them all out in the middle of the room. I can enjoy him and sleep late with him. We can cuddle up on the couch and watch cartoons. I can enjoy him because it's just him. My oldest is 24 and is in a world all by herself.

My hope in sharing this with women is that we will begin to be honest with ourselves. So, princesses, when you are dating to get married, it is essential, to be honest with yourselves. When choosing a mate, it's like making a cake. There are many ingredients in making it delicious. You can't go to the supermarket and buy flour, mix it with water, and say that's a cake. LOL!

Accordingly, in your period of dating, think of the men you date in this way: He is tall and good-looking, but what else? Is he saved? Does he love the Lord? What does he think of being celibate? And ladies, wisdom will tell you, you shouldn't question guys like you're a drill sergeant. Pay attention to his mannerisms. Is he kind to the waiter while you're out having dinner and so on? Remember, actions speak louder than words. I stopped dating a guy because he was mean at the waiter and threw the tip at him. How rude and disrespectful!

Sometimes, it takes time to get essential data. You don't have to ask your ten questions on the first day you meet a man. As mentioned earlier, I got so good at collecting data that I could tell from talking to a guy for a few minutes whether I wanted to see him again. That's how it was with my husband. When I met him, I knew I wanted to talk to him again outside of the event.

Princesses, by spending time in prayer, reading your Bibles, books like this, praying in the Holy Ghost, asking God to open your eyes and ears, you will be able to see beyond the surface stuff. Don't fall for the one ingredient that attracts you to a potential prospect. Allow him to talk so that you can go beyond the surface presentation. Pay attention to what he says but pay closer attention to his actions. How saved can he be if he is trying to get you into his bed? He says he is a gentleman, but does he have gentlemanly qualities?

2. A Man's Physique/Health

Church folks are so full of crap that it makes my stomach turn. They will tell you, "Oh, the outside doesn't matter; it's the inside that does." In the meantime, many of these men who teach have wives who look like Barbie and wouldn't dare marry an obese woman. A person's physical appearance is critical to who they are. The Bible talks about taking care of our bodies because we are the temple of the Lord. So are we to overlook the physical while dating to get married? No! And the truth is, what's on the inside always manifests itself on the outside.

As a young girl, I ran track, so I prefer athletic men. But this was a negotiable for me. I was open. He didn't have to be an athlete but must be conscious of his health and do some form of exercise. I would NEVER marry an obese man! I think our health is like our faith; it's a personal decision. And I don't want to have to force a man to eat healthily or exercise. Some might say, "You can marry him and get him to change his diet, eat, and exercise and so on."

Question: What if you marry him and he doesn't want to change? Then what? That's going to breed resentment, frustration, anger, and it will bring up a lot of issues in your marriage, all because you had unrealistic expectations. Also princesses, never try to change a man! Instead, marry the man in front of you. If you need to change the man in front of you to become someone you want him to be, then he is not the man for you.

Don't be fooled, ladies; a man will only change if he wants to. You cannot force him to do what you want him to do. That's why a husband is a choice. Marry a man you have common ground with, so you can work together. I am working on a book about women and wives trying to change their men to do what they want. Trying to usurp someone else's will with yours is witchcraft. You can read more in my upcoming book. The only people God has given you the power to impose your will over are your children because you are to train them in the ways of the Lord.

Okay, ladies, that is all I will share for now on my non-negotiables and negotiables. I once shared my whole list, and someone copied it to the "T," so I don't share my entire list anymore. Lol! Just enough for you to understand what I mean.

Three Guys, I Met Online

While Facebook, Twitter, Instagram, Snap Chat, and so on are new, there have always been ways to meet people online. I know a few couples who met online in AOL chat groups and online dating groups. I have met a few guys online who I dated and gathered data on. Let me tell you a little about how I got data on them without going out with them. Princesses, please remember that dating means to gather data. You can date aka gather data on guys without going out with them. This will save you lots of wasted time.

Guy #1: Let's call him Mark. Mark lived in my state but a few hours away. I often exchanged info with guys who lived in my state, since I wasn't going to move. He seemed sweet. We talked on the phone; he was a Christian, single, never been married, no kids, and worked in the sports field.

Yes, he was tall and athletic, but from what I could gather, he was cheap. He didn't want to make the 2-3-hour drive to come and take me out. So after a few months of going back and forth, it dried up on its own. I moved on and stopped accepting his calls.

Guy #2: We'll call him Paul. Paul was a brother in a local church, and we knew some of the same people. We connected on FB; he inboxed me and started up a conversation. Knowing which church, he attended gave me some comfort. We talked a few days on the phone consistently. One day, Paul didn't call, and I wasn't gonna call him. Next day, he didn't call, and neither did I. Lol!

Eventually, he called and asked why he hadn't heard from me in a few days. I asked the same thing and gave the excuse that I was busy studying. He asked, "So if I don't call you, you're not gonna call me?" I asked him the same question, and he said, "Well, it doesn't mean that I should be the only one calling you." I looked at the phone like, "Bro, I just met you." He wanted someone to pursue him, and I wasn't going to do that. We talked another time, but that was that. He got married a few years later and is now divorced. We are still friends on Facebook. Lol!

Guy #3: I'll call him Mr. Crush. Did I have a crush on him? Oh no honey, I was too old for crushes. Lol! He had a crush on me and referred to me as his "CRUSH!" Oh, I really, really, liked this guy. I just knew there would be something between us. However, I was careful to keep my emotions in check and leaned all the way back. HINT, HINT: Did you catch that? "*I just knew there was going to be something between us?*" Here it is princesses. Meeting a guy, knowing nothing or enough about him, but putting our marital hopes and dreams in their flimsy, full-of-holes basket. Beware!

I met Mr. Crush on Facebook via another friend. He was a born-again Christian, funny, and charismatic. He was 6'5", and y'all know I love a tall man. He was never married, no kids, came from a good family and worked in finance. Finance is one of my favorite topics, so I was happy with the connection. And I often said there must be a saved, black man on Wall Street who was looking for a wife.

Mr. Crush often liked my comments on our mutual friend's posts. Eventually, he sent me a friend request, and I accepted. He continued to like my comments and talk on our mutual friend's posts. One day, I posted a funny picture of me with bulging eyes, and he loved it! He jumped in my inbox and said how much he loved the funny pic and that a lot of women wouldn't have posted a picture of themselves like that.

We talked via inbox for a few months in a platonic form, just getting to know each other. Then he asked for my number. We talked a few times, and he said he wanted to take me out. "Great," I said. Only one problem: He lives in New York, and I lived in New Jersey. He claimed he didn't know New Jersey and that I should come to New York. My response was, "Well, I don't know New York either, but it's only two trains from where you live to me, and I could meet you in downtown Newark." I wanted to meet him there mainly because we would have to go back downtown anyway for dinner, plus I didn't want strangers knowing where I lived. His excuse was still that he didn't know New Jersey, and my response was I still didn't know New York.

There were times he would call me, text me, or inbox me that he was at a restaurant or event and for me to meet him there. My answer was always, "Nope." My thinking was if he is a man who is interested in me, but he doesn't want to get on one or two trains to come and take me out? But he expected me to figure out how to get to Manhattan to meet him? Not! Additionally, I did not accept the same day or the next day dates, so that was an absolute no, no.

Lol! So, I guess he realized that after a while of this back and forth, I wasn't going to go to New York to meet him. Then we were in this Christian Singles Group, and he became infatuated with the founder. But there were a few other guys who were also interested in her. She posted something about wanting to go motorcycle riding in the desert of California.

Mr. Crush posted a motorcycle and a basket with wine and cheese and commented that he could be on the next plane to California tomorrow. So there I was thinking, "Wait for a second, he couldn't get on two trains to come to Jersey, but he was ready to jump on a plane and purchase a motorcycle to go on a date with our fellow sister all the way across the country? Hmm? Okay.

Mr. Crush thought she would be impressed, but she shot him down, along with the other guys who "were shooting their shot." He continued to shoot until she plainly stated that she wasn't interested in him or any of the guys in the group. LOL! Next thing I know, he posted a picture of another girl who came from across the country to go on a date with him. In no time, he packed up and moved to the middle of nowhere to be near this woman. That was a bit shocking because he swore up and down that he would never leave New York since he loved it so much.

Soon he posted that they were getting married. Then they broke up, made up, broke up, made up, and got engaged. Then they broke up, and he returned the ring. Then about a year later, they made up. He bought another ring, got engaged, got married, and in about two or three months, they broke up and got a divorce.

In the meantime, I was dating, courting, engaged, married, and building my beautiful family. Recently, right before I wrote this book, the mutual friend of ours, both of whom I had unfriended, messaged me. She stated that he said he messed up with me and how he should have married me. "Oh, well, guess it wasn't God's will!" LOL!

You see ladies; I believe if a man wants you, he will climb mountains, swim across the ocean, take ten trains and six planes to see you. Mr. Crush didn't want me. If he did, he would have gotten on the two trains for a half-hour ride to come across the bridge to see me. He could have even taken a cab.

The truth is, he didn't want me! He was willing to fly to California to see the other girl. He moved across the country to the middle of nowhere to be with another girl because he wanted her. He didn't want me! And that's what you must accept when men don't want to put forth the effort. He might have wanted my body, but he didn't want me. And that's why, ladies, you must sit back and allow a man to pursue you to show you that he wants you. Let's look at the pros and cons of Mr. Crush, and I will show you how many of us mess up with men.

Pros: He was born again, never married or have any children, wanted to get married and have kids, tall, dark, handsome, established with a great job, spoke well and was well versed in several topics.

Cons: I liked him, hoped that there would be something between us, shaky on tithing, didn't want to move from New York. Most importantly, HE DID NOT PUT IN THE WORK TO HAVE ME.

I know many women who would have gone to New York to see him, meet up with him every time he was out, and wanted company. Princesses set your standards and stick to them. My father said for me to allow a man to pursue me because even in marriage, he needs to continue to pursue me. But it's a two-way street, ladies. Not only does my husband need to continue to pursue me during the marriage, but I need to keep him chasing after me. In short, I don't know about you, princesses, but I refuse to pursue any man!

Additionally, Mr. Crush didn't know that four other guys flew across the country to come and see me because they thought I was worth the trip. Of course, there wasn't any love connection, mainly because of me and I didn't want to move. But at least they came to see about me. And they were well off guys. The last one was an engineer who had purchased his first home cash as per him. Another was in the military, and another was a divorced father of two, businessman. And I don't remember with the other guy did. All were Christian men who were looking for a wife.

On the other hand, Mr. Crush was only about 15 minutes away, two trains for less than $5 or a taxi ride for $25 but he didn't come and see me. But instead, he wanted me to go and see about him and pursue him? No Bueno!!

Stop Being a 'Pick Me' So That He Can Pursue You

Princesses, please stop running men down and allow the ones who want you to pursue you. Stop calling, texting, messaging them, and let them call you. Lean back so that you can see if he wants to do the work to have you. You are the prize, the gift, and he needs to put in the work and run you down! But some of us are so desperate that we feel the need to prove that we are wife material. We feel like if we don't compete, he won't choose us. There's a new word for that on social media called "Pick Me." Stop being a "pick me," ladies.

When I think about a man pursuing me, I think about the scripture in **Deuteronomy 28:2**, that says, **"...the blessings of the Lord will overtake me."** That's what you want, ladies. For the blessed and prepared man to pursue and overtake you so that he can profess his love, provide for, and protect you. Remember also the Psalm 23 Shepard.

Unfortunately, many women have become the pursuer and the aggressor. Many women have become like men; as a result, some men have become like women. You are pursuing him, washing, cooking, cleaning, sexing him, moving him into your home, taking care of him, working two or three jobs, while he sleeps until midday and plays video games the rest of the day. You come home from working several jobs, wash, clean, cook, bring him his plate, sex him, and do it all over again. And then you want to cry that he doesn't want to work or help you around the house. Why should he? You're doing it all! You were so desperate to have a man that you are making yourself a man!

I want to scream every time a WIFE asks for prayer because she doesn't know how they're gonna pay rent, 'cause she was sick and couldn't work. In the meantime, she's got a grown-behind man in the house. No, ma'am! Ladies, my husband has never asked me how we are gonna pay the mortgage or eat. Do you know why he's never gonna ask me that? I didn't marry that type of man. I married a man who was a "prepared husband." A man who understands that it is his responsibility to provide for his family. I married a Psalm 23 Husband, and he plans and makes sure that all of our needs are met.

Someone asked, "What if he loses his job?" Question: Did you ask him that while you were dating and gathering data on him? Did he convince you to trust him with your life? When a man has already lost his job, that is not the time to ask, "What we goin' do?" Where are your emergency funds, savings, and so on? Did you marry a marketable man? As women, we need to make better choices in husbands. Ask the question, "If you lose your job, how soon can you get another one?" Now you need to judge his answer based on who he is as a man.

Remember, count the cost before you build ladies! Marry a man who can walk into any place of business and walk out with a job! Furthermore, remember that death and life are in the power of your tongue. Rise early and pray for your husband. Declare the word of the Lord over your husband and your family and finances. Speak favor and the blessings of the Lord over your husband.

A few years after we were in our home, our boiler broke in the middle of a snowstorm. My husband called the plumber, and he said there was a leak and it would be a waste to fix, so we needed to replace it. My husband then called PSEG, who came out and checked it, and they said the same thing. Right there and then my husband signed the paper for us to get a new boiler and told us to pack our things because we were going to a hotel until it was fixed.

Usually, it would take about two days to replace a boiler, but because of the storm, it took almost a week. Princesses, that's what Psalms 23 Husbands do. They plan, and if there's an issue, they fix it. A prepared husband, don't turn to the wife and ask, "What we goin' do?" A Prepared Husband was created to solve every problem his wife and family have that God created him to address.

When stuff hit the fan, a prepared husband doesn't freak out. A husband is to take control of every situation, fix issues, and make sure his wife and children are comfortable. When stuff happens, a wife needs to be able to rest in her husband's ability to calm the seas. It breaks my heart when I read a wife post on social media that she doesn't know what they are going to do about a situation! Ma'am, your husband, should be telling you the answer, not you are asking others for prayers because you have a male child as a husband.

Get up, Get Out and About, and Date Up

Princesses, even though this book is entitled *23 Types of Guys You Might Meet on Social Media*, you can meet these same guys in your community. You can meet at the supermarket, a diner, a museum, community events, or church. The whole idea is to get up, get out and about, and date up. You can't say you want to meet someone, but you stay in the house 24/7 or don't change your routine. That is called insanity: doing the same thing while expecting a different result.

If you are a woman waiting in expectation, then you need to expect to meet your Boaz. Any of these guys could be a good guy. However, it goes back to intent. Don't get with a guy because he passes just one of your requirements. If you desire a husband, then don't waste time with the guy who told you he doesn't want to get married. See, we think we can convince him to change his mind and marry us. But as women, we need to stop thinking that. If he wants to marry you, he will. You won't have to do any convincing because you are what he wants.

As I was finalizing this book, I was talking to a dear sister who has been dating a guy for two years and has reached her breaking point. She said she is trying to give him more time to get himself together. He is in his forties and hadn't kept a stable job since they met. More time? For what? For him to waste your time? This man is not a prepared husband. See, our issue is, we meet a guy and try to turn him into a husband. In the meantime, other men are husbands and want to pursue us, but we are tied up, tangled up, and shacked up with a fool. No ma'am, if you meet a man and he is not prepared to be a husband, NEXT! Move on!

Therefore, ladies, it's important not to get emotionally entangled with these men who you know are not husbands. It makes it that much harder to walk away and move on. They pull on your heartstrings, and suddenly you're marrying them because you feel sorry for them. How could you marry a man you feel sorry for? A man you must profess your love for, provide for, and protect? Boy, bye!

Princesses, if you have been waiting for Jesus to send your husband to the church to sit next to you or to ring your doorbell, it's time for you to make a change. I had turned 34 and realized that I hadn't met my husband or even a prospect. I heard the Lord spoke to me while I was lying on my futon. He said, "Get Up and Get Out!!" Honey, I jumped up, looked up for any events in my area, found the First Friday Event, got ready, invited a few girlfriends and I went and boom! Met my husband! So, I'm saying the same thing that the Lord spoke to me! Get up and get out dolls. Your husband awaits you! And guess what? The Lord sat him right next to me!

Why You Must Reposition Yourself to Be Found

O nce I was married to my husband, I realized that the type of man I liked was not attending the churches I attended or associated with. For years I was waiting for God to send my husband to my church. In my father's little church with a handful of the same people, there were no men who I would even go out with. When I attended other churches like my family church, it was the same thing. My husband attended a Baptist Church, and we didn't associate with Baptist Churches. Thankfully, I went to that event and met my husband.

Proverbs 27:17 states *As* **iron sharpens iron, So a man sharpens the countenance of his friend.** Men like my husband didn't attend my little church with a handful of the same folks. My husband's pastor is a lawyer, and his frat brother also. I realized after I got married that the type of men that I liked, associated with men who are like them. No wonder all those years they never came walking into my little churches! I realized that to be found by the type of man that I wanted; I needed to reposition myself and put myself in the environment that those types of men were. Can I tell you that in all my life in the church, my husband's church is the first church that I have attended that the men seem to equal the number of women in attendance?

My dear princesses, if you have been sitting in your church for forty years, waiting for God to send your husband, perhaps God is waiting on you to reposition yourself so that you can be found by your Boaz.

How Are You Perfecting Yourself?

*B*eing a pretty face is not enough to keep a Prepared Man interested. Men of substance are looking for women who have more than a pretty face and a nice body. There's more than Botox, fillers, extensions, a chiseled nose, and butt fillers. Cultivating and nurturing is vital. Read the stories of Rachel, Rebecca, Ruth, and Esther again. They were more than pretty! To this day, my husband tells me all the time how he was attracted to me because he thought I was smart for networking my book.

Yes, he thought I was pretty and sexy, but it was more than pretty he says. Think about it princesses, how many said you were beautiful and took your cookie and left you? Moreover, he loved how much I talked about my daughter and my motherly instinct. Presently he compliments me almost daily on what a great mom I am to our children and how I sacrifice for them. Men want more than a pretty face and cute waistline. Now, men who want to screw you might only care about your pretty face and nice waistline. However, a man who is looking for his helpmate who will help to fulfill God's will and vision for his life is looking for a woman of his heart's desire.

Recently, I was talking to my husband about what took him so long to get married. Remembering that I'm a writer, so I speak to him a lot about what I write. He said he has never met a woman that he wanted to do all that he is doing for me, for. He continued that when he was looking for a wife, he was not looking for an Instagram model.

Additionally, he stated that he loved smart women. Ironically, he has always told me that he thought I was brilliant because I was marketing my first book at the networking event. Furthermore, he stated that the woman he desired didn't have to be like Condoleezza Rice, but she had to be like Michelle Obama. Then he said that I'm like Janet Jackson and Mary Poppin all mixed up in one!

My princess sisters, can I tell you I was shocked? That made so much sense to me for what men look for in their wives. You must be what he is looking for. If you are not who he's looking for, there' nothing you can do to be her. Remember, many men might sleep with you if you give up the cookie, but that doesn't mean they will marry you.

Men are calculated about what they want. At the same time, it's essential to maintain a virtuous woman's persona. Do you have a spirit of gracefulness, servitude, and compassion? Prepared men of substance don't need you for your money or 50/50. That's why men who have prepared themselves to be husbands never ask you want you bring to the table because they provide the table, all the food on it, and will turn around and serve you on a silver platter. They want a WOW-MAN. They are looking for their missing rib!

You need to be well informed, equipped, empowered, and mysterious to keep a Prepared Man interested. He will eventually get tired of looking at your pretty face and waistline. Talking about how you're gonna lick him up and down gets boring after a while. Prepared Men want your opinion on a subject matter or current events. And for God sakes, please turn off the rachet housewives and watch the political news occasionally. Can you hold your own on the topics he talks about?

Think of some ways to perfect yourself, your skills, and presentation. Have you thought about taking any etiquette courses? You will seem unattractive to a prepared man because you don't know how to act. My spiritual father always told me that I was a little rough around the edges. It finally hit me when I realized that that's why I lost my college sweetheart. I was harsh and yelled at him. So, I got around ladies who were soft and graceful and who could teach me how to be a lady.

Sure, I was young, but I've been on my own since 16 and lived with my father since I was 12. I had a lot of learning how to be a lady and how to be soft and graceful. No, I am not saying something is wrong with you. I am only asking and suggesting that you might want to polish up a bit. And please don't get offended. We are so quick to get offended verses saying, "you know, I could tighten up a bit." Just remember Esther was bathed in milk a whole year before she met the king. Lol!

Can you take a Toastmaster International course to improve on your public speaking skills? This will help during networking events. I've also heard of women going to finishing school. Perhaps take a cooking class; this is something I've always wanted to do. Are there any local history groups to improve your knowledge of it? If you are interested in art, how about taking a painting class? How about a flower class? You could take a photograph or sculpture class.

Another skill I want to acquire is to learn a new language. It's one of my goals for 2019. Think about enrolling in a wine tasting and appreciation course. I did not say to get drunk! When you go to those upscale restaurants, you need to learn how to hold a glass and protocol and so on. And don't forget to continue to read as much as you can. Volunteering is always a great idea. And what about dancing? How about burlesque or ballet? These will help you to be more graceful. What about learning to play an instrument? I have always wanted to learn to play the piano.

Also, I have always wanted to learn to play golf and chess and learn how to use a sewing machine. I used to sew back home in Jamaica in school. I would also like to learn sign language. One thing I keep perfecting over the years is my writing. I've also wanted to take a course in interior design. Investing, too, is another one of my passions. Blogging is another one of my interests, and I have started that in the last few years. You can read more at www.janicehyltonblog.com. Do you see how many interests I have? Do you think that would make a great discussion?

Brush up on your vocabulary; sharpen your knowledge, intelligence, and mind. Join a nonprofit to help broaden your network. I am a student of the Bible, so I had started a Bible study group while I was single, and it did very well. Listen to other types of music, go horseback riding, get involved in politics. So, my dear princesses, perhaps you haven't met your husband yet because you need to reposition yourself? Maybe you need to put yourself in the environment where the type of men that you like are. Remember, how can you perfect yourself?

What Are You Saying?

Princesses expect to meet your husband today! As I mentioned earlier, for years, I would say, "There must be at least one black, saved, single man on Wall Street who's looking for a wife." You see ladies; I wasn't interested in dating a broke, struggling man who needed to count pennies to pay the rent. I wanted a man who was a high earner and didn't need my income to make ends meet. Also, I have always said I wanted a husband who understood that he was a provider and loved providing for his wife and kids. Additionally, I wanted a husband where I worked because I wanted to, not because I had to work to help him pay the rent.

I mean if I'm believing God for my Boaz, he might as well be a Boaz in every definition of the word Boaz. Ruth and Naomie needed someone to protect and provide for them. Ruth was not about to get with one of the fellow guys in the field, picking up grains to save their lives. Ruth was not trying to marry a man who was in the same position she was in. Ruth wanted the owner of the field.

Once married, Ruth didn't have to worry about how they were going to eat or protected. Ruth didn't have to worry about her 50% because Boaz was a prepared man. Well, like Ruth, I wanted a Boaz who was a prepared man who provided, and I didn't have to worry about anything. Some have said Boaz died the night of the wedding.

But look at God. Ruth got pregnant that night if Boaz did die, everything went to Ruth and Obed. So be mindful of folks trying to rain on your parade. All that God did for Ruth and all they can say is "oh but Boaz died on the wedding night."

Do not allow people to make you feel bad because you don't want a struggling man living off pennies! Now, if you want a struggling man, then that's on you. But if you're like me, you want a man who can provide for you and your household, and you don't have to worry, stress, and be trembling in your stilettoes every month. If you don't want to hide from the landlord 'cause you ain't got the rent money, then say no to broke, struggling men who have not prepared themselves to provide for a family. Remember ladies; we want a Psalm 23 Husband. Not a build-a-male who needs your help to put a roof over your head.

Princesses, if you're reading this and you're married, and your husband is not able to provide adequately, PLEASE DO NOT NAG THAT MAN TO DEATH! The only thing you can do now is to pray that God will influence him and give him the vision to work so that it can manifest more income. Married ladies, this is NOT for you. This is for the single ladies who can choose their husbands.

Where to Meet High-Quality Men

One of the questions I get asked a lot is how and where to meet good, high-quality men. I still prefer meeting guys while I'm out and about rather than on social media. When I was ready for dating, after I worked on myself and was sure that I knew what I wanted in my Psalm 23 Prepared Husband, I began to make daily confessions. Also, I fixed myself up, dressed better, wore more dresses, skirts, and bright colors. I was more open and gracious and embraced my femininity. I wanted to attract a high quality, prepared man of God.

Contrary to what we were taught in the church, the church is not the only place to meet your Boaz. There are saved, prepared Psalm 23 men all over this world, looking for their wives. So, get out there and meet and date up. I used to confess before I left my house, "I will meet my husband today! Something good is going to happen to me today! A nice, rich saved man is gonna see me and ask me out on a date!"

When I met a man that didn't have a prosperous and positive financial future and roadmap, I would drop him. I don't do broke and struggling men period! And ladies, you can learn a lot about a man by allowing him to talk. One of the things I had to do as a single woman was to expand my network. Remember when the disciples were fishing all night, and they caught nothing? Jesus came to them and said cast your net on the other side. If your network only includes the same old folks at church, Hakeem down the street, Big P, up the road, and the same sharks on your job who's trying to get ya cookies, honey, you need to cast your net on the other side.

So, to meet high-quality men, find where those men attend events and place yourself in that environment. Remember, I met my husband at a networking event. I love businessmen, so that was the perfect place for me. The men who attended had a certain mindset. I even went to expensive restaurants and sat alone and ate. And I had guys come up and chat and ask to share a table with me. I have been to restaurants that had a bar and sat there and watched the game along with the guys. Great conversation, opportunity to meet guys, and fine-tune your knowledge. Saved men are not only in our churches with 20 members. God has his people all over and everywhere.

Our home is in a beautiful community, and I was amazed when I went to the supermarket that I attracted guys. I'm married now, but if I had thought about that when I was single, I would have shopped at the upper-class supermarkets. Recently, I woke up late and needed to drop the baby off and I had on my winish color robe, sunflower rain boots, some shades, and my hair was standing up. But honies, when I went to the supermarket, I was walking like I was on a runaway.

Three men approached me and complimented me, and two guys asked for my number. I was shocked! The second guy said, "You are beautiful, and your husband is a lucky man." Lol! I even took a pic and posted it on FB because I couldn't believe that I was attracting guys in my bathrobe. Lol! The guys said I was radiant, and there was just something about me that drew them to me. I do feel as if now that I'm married, I have become more gracious and confident. My husband tells me often how I am beautiful and gracious. So, ladies, he causes me to feel graciously beautiful and feminine from the inside out. He brings out the best in me! I'm so grateful!

Now princesses, please don't go out in your robe! Lol! But what that spoke to me was that I was gracefully beautiful and feminine from the inside out. Princesses dig deep down on the inside and let your inner princess come out. Keep your standards high and never settle. Remember that you are in Christ, and you are a new creation. You are walking in your royal anointing.

Another example was after about three months of dating; my husband invited a few of his frat brothers and other friends to an elegant black-tie affair to meet me. He had to get there before I did because remember, I had my daughter, and I had to get her settled. Plus, he was speaking at the event. I remember walking in the entrance, and he was standing with his frat brothers all lined up. I was staring at him, thinking, "Does he see me?" I gave him that little sexy smile and that finger wave that we do. Lol.

At the same time, a few of the brothers were looking at me and nodded to each other smiling and then shook his hand. He smiled and walked over and greeted me and whispered to me how beautiful and different I looked. Lol! Oh, honey, I clean up very well. Lol! He happily introduced to me to his frat brothers and guess what princesses? It was that night he told me that he loved me. Lol! He also has said to me that he knew about two months for sure that he would marry me. That means he was thinking about it. I knew about two months in too that I wanted to marry him.

There's an upper-class city a few cites over that I love, love, love! It's like a version of New York, and often I would have lunch in one of the cute restaurants. When I went for my massage, that's where I would go. When I had to take my daughter to the dermatologist, I choose a doctor in that community. Plus, that's where I would like for us to purchase our dream home and for our kids to attend schools, once they are finished with elementary school. And princesses, hubby has already agreed that we can move there, once we get our babies through the early years of school. Yah!

Also, search the events in and around your community. Try neighboring cities and see what events they have. I was a bit limited to what I could do because I was a single mom, and it was just my baby girl and me, so I couldn't go far and for too long. You can try conference centers, clubs, golf clubs, art galleries, wine tasting, performing arts centers, Broadway plays or plays in your community. As an author, I have met a ton of guys at book signings and bookstores. And you know I love men who read!

Go to bookstores that have cafés and sit and read. Be poised, sit tall, smile, wear bright feminine colors. There are fewer brick and mortar bookstores today, but find a few where you can relax, read and have coffee. Some men like my husband love to read and visit bookstores often. Sure, many people read books on tablets today, but you never know. Remember, the idea is to live and enjoy your life. If you are enjoying living your life, it will radiate through you, and you might meet your Boaz.

What about luxury hotel restaurants, not only when they have events but in general and read a book or work on your tablet or laptop. You might not want to go in the evening because you don't want to be mistaken as a working girl, so go in the day. I have done this. A very luxury hotel in my city has an escalator that gives a view of the whole downstairs. Dress up pretty, be chick, smile, and be gracious and friendly.

Find all the best restaurants and see if they are hosting any events. Look pretty, polished, and classy. Be polite and let your beauty and femininity come through you. Remember, I met my husband at a networking event that was hosted by a restaurant that turned into a lounge on Friday nights. I invited two church sisters, but they were too deep, and almost ten years later, they are still single. Don't be deep! Also, there's an upscale restaurant in New York that I had planned to attend an event a few months later. I didn't go to the event, but I asked my husband about it, and he was aware of the restaurant and said he would take me there.

Do you have any upper-class female friends? Do you like yoga? Many upper-class women go to yoga in their community. If you like yoga, then go to yoga in an upper-class community and make friends. They might be able to introduce you to friends of theirs who could be potential husbands. Instead of going to the broke-down gym around the corner, invest in a good gym membership where high-quality men work out.

Side note: my husband just brought me my coffee, and I asked him, "If a single woman wanted to meet a man like you, where would you tell her to go?" He said, "Cultural events, fraternity events where they are feeding the homeless and doing community events. Toy drives, film festivals, professional networking events."

No, you are not just going to possibly meet someone. This is about living and enjoying your life, and in doing so, you strategically place yourself to meet a possible prospect. High-quality men can see through you if you're faking. Therefore, find what you love and enjoy and participate. Get up and get out of your house, your job, and your church with the 20 members.

Do you like operas? Are there any art exhibitions at your local museum? When was the last time you went to a Broadway play? My husband went on to say, "Find organizations that host annual events and attend. If you want to meet an accountant, then go to the Black Accountants Conference. If you want to meet someone with an MBA, then attend the Black MBA conference." Of course, this doesn't mean to only go to black events.

If you begin to build your network, you will strategically place yourself in the right places. Also, you will align yourself with people who have common interests. Always be sweet as pie, gracious, and feminine, carry yourself like a Princess, and you will have no problem meeting high caliber men who want to date and marry you. Remember that guys love and adore rarity, so be rare and different. And please princesses, please do not sleep with any of these men. My father has always said some guys might sleep with fast and loose women, but they most likely won't take them home to meet their mothers or wife them. See, they will lay with you, fill your head up of sweet promises of lies and get up and marry the girl that won't give it up. Remember that, please!

Recently my husband and I were invited to dinner at a friend of his home. I was shocked at the caliber of single men who were there. As a single woman, I was never invited to any of those events. Why? None of those people were in my network. My husband has opened a whole other world for me that I didn't know existed as a single mom, sitting in my little church with 20 folks praying for God to send my husband. The cookouts I was invited to had the same old broke guys with empty promises, still living in their momma's basement looking for a woman to take care of them. Lol. Princesses, all of this takes self-improvement and stepping out of your comfort zone. Remember to cast your net on the other side. If what you've been doing has not yielded the results you seek, then it's time for a change. In the meantime, you need to become a wisdom magnet. Improve your knowledge of current events and politics. Read various books, get a little knowledge of sports. Honey, when you meet these high caliber guys, you need to be able to hold a conversation. But if you don't know anything, then what exactly will you talk about?

That was one thing my husband loved about me. Whichever topic came up, I could hold my own. And we both love politics, history, and reading so honey; we had a lot to talk about. I even had the guys at my job teach me about sports and all of that, so if I met a guy who was into sports, I could have a conversation with him if the topic came up. However, princesses, please don't try to outshine any man you're dating. Give your two cents when necessary but never take over a conversation and act as if you know more than he does. Even today, when I ask my husband's opinion on something, I shut my pretty li'l lips and allow him to talk.

Princesses, I was very limited in time, place, and finances because it was just me and my baby girl. But I found events that were free or affordable. A friend brought me to a lovely boutique in an upper-class neighborhood where I bought gorgeous and feminine dresses. I had about three other stores that I shopped when there was a sale and bought beautiful dresses. And I always shopped clearance. I knew when the stores had sales, and that's when I shopped.

When I was in community college, I remember there was this lovely pair of shoes I wanted. Oh, they were so pretty, but I could not afford them. Would you believe I prayed over those shoes and commanded the price to go down? I went and checked those shoes every week until I could afford them. I still have those shoes, some twenty years later, and they are still my favorite pair. Something comes over me when I wear those shoes. I feel sexy and free, and I feel like I'm walking on a runway. Get stuff that makes you feel good.

Sweeties, if you want to attract a high-quality man, then you must be attractive. Remember that men must be attracted to us. Often I would fix my hair up, get my nails done, put on some cute stilettos or sandals, and make myself available to be found. And guess what? It paid off because he found me and I'm living my best life.

Wishing you, Grace! Again, ladies, this is not for every single woman. Cause I can hear someone is saying, "Chile if that's what I have to do to meet a man, that's too much." Finally, remember, if you're not having fun doing this, then please stop. You can't fake being happy and having fun. It will radiate through you like rotten cabbage. Lol!

The idea is to find your passion and work it! I met my husband because I was passionate about my gift of writing. But I also love to dress up, go out, and have a good time.

How Bad Do You Want A King/Husband?

As I was getting ready to go out and about this morning, the Lord reminded me of the stories of Saul and David. I was wondering how some women say they want a man, and the only requirement is that he has a penis. They don't care if he works, has ten kids, a deadbeat, looking for a woman to take care of him, or anything. They only care that he is a "male."

The Bible said the people of Israel went to the Prophet Samuel and told him they wanted a king like the other countries around them. They wanted a king they could see and insisted that Samuel get them one. Finally, the Lord gave them Saul. But God rejected Saul because he didn't obey the Lord and broke Samuel's heart. But most importantly, King Saul did not have a heart for the things of God.

While Samuel was grieving King Saul, God asked him why he was mourning. Because you see, God had already chosen a new King from the sons of Jesse, a man after His own heart. So you see, ladies, your husband can't just be any man. He must be a man after God's own heart, a man that's called to be a husband. Your husband must be a man who has the anointing to be your king, not just any male who comes in your life, declaring that he is your king.

Do You Know That Men Are Hunters?

It is essential to know that all men were created by God to hunt; therefore, all men are hunters. Are most men looking for wives?

Not sure about that. However, I do believe that all men are hunting for something. Be it sex, a wife, money, a nurse or a purse, a baby momma, or somewhere to live. All men are hunting for something. They are looking for someone to wash, cook, clean, sex them, take care of their kids, and stroke their egos.

But, praise the Lord, some good men have prepared themselves and are looking for wives. Men like The Psalm 23 Husband! Good and prepared men who want to profess their love to you, provide for and protect you, and yes ladies, adore you. Choosing a husband is like an algebra equation, and all mathematical concepts must be used to bring you to your final answer.

Not all men have prepared themselves to be husbands. Additionally, not all men are looking for wives who they can profess their love to, provide for, and protect. Likewise, some men are looking for women who can take care of them and provide for them. Here's a thought. Some men are looking for women to take care of them because they are women! Those are the men who seek out extraordinarily aggressive and independent attitude women. Since they want to act like men and take on masculine roles, it's only fair they attract feminine males.

On the other hand, some men are looking for women to use and abuse. Also, some men are looking for women with kids to victimize because they are predators looking for prey. One of my favorite verses about hunters is **Psalm 10:9: "Like lions crouched in hiding, they wait to pounce on the helpless. Like hunters, they capture the helpless and drag them away in nets."**

Please understand that I am not saying all men are like this, which is why I preface with "some." Not all men want to protect, profess, and provide for us. Consequently, ladies, it is your responsibility to familiarize yourselves with various types of hunters by arming yourselves with the necessary tools, such as being prayerful, vigilant, alert, and on guard. Additionally, this book is a great tool to help you familiarize yourself with various men.

Terms such as being gullible, desperate, thirsty, and naïve have been used to describe us as we wait to be found because we project gullibility and desperation. Let us cast off those terms as Apostle Paul encouraged the believers to "cast off" every weight and sin that so easily beset us. Instead, let us clothe ourselves with wisdom, grace, femininity, godliness, and most of all, be wise as serpents and harmless as doves.

How to Be Wisely Vulnerable

As women, we are encouraged to be vulnerable. And I agree to some extent. However, it is foolish to meet a man and be utterly vulnerable to him. For some, women being vulnerable means that they should open up the tabernacle and let him all up in the holy of holies. Give him your purse with all your information, and while you're at it, give him your social security number and access to your bank accounts. Oh, and of course, let him move in with you and your kids! But wait for a second, ladies! You don't know him! You don't know what his intentions and motives are. So you need to find out who this man is before you can be "vulnerable" with him.

Remember, when we were children, our parents taught us "stranger danger." The same applies to adults. You can't trust a stranger with your heart and life. How do you know you can trust this man, and how do you know he wants to protect you vs. be a predator? How do you know this man sees you as his wife vs. his prey? Therefore it baffles me when women go to a guy's house for Netflix and chill on the first date? ARE YOU KIDDING ME?

Don't rush it, ladies. Take your time to get the data you need. It takes time to build trust, vulnerability, and respect. I know so many women who meet men and automatically get into a "situationship" with them without having the data. Next thing you know, three months later, they begin to post negative messages about these men. Think of the parable about the foolish man who builds his house upon the sand. But the wise man builds his house upon a rock, **Matthew 7:24-27.** If you want a good foundation, it takes time!

Why? Because it takes time to get to know a person and gather the data, you need to make an informed decision. If you continue to do the same dumb stuff, you have yet to learn. And until you learn, you will continue to waste time and effort because you fail to sit your hips down and become wise! Discipline yourself to stop the insanity of doing the same foolish things while expecting a different result.

Please, please princesses, I am not saying for you to be like Zena the Warrior Princess. However, the Bible talks about guarding your heart, eyes, and ears. That means for you to protect what goes in through your eyes and ears. Why? Out of your heart flow the issues of life, according to **Proverbs 4:23.** I believe in being 100% vulnerable to the man who has been through the process to profess his love, provide for you, and protect you. Have some emotional and self-control.

Proverbs 25:28 states that **a person who doesn't have control over their own spirit is like a city broken down and without walls.** That means anything and anyone can walk in and out because there are no boundaries, standards, or self-control. Yes, be open to meeting, talking to, and getting to know guys. Share information carefully and wisely. But you don't need to be on the phone all night telling some strange man you just met all of your HEART'S desire. Remember to guard your heart with all diligence.

And for those of you moms who have children, please protect them. Do not expose them to every man you meet. Why? You are not going to marry every man you meet. Therefore, every man you meet does not need to meet your most precious gifts and prized possession. Neither do you need to share every detail about your kids to every man you meet. Some men are predators who marry women with children so that they can have access to them. Remember to be wise as serpents and harmless as doves.

How to Wisely Go Out on Dates

Every time I hear or read on social media about women demanding that the men they just met, probably spoke to a few times and don't know much about, take them to the most expensive and upscale restaurant in town, I CRINGE!! It's as if he should have gotten a download from God that they are the best thing on God's green earth. And princesses, you might be, but guess what? He doesn't know that YET!

See, you think that you're all that, and he needs to show out for you on the first date. And again, sweetie, you *are* all that, but he doesn't know that! He's trying to get to know how great you are and if you are worth his time, money, and effort. That's the same thing as women asking men on the first date what their intentions are towards them?

Princesses, please stop rushing the process. Sit back, relax, and get the data you need. At the same time, please remember that these men are gathering data on you, too. Your snobbish and entitled attitude will run a possible prospect and a good man away. The story of Esther and the King, along with the other prospective queens, is a perfect example of why we need to have a humble, graceful, and thankful spirit when we go out on dates. I will be writing more about Esther in an upcoming book.

So, meeting a guy, probably via social media, talking via text, phone, or messages, and demanding that he takes you to the most expensive restaurant and spend his whole paycheck on you is not something I encourage. Remember, the same way you're gathering data on him is the same way he's collecting data on you. You don't want to come off as unappreciative with an ungracious spirit. Now if he chooses to do so, then that's even better. But to demand? No Princesses, that's not ladylike.

I am not saying to accept a fast food restaurant date. Lol. All I am saying is that don't demand that he takes you to the most expensive restaurant in town. My husband and I first date were to be at an upscale, fancy restaurant that you have to make reservations for. He also planned to propose to me at this same restaurant and is one of our favorite places to eat.

I believe my husband' and my fourth date was an early morning walk in the park. Others are usually out during that time running and walking. The trail is about an hour or two walk if you stroll and enjoy the scenery. It has a vast pond, often with ducks in it, and it's just a beautiful sight to see. Afterward, he took me to breakfast.

Also, I don't mind a coffee or tea date, where we can sit and talk if I was already out and about or coming from work. But here again, I love coffee and tea, so I don't mind. And what about a drinks date? Sure, why not? I didn't drink while I was dating, but I'm ok with a man who enjoys a glass of wine or a beer. And usually, those places have a place to eat. So while I didn't drink alcohol, I would have a virgin Pina Colada or cranberry juice or anything non-alcoholic.

Now that I think back, I believe my husband's and my first date was a drinks date. It was at the event where we met. He asked if I wanted to share a drink with him. I said sure, and I went and sat at the bar with him, and I had cranberry juice. That is where he said that he would call me to take me out on a date.

My husband's and my first real date and many others were at Applebee's. Ladies, my husband is far from cheap. But it was more of a distance thing for me. I needed to be close to my home in case there was an emergency with my daughter, who was 18 when I met my husband. But remember she was a special needs child, so I could only go so far. Other times, we would go downtown when I had a little more time to be away from home. In the downtown area, there are lots of cute little romantic spots to go for a date. Also, my husband used to be in the restaurant business, so he knew many of the establishments.

Remember though, for our first date he wanted to take me to this very nice, upscale and expensive restaurant. When my daughter was busy with other activities or during the day, he took me to charming upscale restaurants. So be open. Don't demand anything but be appreciative of everything your prospect does for you. I can't stand women with entitlement spirits. Lol! It is so unladylike and is not godly and virtuous at all.

Can I tell you that my husband mentions that walk in the park date all the time? When he asked what I wanted to do, I said that we could go for a walk in the park. Simple, beautiful, free, and lots of uninterrupted time to get lots of data you need. He tells me all the time how that set me apart for him. Additionally, he has said that suggesting a walk in the park told him that I wanted to talk, and he was good with that. Picnic dates, oh I love those. I've had a few dates with guys who wanted to cook for me, but I didn't feel comfortable going to their homes.

Another thing my husband has said to me repeatedly is that, while dating, he watched how I was with money. I think I mentioned earlier that I had an excellent job but kept my one-bedroom apartment while saving for my first home. So, ladies, be sweet, gracious, kind, and appreciative. I'm going to write more about this soon.

What About Netflix and Chill Dates?

Please princesses, NEVER accept a Netflix and Chill date! Why would you go to the house of a man you just met to watch a movie and chill? I don't even like to go to the movies on the first date. I want to sit and talk and look at a man. I don't care if it's at the local coffee shop! At least you are in an open space where there are people present! Netflix and Chill dates for a guy you just met says one thing: SEX!

Let me touch on this while I'm talking about first dates. Princesses do not assume that a man you just met and are going out with for the first time is what I call a 100%. Do not assume that he's a gentleman, will pick you up, open the car door or other doors. Neither that he will pull out chairs and pay for the whole date. I hear a lot of women being mad that they went out on a date and he asked for her to pay half or tip. She's mad that he would dare ask her to pay. But ladies, did you discuss that before? Did you take time to GATHER DATA before you went out with him, assuming he's a 100% gentleman?

Are Your Words Flavorful & Attractive?

$\mathcal{P}$rincesses, please, I graciously ask you to note that I am not promoting toughness, aggressiveness, hardness, and callousness. Instead, I want to encourage a spirit of grace, softness, kindness, graciousness, wisdom, and femininity. God already put everything in you that you need to attract your Psalm 23 Husband. You need to fan the flames of the graciousness that God has placed within you and stir up those gifts. The subtitle of this book is *How to Be Wise as Serpents and Harmless as Doves in Dating*. Doves are soft, loving, kind, and graceful. So while you need to use lots of wisdom as you date, please be sweet, feminine, kind, and gracious.

One of my favorite verses I thought about when I was dating was **Colossians 4:5-6.** Even though it is not specifically about dating, it's applicable. It states, **"⁵ Walk in wisdom toward those *who are* outside, redeeming the time. ⁶ *Let* your speech always *be* with grace, seasoned with salt, that you may know how you ought to answer each one."** Based on this verse, you will see that Apostle Paul encouraged us that we ought to communicate with people, especially those who are outside the body of Christ. However, applying it to how our speech needs to be while we date and gather data makes it a great scripture to remember. Let's break it down a bit.

First, it talks about walking in wisdom, which means all that you do needs to be done with wisdom. What is wisdom? Simply knowing what to do when you don't know what to do. **Proverbs 4:7** talks about **wisdom being the principle thing and in all your getting get understanding.** The way you speak, dress, carry yourself, and everything about you needs to be strategic. **Colossians** goes on to talk about redeeming the time. Redemption means to buy back. Think about all the time you wasted trying to get a man to choose, love, and marry you. Now, you don't have to walk around blind because this book is full of wisdom on how to gather data. In verse 6, it says to let the speech-he way you speak or post on social media—be with grace.

When you hear the word grace, what comes to mind? Grace is God's free and unmerited favor to mankind. Be kind to all; be pleasant and welcoming. Then it goes on to talk about our speech being seasoned with salt. Think about salt. What does salt do? It gives food flavor, but it also purifies, and it's sustaining. In other words, Paul is saying let the words of your mouth be flavorful and full of wisdom. Additionally, I want to stress to you that, in the book of Proverbs, several scriptures talk about not talking too much.

Finally, Paul said he stated the above so that you will know how to answer everyone. So, when some dirty freaky man jumps in your inbox and sends you dingaling pix, remember this verse. You will know how to answer by exercising your blocking authority! When another man says, "Sister Ice Cream, God told me that you're my wife," you will know how to answer him. When a hobosexual wants to talk you into moving him to your house so you can take care of him, God will give you how to answer him. And I know some women curse like sailors. Be mindful princesses! Not every man likes a cussing woman.

Allow me again, princesses to remind you that this book is not about being tough and hard. However, it's about wisely, softly, graciously, lovingly and skillfully extracting the data you need about any man who approaches you with interest so that you can make an informed decision.

Finally, princesses, before we gently twirl into *23 Types of Guys You Might Meet On Social Media,* I want to once again express that this book is not for every woman. But it's ONLY for women who want to get married.

23 Types of Guys You Might Meet Online

As women, we need to understand that though men are different in some ways, they are a lot like us. They advertise what they have in hopes of getting an unsuspecting young lady's attention the same way we might show a little cleavage or leg or comb our hair a certain way. We know what men like therefore we dress in a way to draw their attention. Well, did you know that some men do the same to get our attention?

But remember the old saying, "Not all that glitters is gold." Here are 21 types of guys you might meet on social media in no specific order. Pay attention, ladies. Be wise as serpents and harmless as doves. Be discrete and wise like Deborah, humble and wise like Abigail, feminine and wise like Esther. Be mysterious and kind like Ruth, beautiful and smart like Rachel, and gracious and kind like Rebecca. Take your time and get the DATA you need before you commit yourself to a man who has no intention of making you his wife.

Remember that you are the King's daughter. Whoever you meet will need to go through the process to get into your holy of holies. STOP making yourself available to every man who says you're pretty or cute, or who jumps in your inbox. While no man is perfect, you want to meet a man who is full of the Holy Spirit and has a heart like Christ. He needs to have fruit that you can see. It needs to be long-lasting fruit, not just the surface stuff, but real and authentic fruits.

Here you have it, princesses, *23 Types of Guys You Might Meet on Social Media.* We will refer to them as Mr. So, and So. When you see a certain mister on social media or in person, it will quickly click in your head that "Oh, that's Mr. Help A Brotha Out or Mr. Jet Setter!" Lol.

1-Mr. Sex

My dad, Pastor Bradshaw, told me a long time ago, "All men want to have sex." Rich, poor, broke, sick, laying up in the hospital or nursing home, the homeless man on the street, presidents, pastors, and bishops, all men want to have sex! This one statement revolutionized my whole life and outlook on men. Ladies, understanding that all men, regardless of age, ability to provide, profess and protect, want to have sex will transform your dating lives.

Please, stop thinking that every man who approaches you wants to profess his love, provide for you, and protect you. I feel so many women get hurt by this, meeting a man and putting all your marital hopes and dreams in his flimsy full-of-holes basket. Sadly, most men who approach you want to screw you. Think about it! Of all the men who have romantically approached you, how many of them wanted to marry you? How many of them did you have sex with and then poof they were gone? Exactly! Men are hunter's dearie, and all men want to have sex! They are not all looking for wives to adore. Mr. Sex is all around you; you need to be aware.

Therefore, be mindful, when a man comes up to you and is smiling in your face, my dears. In the back of your mind, remember that all men want to have sex. "But I stand on the word of the Lord because I am rooted, grounded, and established in the promises of the Lord." Why? Ok sure, you don't know for sure if the man who's standing in front of you wants to "screw" you because you don't know what his intentions are for you. But just in case he does, you have the word of the Lord to stand on.

Slowly, Mr. Sex will begin to try to make his desires your desires. The Apostle Paul talks about fiery darts of the enemy, encouraging us to put on the Whole Armor of God according to **Ephesians 6:10-20**. Be watchful, vigilant, and prayerful always. Stand in the truth of the promises of God. The exciting thing about the Whole Armor of God is that it's all about the Word of the Lord. 1 will be writing about this soon, but in the meantime, immerse yourself and be rooted and grounded in the word of the Lord daily.

Mr. Sex: His first, second, third, and last name is sex! All he talks about is sex. He looks, smells, and sounds like sex. If you are on your guard, Mr. Sex is easy to spot. He comes in your inbox with pictures of his dingaling, telling you how he's gonna give it to you and all the positions he wants to do with you.

He begs you for a chance to prove himself to you and tells you that, after him, you won't want anyone else! Now, c'mon ladies! Lol! What more do you want? I mean, he is telling you plain as day what he is about. Is that what you want?

Mr. Dingaling Print: Oh, Mr. Dingaling Print! There are all types of dingalings. There are good, healthy, rich ones who are looking for a wife. On the other hand, there are broke, sick, lame, and limp ones who are only looking for their next place to make a lousy deposit. And many women are fascinated by dingalings! However, men are even more intrigued because many allow their dingalings to make decisions for them.

Some women get caught up with Mr. Dingaling, unfortunately to their demise. I have known women who have stayed in unhealthy and abusive relationships because of this guy. Some women have worked two and three jobs to take care of Mr. Dingaling while he stays home and plays video games all day. Others sleep all day, wake before the streetlight comes on, dress up to go out, and drink and party the night away with your money in their pockets. Comes in your apartment around 4 a.m. and sleeps all day while you get up at 5 to begin working three jobs to keep Mr. Dingaling Print happy.

Some women are mesmerized by dingalings, especially if a guy has a "big" or a "good" one. Well, at least he says it's big and tasty. On social media, Mr. Dingaling Print is the type of guy who takes pictures with the print of his dingaling showing. The way he sits and stands, the kind of pants he wears, and how he positions himself just right for the camera to snap a print of his dingaling.

You need to be careful about Mr. Dingaling Print because he is showing you what he is about. He knows that some women love a big dingaling. As a result, he is showing you that he has a big one with the hopes that you will jump in his inbox and drool over his dingaling. He hopes that you will ask him for a picture. If you don't ask, Mr. Dingaling Print will offer to send you a picture of his dingaling and offer you a ride on his pony. Most times, Mr. Dingaling Print will send you a picture without you asking. Beware, ladies. Remember, you desire a godly man after God's own heart.

Mr. Big Dingaling: Like Mr. Dingaling Print, this guy is known for having a big dingaling. I am amazed at the number of women who said they either got with a guy or married him because he has a big dingaling. Many women put up with and deal with a lot of mess and foolishness from him.

He doesn't work, can't provide for her and the kids, but she is still with him because he has a big dingaling. Like Mr. Dingaling Print, he will send unsolicited pictures because he knows that many women will go crazy over his big dingaling.

At the publication of this book, there is a well-known couple who broke up, and she is dating another man. Her ex-boyfriend posted pictures and a video of his dingaling. The internet was going wild, and many women were asking why his ex-girlfriend broke up with him. Many women said they would have stayed with him and put up with any issues he had just because he has a big dingaling.

In the meantime, other women said Mr. Big Dingaling is annoying, but after seeing his pictures, they would put up with him. Others said he could get their cookie any day. I thought this was funny, but it's unfortunate at the same time because many women choose a man based only on the size of his dingaling and tolerate a lot of mistreatment. This Mr. Big Dingaling treated his ex-girlfriend terribly, and now people are saying they can see why she stayed with him for such a long time.

Ladies, please do not choose a man solely on the fact that he has a big dingaling. There is so much more to marriage! If you take away his big dingaling, who is he? Can he protect and provide for you? If his big dingaling doesn't work, what's left of him? Sitting on the couch with nothing, do you like him? These are questions, as women, we need to ask about our potential suitor.

Mr. Dingaling in Your Inbox: Apparently, there's a new phenomenon on social media. Guys are jumping in our inboxes, sending pictures of their dingalings. I also refer to him as the dingaling slinger. He slings it in everyone's inbox and sees where it hits. It's as if the dingaling picture is the new selfie. This guy is different from the other Mr. Dingalings because it doesn't matter if it's big or small. For some reason, he thinks you are interested in seeing his dingaling, so he takes it upon himself to introduce you two.

Mr. Dingaling in Your Inbox has nothing else to offer. Sending you an unsolicited picture says he lacks self-control and doesn't want to have any meaningful dialogue. He thinks he's competing with other dingaling slingers, so he tries to beat them to the punch. Princesses listen: any man who would disrespect you by introducing himself as a picture of his dingaling deserves one thing: #BLOCKED!

Mr. Ghetto Dingaling: I have always wondered why ladies layup with guys who have no job, no house, no car, and no means of taking care of himself, much less a woman. Well, it's because he might be a Mr. Ghetto Dingaling. It's been stated that Mr. Ghetto Dingaling doesn't work but spends all his time being taken care of by a hardworking woman. He has a good dingaling.

Mr. Ghetto Dingaling will jump in your inbox and tell you how good his dingaling is. He tells you how he can make you have multiple orgasms every seven seconds. Mr. Ghetto Dingaling insists that you're missing out on the best dingaling of all time.

Many women foolishly allow Mr. Ghetto Dingaling to get in their heads. Next thing you know, Mr. Ghetto Dingaling is sitting up in yo' house, eating your babies' cereal, and drinking their milk. He sleeps all day while you work several jobs so that Mr. Ghetto Dingaling can be a kept dingaling. Because of this, I'm all for taking the cookie off the table. If you don't give Mr. Ghetto Dingaling yo' cookie, you won't know how good his dingaling is. Honey, baby girl, you deserve better. Please let Mr. Ghetto Dingaling go.

Mr. Grey Sweatpants: He is like Mr. Dingaling Print. However, he intentionally wears grey sweatpants when he wants to catch the eye of women or get attention. Like Mr. Dingaling, he is telling you what he is about and what he wants.

When some man wears grey sweatpants, to some women, that is a message. It could be a message that he has a big dingaling or that he wants to "play" or he wants to flirt. So, ladies, be on the lookout and beware that this might be a silent message for you to look in his direction. Now, this does not mean that, when all men wear sweatpants, this is what they are saying. But I'll go out on a limb and say "most." Watch out, princesses. Don't get caught up with Mr. Grey Sweatpants. Lol.

Mr. Long Tongue: He takes pictures showing women how long his tongue is as a sexual suggestion. He understands that a picture is worth a thousand words. Women, in turn, flood his inbox with the desire to experience his "long tongue." This mister is like Mr.

Dingaling. He is showing you what he is about. All he has to offer is his long tongue. Mr. Long Tongue swears that he can make you levitate to the seventh heaven, as your body goes into shock from ecstasy. Mr. Long Tongue is easy to spot, ladies. Just look at his pictures, where most of them are showing off how long his tongue is.

Mr. Long Tongue wants to give you a vision of what his long tongue can do in hopes of having you daydreaming about it. He wants to get you salivating about how long his tongue is. And the thought of it caressing your body will make you jump in his inbox begging him to give his tongue a run over, in, out, and around your most sensual parts. It's a trap, princesses.

Mr. Fruit Eater: Oh, my Lawd! This mister will have you screaming and pulling your hair out because of how he eats a "peach." He posts videos of himself licking, sucking, swallowing, and eating various fruits. He knows that women love to see it and that his inbox will always be full of thirsty women, wanting him to "eat their fruit." Princesses, this guy is letting you know what he's about. No decent man of God looking for a wife is going to be on social media licking and sucking fruits and writing sexually suggestive posts.

In the same way, ladies, a man who is seriously looking for a godly wife is probably not going to be interested in the woman who is posting sexually suggestive posts, videos, and pictures. Remember, ladies, the same way we are watching them, they are watching us. I often say dress and carry yourself like you're going to be the wife of a future president. Now, I'm not saying you can't show a little cleavage—of course you can! All I'm saying is keep it sexy and classy.

2-Mr. Take What You Can Get

Princesses, men are often straightforward and sometimes honest creatures. They will tell you what you can get from them. But it's up to you to accept or pass. Why do you think there are so many married men having several affairs while married? Sure, some hide the fact that they are married.

However, some will let you know they are married and just looking for a little something on the side. So beware, ladies. If you want to be married, don't settle for a Mr. Take What You Can Get. And it doesn't have to be that he is married. It could be that he's not ready or maybe he's just looking for sex. I was told this by my Mr. Drop Yo' Drows Gorgeous, and guess what I did? Mr. Take What You Can Get is more about you than it is about him.

Mr. Cuddle Buddy: Ooh la la! Mr. Cuddle Buddy. This guy is just what his name says. Cuddle Buddy! He advertises himself as a cuddle buddy and will come over, cuddle with you, or give you the "buddy!" First, how do you even cuddle up with just any man? Yuck!

You call him when you're having a bad day, when you need a hug, or when you want to talk, or to get your itch scratched. Like Mr. Friends with Benefits, ladies, you know he's not a man you would marry, so why are you wasting your time? Buy a body pillow and get a notebook to write in. Stop spending your time with males who are not marriage material.

Mr. Friends with Benefits: There is a thin line between friends and benefits. This guy can be your friend and give you a l'il benefit. Rumor has it that lots of women have a "friend with benefits." I don't know how true it is, but I didn't have one when I was single. "Ain't nobody got time for that!" I wanted a husband, so I didn't have time to be dishing out my cookies to Mr. Friends with Benefits, blocking my blessing of a godly husband. Plus, I hate to waste my precious time!

Mr. Friends with Benefits is the guy who you are keeping around and hanging on to. However, what you don't realize, ladies, is that you could be blocking your blessing. Your real husband might be held up because you are giving all the benefits to Mr. Friends with Benefits. Drop him like a hot potato and make space for your husband.

Also, many men who keep you as a "friend with benefits" often wife the other girl. Next thing you know, he's married, you're in your feelings 'cause you're gonna tell her that y'all been sleeping together. Newsflash, Sistas! He asked her to marry him and not you! You were just kitty to him. You were not worth professing his love to, providing for, and protecting. The only thing you were to him is a toilet that he could release himself into. Now, think about that before you sign up for FWB! Say no to Mr. Friends with Benefits!

Mr. Drive-Through Dingaling: I laugh at this guy because I know a few like this. He is just what his name says, Mr. Drive-Through Dingaling. The same way you go through the drive-through at your fast food restaurant and get a meal in a few minutes is the same way this mister is.

He will text a few ladies and say, "Drive-through." His purpose is to get his needs met quickly. Don't plan to stay long, spend the night, or bring a weekend bag. Once you have serviced him, he will ask you to leave or even call an Uber for you. Sis, don't you think you deserve better than a pit stop? Is that what you want?

Mr. Come Through: Lol! Mr. Come Through is like Mr. Drive-Through Dingaling. The difference is, he is the one who texts to say he's coming through. He wants you to get a meal prepared, put on his favorite lingerie, and be ready to service him. It's like you're a pit stop!

You, trying to prove to him that you are wife material, will get to cooking and being sexy because Mr. Come Through is on his way. You are hoping he will see how special you are, and he will finally make you his wife. Girl, please stop it! You know this man ain't never gonna marry you! Please stop allowing Mr. Come Through to go through and come in you. Stop blocking your blessing, ladies, and put a stop to Mr. Come Through from coming through so you can have your breakthrough!

Mr. Bang Bam Thank You, Ma'am: Mr. Bang is like Mr. Friends with Benefits and Mr. Cuddle Buddy. All he cares about is banging you. That could be because you want it, or maybe that's what he's talked you into. This mister is the guy who gets in your ear and tells you how well he can bang you. How he can have you climbing the wall, calling Jesus, and having your toes curl. Only if you let him hit, bam, bang, bam the kitty.

Mr. Bang Bam Thank You, Ma'am tells you how he's gonna spread it wide, flip it, hit it, spank it, and split it! Ladies, that's all he has to offer. Banging you? You see, the lingo is a bit different, but when you get down to the nitty-gritty, it's all about them getting what they want under the disguise of you possibly getting what you want. Don't you dare fall for the games!

Mr. Wrong: Ladies, have you ever met a man that you know is just plain wrong for you? Raising my hands and saying, "Amen sisters!" You gave him the time of day, holding your breath, hoping and praying that the frog standing in front of you will eventually turn into a prince.

Like you, I have been there, but eventually, I had to walk away because I had to look at the end, and what I wanted was my Mr. Right and not a Mr. Wrong. Stop entertaining Mr. Wrongs and make time for your Mr. Right.

Mr. Right Now: Oh, Mr. Right Now! Who will be honest enough to say, at one time or another, we have dealt with Mr. Right Now? Be it for sex, company, companionship, or help with a situation, you know he's not your Mr. Forever, but for right now, he will do. Ladies, beware of this man wherever you meet him, be it online or face to face.

Do not allow Mr. Right Now, to be all up in your inbox, telling you his sacred lies, stroking your bruised heart while he tells you how he can scratch your itch. Don't even use Mr. Right Now, to try to get over the last guy who hurt you or allow him to be your rebound. Mr. Right Now is a waste of your time, but if you are not careful, he could take you off destiny's path.

Once you recognize that he is a Mr. Right Now, block him, delete him, stop talking to him, and anything else you need to do for him not to have his claws in you. Why waste time with Mr. Right Now, when you're Mr. Forever is waiting right around the corner? Unfortunately, some women make the foolish decision of making Mr. Right Now, their Mr. Forever!

Mr. Hang Out: What does this mean? Mr. Hang Out jumps in your inbox and says, "Hey, let's hang out." Your response is, "Okay." But two weeks later, he hasn't set a date, time, or place to "hang out." You sit at home foolishly, waiting for Mr. Hang Out to message you. Question: Why are you sitting at home waiting for Mr. Hang Out when you need to be hanging out meeting and dating other guys?

You then jump in his inbox, leaning all the way forward by setting up the date and even offering to pay! Gurl? He nicely brushes you off because he has "other plans." A week or so later, he jumps in your inbox late in the midnight hour out of the blue and says, "Hey, when are we gonna hang out?"

Mr. Hang Out offers to come over or for you to come by and "hang out." You, in all your desperation, welcome his invitation. The next thing you know, you're hanging on to the ceiling fan as ya'll are knocking boots, because Mr. Hang Out has already classified you as a booty call. You see, ladies, when men meet you, they automatically put you in a category.

Mr. Vague: I have no time or patience for this guy. He is so vague that you don't even know his name. Lol! I think that, if you are an authentic person, there's nothing to be vague about. Yes, be wise with your answers. Don't reveal too much; there's a way to answer questions without dishing out all your business.

You try to ask Mr. Vague questions, and he gives you non-answers and nothing specific. That way, you don't have enough data to make an informed decision. You ask him about his employment, and he says, "Well, you know, I work in the automobile industry." Or he says, "I work in the security and protection industry." You think, oh that sounds nice. But what does it mean? How about this one? He says he is in the entertainment business. Chills go up to your spine, and the butterflies in your heart begin to flutter with joy.

Fascinated by his words, you find yourself wanting to lock him down. You give up the cookie, and while having a "heart to heart" in his momma's dingy basement on a mattress on the floor, he tells you that he's not looking for anything serious "right now." Additionally, he goes on to say that he is a mechanic who doesn't have a stable job, or that he is a security guard doing the graveyard shift fill-ins. Come to find out that he makes bootleg DVDs and sells them. Do you know that's stealing? Ladies, I keep stressing to you to get the data so that you can have more than enough info to make an informed decision.

3-Mr. Sexy, Mr. Eye Candy & Mr. Physical

Lie if you must, but we are all attracted to something about a man. Either he is eye candy, incredibly sexy, looks good physically or something else about him. I know church folks say it doesn't matter what he looks like. Liars! Can you name one well-known pastor whose wife is ugly? I'll wait. Go ahead.

Ladies, there's nothing wrong with wanting a man who you find physically attractive, good looking, or sexy. However, what is the #1 rule? Don't choose him because of one thing! My husband is a very handsome man. I remember sitting across from him on our first date and thinking, "My lawd, he's good looking!" But that was not enough for me! I had to make sure he added up to what I desire in a husband. So, as you gather data on the guys you meet, please beware of your weakness for the following guys.

Mr. Tall Drink a Wata: (Please note that it's not water, but wata. Lol!) Like Mr. Status, he leads with his body. Am I the only woman who loves a tall man? I know I'm not. Yes, Lawd! This mister is taller than the average guy, and he knows that many women love a tall man.

Craftily, he uses his height as bait to get women in his inbox because he's fully aware that many women love a tall man. Please, ladies, don't be thirsty by jumping into Mr. Tall Drink a Wata's or anyone else's inbox without him contacting you first. I know we are living in the "age of the woman," where we say and think that if a man can do it, then we can too.

Well, if that's where you are, that's on you. But my father has always told me that if a man wants me, he will come for me. If he's interested in me, then he will make his interest known. Please stay out of the menfolk's inboxes. And if a man sends you a message, be on alert. Don't get all desperate, impatient and thirsty. Let him lead.

Mr. Big, Tall & Husky: Like Mr. Tall Drink a Wata, you might be wondering if they aren't the same person. Somewhat, but not precisely. You see, some women love a tall guy who is of average weight. On the other hand, many women love a husky man. He is comfy, feels like a teddy bear, and gives great hugs.

Some women might love a tall man but not necessarily a husky man. Whatever your taste calls for is alright with me. However, rules and guidelines still apply. Make yourself pretty, feminine, and stand out in open space so he can see you, but never jump in his inbox telling him how sexy he is and how you need a bear hug. Lol!

Mr. Tall, Dark, & Handsome: This mister is like Mr. Tall Drink a Wata. However, he is a triple threat. He is tall, dark, and handsome. Beware, princesses, the same way as ladies we hope to attract guys by fixing ourselves up, they use what they have to try and draw us, too.

Please, remember that I am not saying every man is out there just looking for women to screw over. Some great guys are genuinely looking for a wife. However, I want you to be aware. If a man is selling his tall, dark, and handsomeness, then more than likely, he is just looking for victims. Be vigilant and remember to vet every guy you meet, be it online or face to face.

Mr. Light-Skinned: Apparently, being light-skinned is back in style. Lol! I know many women of color who would not date a dark-skinned man. Yeah sure, that can be considered shallow and hateful of one's race. And yes, I know that God only created one race, the human race. But I also know that you know what I mean! However, let's be honest here! We have a right to like what we like. I, for one, love a chocolate man, but if you see my husband, he ain't even close to being chocolate. Lol! But, while I loved chocolate guys, I was open to whatever complexion my African King could be.

Ladies, if you love Mr. Light Skinned, be careful that you don't allow that to take your mind off the things you need to pay attention to. Mr. Light-Skinned is no different from any of these guys I've mentioned. No matter who he is, or what wrapping he comes in, get all the information you need before making a lifetime decision.

Mr. Phine Like Devine Wine: This mister is so "phine" with a "p" that he's pretty! Mr. Phine Like Devine Wine is like Mr. Drop Yo' Drawers Gorgeous. He's so fine that he has women staking out his house to get his attention. He spends a lot of time in the mirror, making sure he's "pretty."

Princesses, why would you want a man who spends as much time or more time in the mirror as you? He could be a man who's metrosexual, who likes to take care of himself. He gets manicures and pedicures, and there's nothing wrong with that because who doesn't love a man who takes care of himself? He might get his eyebrows waxed, and that is a bit questionable but okay? He might have curly hair or walk around with a brush so he can brush it often. Every time he passes a mirror, he checks himself to make sure he's looking "pretty." Lol! Be mindful, ladies. What you see is what you get!

Mr. Sexy Wet Lips: Yuck! I was never into a man that licks his lips. All I can think about is, do his lips smell, or is he licking them because they are dry? But some women love a man who licks his lips because they believe it's very sexy.

Now, I love a man with beautiful lips, but I would never be with a man who licks them all day. I think they are too caught up in being "sexy."

And it's a turn off for me. I remember sitting across from my now husband on our first date, thinking, *"Wow, he has nice lips."* I remember it like it was yesterday and texted my girlfriend about how handsome he was.

Mr. Salt and Pepper: Who doesn't like a mature man with a little salt in his beard or hair? Not me! At least not when I was in my 20s or 30s. LOL! But this is a turn on for some women. Some younger ladies love an older guy because it suggests that he's established, mature, and is finished with his dog days. Ladies, older doesn't necessarily mean more mature. Only time will tell, so pay attention.

Do not make assumptions about anything. Words and actions need to align. Look for the fruits of his life and please avoid trying to train a grown man to be more mature. That was his mother's responsibility, not yours!

Mr. Facial Hair: Note: I wanted to call this mister, Mr. Beard. However, because "beard" has several meanings, I wanted to differentiate between beard on a man's face and the other "beard," which we will discuss later. As for Mr. Facial Hair? Oh, I am sure you have heard of the new beard craze! I don't care for beards, especially those wild, out of order ones. My husband wears a beard sometimes, but I prefer a nicely shaved face or a goatee. That, to me, is incredibly sexy, and every time he comes home with a goatee, I want to jump him. Lol!

My husband's goatee is an automatic turn on for me! So, because of this beard phenomenon, just about every woman is trying to get herself a bearded man. Nothing wrong with that. If it floats your boat, then let it drift on. But remember, don't allow the beard to distract you from the data you need to extract to make an informed decision.

Mr. Zaddy: Ladies, please leave those older men who are trying to act twenty-one alone. Mr. Zaddy is an older man who dresses as if he's twenty-one. Zaddy knows his time has passed and is trying to get it all out before the clock strikes midnight. Zaddy works out, has bulging muscles, and looks good for his age and is still trying to play the field. Zaddy often doesn't want women his age but wants younger because he thinks he has something to prove to everyone, including himself.

Princesses, a Zaddy is a Zaddy! Mature men embrace who they are and enjoy their lives where they are and marry women they can grow with, not women who are young enough to be their granddaughters! Leave Zaddies alone because if he doesn't want to embrace himself, he won't be able to embrace you as you grow in grace. Mr. Zaddy is not ready to accept responsibility and establish a life with a wife.

Mr. Sexy Old Man: Mr. Sexy Old Man is different from Mr. Zaddy. The sexy old man is one who has embraced his age and is sexy. Mr. Zaddy is the fifty-year-old man, acting, behaving, and dressing like he's a teen. Even though Mr. Sexy Old Man has embraced his age, this doesn't mean he is the man for you. Many young women fall for Mr. Sexy Old Man, thinking he is ready to settle down, only to find out that he was looking for another notch on his belt. Beware, princesses. Just because he is older doesn't mean he is mature or ready to get married and settle down.

Neither does it mean that he is finished playing the field. I know many younger women who married older men, thinking they were mature, ready to settle down, and finished with their "dog" days. Don't be fooled, ladies. Actions speak louder than words.

Mr. Bald Head: Lots of women love bald men. Some women think that a bald man is just sexy, and it is a turn on for them. I say, if it floats your boat, then float on, doll! However, make sure the words line up with the actions.

I also believe that you need to be attracted to your mate. You need to find something sexy about him. But again, ladies, don't decide solely based on him being bald. Remember, men know what we like, too. He could be using his bald head as bait. Mr. Bald Head needs to go through the process also. And if, while going through the process, there are red flags, don't be afraid to drop him or any other man and move on.

Mr. White Tee and Pecs: Who doesn't love a sexy man with a little muscle and those pecs? He is perfectly framed, works out just enough. Not overly buff, but simply in shape and sexy. His shirt fits perfectly, no fat, flab, or rolls.

Mr. White Tee isn't necessarily doing this to get women, but he might be. I will go out on a limb here and say most women love a man who works out, stays in shape and is healthy. Likewise, ladies, most men like women who stay healthy and fit. However, here again, ladies, because he looks good on the outside doesn't mean he is right on the inside. Neither does it say he is right for you. Flip through that book and see if the pages are as good as the cover.

Mr. Athletic: Can you say "sexy?" I love an athletic man. As a young girl, I ran track and always preferred men who had a workout ethic. However, I was flexible when it came to my husband. He didn't necessarily have to be a gym rat but should be mindful of his health and have a regimen regarding exercise.

Mr. Athletic knows that women love a man who works out. He often posts asking who wants to go to the gym with him or meet him there. Here again, he knows his inbox will be full of women wanting to go work out with him. Ladies, beware! If you are not a woman who loves to work out but is working out with a man to get his attention, it will only be temporary before the real you come out.

To me, working out and being healthy is like your faith. It is who you are, and you can only fake it for so long unless you have been truly converted. First, if a guy is asking on social media who wants to go work out with him, a little bell needs to go off in your head that says, "Issa a trap."

Let's say you jump in his inbox and agree to go work out with him. And then afterward he offers to come over or vice versa. Can you say "trap?" He comes to your place, one thing leads to another, and the next thing you know, he's working you out and has you doing legs stretches to touch the ceiling, yelling wider baby, open dem legs wider!

But here's the thing. Next week, when Mr. Athletic wants to layup with someone else, he will once again post his bait question, asking, "Who wants to go work out with me?" To your surprise, because you gave up the cookie, you think you are in a relationship. You get all in your emotions, jump in his inbox to give him the fifth degree about why he didn't ask you to go and work out with him. He then blocks you on all his social media platforms. Why? Because he was only using his athleticism as a bait to catch women.

Once again, I am not saying that every man is like this. What I am saying is to be alert, be wise, watch, and pray. Pay attention to the red flags, and for God's sake, please don't be thirsty. Remember that men are hunters, and they hunt with good or bad intentions. Lastly, Mr. Athletic could also be classified as Mr. Bait.

Mr. Good Hair and Hazel Eyes: This mister is like Mr. Pretty Boy. He might be caught up in himself and think that his looks will get him in every woman's panties. Why? Mr. Good Hair and Hazel Eyes know that some women love a man with "good hair." So, in the event, they have kids together, they will come out with good hair and hazel eyes.

Here again, ladies is a perfect example of not choosing a husband based on one thing. On your list of desires for a husband, Mr. Good Hair and Hazel Eyes might score a one, but you decide to go with him anyway? Lol! Beware, ladies. It takes more than one requirement to live a good life.

4-Mr. Baits

$\mathcal{I}$f I hear another woman say they were baited, I'm going to scream! That's why this book is so essential, ladies! Men are hunters. Men play games. Men say what they need to say to get what they want. Men and women communicate differently. However, there are many times when men are extremely honest. So we need to listen to them carefully. I'm working on a little something about how we need to hear when men speak.

What men say often doesn't mean what we think it means. Be alert and vigilant. Be wise as serpents and harmless as doves. Stop, slow down, settle down, think, and focus! Remember that all men are hunters, and they are hunting for something!

Baiting and bait-and-switch happen all the time in the church, also. You wouldn't think that about men in the church, but men are men, and what did my father teach me? All men want to have sex! Women need to stop being desperate 'cause, in the end, we will be the ones to suffer and left picking up the pieces. So be mindful, princesses, as you go about your life and socialize either on social media or face to face. Men are hunters. And there are traps everywhere! Stop allowing yourself to get into baited "situationships."

Mr. Bait: You've heard the saying, "Everything that glitters is not gold." How about, "Don't judge a book by the cover"? Well, Mr. Bait is the guy who baits you with "something." It could be money, his good job, gifts, jewelry, or even his good looks. Or the idea that he has "good dingaling!" He could be a gentleman on the surface but an abuser down below.

Mr. Bait is the perfect example of why, as women, we need to get all the information before we jump into a full-blown relationship with someone. I've often wondered how women know that a man is abusive before they marry them but go ahead and marry them regardless.

Ladies, having your list and being prayerful and wise about it is crucial. Do not allow anyone to bait you because your life and destiny depend on the man you marry. Here's another thought: If a man must bait you to have you, why is that? How does he plan to keep this up? Why isn't he being himself? Doesn't he want you to love him for who he is?

Mr. Boyfriend: Would you believe that I have never had a boyfriend? Nope, didn't believe in them. Other than my childhood boyfriends when I was five or six years old, I refused to be anyone's girlfriend because I wanted a husband. Some have asked, "Well, aren't you supposed to be a girlfriend before you become a wife?" Says who? Girlfriends are not biblical, but a wife is. I remember reading that Mary was engaged to Joseph. There is no boyfriend in the Bible. And as long as I have known myself, I have always wanted to be married.

Therefore, I decided not to entertain boyfriends. When I was dating, I was gathering data for a husband ONLY! So, if the guys I was collecting data on weren't marriage material, didn't want to get married, or weren't ready to get married, I would move on. I have heard so many women say, "Oh, we've been dating three years, and he has not asked me to be his girlfriend." So, in three whole years, the conversation about your future didn't come up? Ladies, please understand the following: Men who have prepared themselves to be husbands are looking for wives and not girlfriends. Little boys and males who want to play with your emotions and your body look for girlfriends. There's a vast difference between a man who's looking for a wife and one who's looking for a girlfriend.

Question: Are you a wife or a girlfriend? Declaring who you are is very important to know. Why? Because girlfriends get boyfriends, but wives get husbands. If you're a wife, why would you settle for being a girlfriend? Mr. Boyfriend advertises that he is looking for a girlfriend. Why sign up for a boyfriend when a husband is what you desire? If you settle for a boyfriend, that's all you might get.

Have "boyfriends" become "husbands"? Sure, they have. But why waste ten years being a girlfriend to one man when you can date and gather data on several guys at once until you meet one who is serious about marriage? But most importantly, meet someone who wants to marry you. Many thirsty and "pick me" women jump in men's inboxes, volunteering to be their girlfriends.

Additionally, these women offer to wash, cook, clean, and sex them until their toes curl. If you want a boyfriend, then be a girlfriend. But if a husband is what you desire, I encourage you to carry yourself like someone's wife. Don't ever settle for girlfriend status with Mr. Boyfriend when your husband is seeking you. Gather data on as many guys as possible until you meet the one who will put a ring on it. Mr. Boyfriend is all about getting his needs met for cheap. He is not about investing in you because he might not be ready to commit to you.

Sadly, many women who accept girlfriend status help to prepare their boyfriends for their wives. Many boyfriends have left their "girlfriends" and married their wives they met three months later. Again, sure, there have been many couples who were boyfriends and girlfriends for years before they finally got married. However, I am against being a girlfriend when wifey is what you desire. Why meet guys, jump into a "situationship" with them, and sign up to be their girlfriends? Shack up, have babies, pay bills together, purchase homes, and so on.

Furthermore, Mr. Boyfriend calls it testing it out to see if they want to get married. Excuse me? I am not a car; no one will test drive me. Say no to boyfriends, ladies. If you want a husband, then date and gather data for a husband and not a boyfriend. Some had asked if I was my husband's girlfriend before I married him. Nope! I don't do boyfriends, period! Neither am I going to tie myself down to a guy I just met with the title of "boyfriend." I will write more about this in an upcoming book on dating.

Mr. Nice Car: When I was a teen, my biological father moved his girlfriend into our home. She had two daughters; one was older than me and the other younger. The older girl had a thing for guys with nice cars. We would be walking in our neighborhood, down the freeway, or wherever, and she would wave at a nice car, they would stop, and we would get in. Now, looking back, it was God's grace and mercy that nothing happened to us. I'm scared just thinking about it now.

1 Corinthians 15:33 says, **"Evil company corrupts good habits."** (KJV says "manners.") Ladies, not only do you need to be mindful of the company you keep but be careful who you allow your children to be around. I often say that I am raising kids for Christ. There is no opening for anyone to come in and sow questionable seeds in my babies' hearts and minds other than what I am sowing. That is why Sunday school, children's church, Bible studies, and vacation Bible school are essential for our children. But most importantly, we teach them at home and live a life that is acceptable and good in front of our children. Keep them around godly people and give them opportunities to grow in the things of God.

Back to Mr. Nice Car. Guys know that some women have a thing for men with nice cars. This mister likes to flash his car. He likes to take pictures with his car, post them, and wait for the bait to take. He offers to take an unsuspecting woman for a spin in his fancy car. Next thing you know, you are in some alleyway, giving it up in a nice car. LOL!

Mr. Chef: Who doesn't like a man who can throw down in the kitchen? I love a man who can cook. That was something that impressed me about my Mr. Wonderful. After a few months of dating, he invited me over for dinner. We sat in his kitchen with the porch door open, and we talked while he cooked, and then we ate.

That meal is still one of my favorites seven years later. Grilled salmon and garlic spinach! Now princesses, notice I said he offered to cook for me after months of us going out, spending time together. He visited my church a few times, and he had met my father. So I felt comfortable. Plus, it was in the middle of the day, and as always, my father and two of my friends knew where I was, along with the address.

But, princesses, as much as I love a man who cooks, I would never accept that as a first, second, third, fourth, or fifth date. For me, going to his house for a cooking date is when our dating is progressing towards courting. Keep in mind that this can also be a ploy. Guys know women like a man who can cook for her. Tread lightly and carefully.

Mr. I'm Looking for My Wife: I've seen countless women fall for this old trick, and it's sickening. He is the man who announces to the world that he's looking for a wife. Mr. I'm Looking for My Wife makes his announcement so that he will not have to go "find" her, as the Bible states. He knows that, by announcing it, many women will flock to his inbox.

The women who flood his inbox offer to wash, cook, clean, sex him, and whatever else he needs. The women who do this are trying to prove they are "wife" material. These poor women don't know that they just get bamboozled, hoodwinked, and taken for a ride. The thing to remember about Mr. I'm looking for My Wife is that a good and wise hunter doesn't announce to the world that he is about to hunt. Because he understands that to find that special one, he needs to plan, be smart, and put in the work to find "her."

A wise man knows that not any woman will do and that a good and faithful wife is from the Lord. Thus, he needs to pray and seek the Lord to give him the wisdom to "find" her. A wise man also knows that a godly woman is probably not going to inbox him because he has announced to the world that he is looking for a wife.

Also, princesses, remember that, when a man wants you, he will come for you. He will initiate and pursue you and overtake you with his profession of love, provision, and protection. You will only need to respond.

Mr. God Said You're My Wife: If you've been in church any length of time, you have met this guy. In the world of social media, Mr. God Said You're My Wife is more prevalent because males can jump in your inbox and say, "Sister Watermelon, the Lord told me that you're my wife." Many desperate women have fallen for this trick. However, women who are wise because they pray, seek the Lord, and pray in the Holy Ghost will not fall for this.

Princesses, any man can come up to you in church, out and about, or on social media and say, "God said." It is your responsibility to check what they are saying against what God has spoken to you. This one trick of men coming up to you and saying, "God Said You're My Wife" has gotten many Christian women in trouble. For this reason, we need to be prayerful as we wait to be found by our God-ordained husbands. Note, waiting on God for our husbands is not passive but active. I will write more extensively about this soon.

How is it that God has told Mr. God Said You're My Wife that you're his wife, but the Holy Spirit didn't reveal that he is your husband to you? Many women in the church accepted marriage proposals from men who claim, "God said," only to get married and realize that God did not say.

Furthermore, I am so against praying that "God show me who my husband is." I can't tell you the countless women who have claimed God said to them that Brother Love was their husband. Yet he married another sister. Somebody is lying on God-beloved! What difference does it make if God shows you who your husband is? This is all emotionalism because your heart is attached to someone. Instead, why not thank the Lord daily that you and your husband will cross paths and he will find you? Here's a brilliant idea. Why not pray and ask the Lord where you need to be so that you can cross path with your husband so he can approach you? In other words, ask the Lord to help you REPOSITION yourself! Even though I am not for meeting one man and assuming that he is the "one." But, hey, it all begins with a conversation.

Additionally, I find that some men use this as a weapon. God told them that you are their wife, so you must marry them! How controlling and forceful is that? I know sisters who have missed out on great guys because they said God told them Brother Sexy was their husband.

Mr. Jet Setter: This mister is like Mr. I'm Looking for A Wife. He announces that he's going to be in a particular state or place, and he would like for someone to show him the sights, best restaurant, plays, events, or where to get a good drink. Here again, he knows that his inbox will be full of desperate women offering to show him around. I have even seen some women offer Mr. Jet Setter to stay at their homes. Can you say DESPERATE?

How crazy is this thinking? You don't know if this man is a rapist, a serial killer, or anything else. And for the women who have children, what about your babies? How could you allow strange men around your children? When you see Mr. Jet Setter seeking his prey, please don't jump in his inbox, offering up yourself and children to him as sacrificial lambs. Guess what, ladies? It's you this week and someone else next week.

Mr. Hookup: His name says it all. He is only looking for a hookup! He'll post asking if anyone wants to "hook up" for the weekend, day, or night. Here again, many desperate women will jump in his inbox, letting him know they want to hook up. He already knows that all he must do is make a job announcement, and the applicants will come running.

Therefore, it's important, ladies, for us to pay close attention. Be vigilant, pray, seek the face of the Lord. Pray for wisdom so that, when the bait is thrown out, you will not fall for it.

Mr. I'm Hungry: You know the saying, "A way to a man's heart is through his belly." Honestly, I think that's a trick from the devil that has been used to get women in a whole lot of trouble. Don't fall for it, ladies. It's a trap!

Oh, this mister almost caught me back in my single days. I was about nineteen or twenty. There was this brother in one of what we call our 'sister churches.' I must admit that I did like him. He was saved, loved the Lord, no kids, a firefighter, and my pastor knew his pastor. And of course, he was tall, dark, and handsome.

He would call here and there but never offered to take me out or get to know me. One Saturday, while on the phone, he said, "Man, I'm so hungry." He said that a few more times during our conversation, and then he said, "I'm so hungry, but I don't want to waste any money on food." Alarm bells went off. Ding! Ding! Ding!

First, my dad had already tipped me off that guys would want to come over and use food as bait. However, he stressed never to allow a man to come to my apartment. Also, I had a child, and I needed to be careful with her. So, when Mr. I'm Hungry kept saying he was hungry, I already knew he was saying that in hopes of me saying, "Why don't you come over, and I will cook you something?" LOL! Nope! I already knew the game!

Additionally, he said he was hungry but didn't want to waste any money buying food. I thought to myself, *"Well, if he doesn't want to feed himself, then he definitely won't want to feed my baby and me."* You see, sisters, you can't be so desperate for a man that you miss all the red flags. Pay attention to everything they say and do because the rest of your life and destiny depend on the man you choose.

Mr. I'm Hungry, and I are friends on Facebook. He finally got married in his mid-forties. And sure enough, he married an older woman who washes, cooks, and cleans to his heart's desire. I was honestly in shock that she was so much older than he is. She has passed her childbearing years, which means they won't be having any children, plus he doesn't have any of his own.

Mr. 1 Need: This thirsty male is like Mr. Hungry. He announces to the world that he needs someone to cook for him. Or he will say, "I need my hair braided, a massage, a foot rub, or my house cleaned. Who wants to come through?" Because we are women, our natural ability is to serve and fulfill needs. Many women jump at this opportunity to satisfy his need.

Mr. 1 Need, knows that, in seconds, his inbox will be filled with desperate women wanting to show him that they are wife material. These "thirsty," "desperate," and "pick me" women will offer to do everything for him, including satisfying his sexual needs. Because you see, ladies, his real need is sex but throwing out "I need a massage" gets the women to offer. Mr. 1 Need knows that if women will offer to satisfy his needs, quenching his sexual desires is just the icing on the cake.

And guess what, ladies. As soon as he's done with you, next week he will post the same thing again, and when you offer, he won't respond because he has already used you up. He is off to the next desperate woman. He will even block you on every social media platform because he doesn't want you to mess up his "game." So, ladies, learn to recognize the game so you will not fall victim to these ploys of the enemy and avoid getting played. Don't forget the old saying, "Don't hate the player, hate the game."

Mr. Celibate: Oh, you need to pay close attention to this mister right here! He says he is celibate, so you're thinking, "Oh praise Jesus, at least I don't have to worry about being pressured for sex." But, it's all a game, ladies. He claims he is celibate by choice yet complains about how miserable he is and how hard it is for him to abstain.

He will often send provocative and unsolicited pictures with the hopes that you will usher him into sex. And when you don't take the bait, he claims that you two are not connected and you need to get to know each other on a deeper level. Mr. Celibate will also ask for naked pictures of you. Question: Ladies, if a man says he is celibate, why is he so focused on sex? Shouldn't he try to get to know you in other areas versus always wanting to talk about sex?

Mr. Credit: I have heard so many horror stories of women marrying men to find out later that they are in a ton of debt. They come to find out that the males marry them for their excellent credit. Ladies, you cannot lead with what you have. Don't lead with, "I have three degrees, a house that is paid off, two cars, and $20K in the bank." That is nobody's business.

You might be setting yourself up to be used and abused. Listen, a man who has prepared himself to be a husband in every capacity doesn't care how much money you make. A prepared man who is ready to be a husband doesn't care if your house is paid off or how many degrees you have. Is it vital that you have taken care of yourself and prepared yourself? Yes! However, a prepared man who wants to provide, protect, and profess his love for you doesn't care about that.

A prepared man cares about you and how you can help him to fulfill God's vision for his life and to help him raise a godly family. Please stop telling these males all you have and how good your credit is. Ask him about his credit and how he can provide. Do not tell him all that you can do for him. Mr. Credit might just be looking for a woman with good credit who can fund his lifestyle.

Mr. Contract: I have known many young girls/ladies who became victims of Mr. Contract. I remember being a young college student, perhaps eighteen or nineteen years old. A man approached me and asked if I have ever thought about modeling and how my freckles would stand out. He then said he could help me become a model because I had the body.

Something within silently screamed, "NO!" Now, looking back, this man could have kidnapped me, sold me into sex trafficking, or something worse. Now, princesses, I am not saying everyone is like this. But if you have a gift, then please find a reputable company to represent you. If you are a model, singer, dancer, etc., please do not fall victim to males on social media who say they can help you refine your gift and get you a contract.

Mr. Father and Son: These two are so funny to me! Lol! Father and son gaming and using it as a ploy to attract and get women. I know a few ladies who got caught up in this game, mainly because the father had a son at a young age, so they look more like brothers.

It is sort of like my daughter and me. I had her when I was sixteen, so we look more like sisters than mother and daughter. And this is one reason I didn't feel comfortable dating guys my age or younger. I needed someone older who could be a father figure to her.

So, ladies, I know you might think it's cute to date the father and son with a friend, but be mindful of what you want. You desire a husband, not a boy toy, or a Zaddy.

Mr. Bae-cation: Yaas, honey! Bae-cation is a word that I recently learned. Let me break it down. "bae" is for bae or baby. "Cation" is short for vacation. So, Bae-cation is a woman a man takes on vacation, but they are only an item when they're away and not at home. My daddy always said, "Beware of men who want to take you out of the country or away so that no one who knows you will see you together." LOL! Don't be a "bae-cation," princesses! How scary is this? You don't know him, but you are going away on vacation with him?

Plus, I know so many women who claim they weren't gonna drop their drows because they have separate rooms! Bull crap! It might work the first night, but don't tell me you're going away with a guy for a whole week and you're gonna sleep in separate rooms the entire trip!

Certainly, I never went away with a guy on vacation, aka bae-cation. I was so determined that no man was gonna get these delicious cookies that I turned down so many weekend trips and bae-cations that my name should have been "No." LOL! Don't be so gullible to go on a vacation that you sell your purity for a weekend fling. If you want to go on vacation, take yourself or get together with a few friends and enjoy ya' self with all your cookies intact.

Mr. Motorcycle: Many women love guys who ride motorcycles. Mr. Motorcycle is in the motorcycle club, and he likes to take pictures on his bike and offer rides to women. It's a conversation starter and attention getter. Some women find it sexy, and that's cool if that's what you like.

However, don't allow the motorcycle to distract you from what's important. Get the data you need to make an informed decision about the man.

Mr. Gym Rat: This mister is different from Mr. Athletic in that Mr. Gym Rat's life is the gym. He is a bodybuilder, drinks and eats protein shakes, and his whole life is about building his body. Might not be a bad thing if that's what you like, but be careful, ladies, when you fall for a Mr. Gym Rat.

Do not allow yourself to fall for this guy because he will want you to become a gym rat, too. Some women start to impress him, but it will only be a short period before you realize that you were doing it for all the wrong reasons. In the meantime, this is a turn on for many women.

If Mr. Gym Rat is what floats your boat, then float on. But remember to get the necessary information you need to make an informed decision. And if you decide to become a gym rat, do it for you and not a man.

Mr. Twins: These two for ones are like Mr. Father and Son. It's a conversation starter, especially if they are identical. They often post desiring a lucky lady to join them for some "fun," aka threesomes.

Here again, princesses, this is a trap. If you desire a husband and not a fling, please leave the two for one special alone. Reminder,

I am not saying that every man is this way. All I am saying is for you to look out for the cunning traps that many set.

Mr. Money Man: Whee, Jesus! I am so glad that I was never a woman who was moved by money. Yes, I wanted the man I chose to have a healthy relationship with money. I wanted him to have an excellent job so that he could provide comfortably for us. Additionally, I wanted him to have a plan in case there' sickness or unemployment.

But I never allowed a man to move me with his money. And y'all, when I tell you that I struggled to provide a life for Lexi and me, I struggled! I didn't have to struggle the way I did because there were men who would do anything for me. But at what price?

And remember, I said I have always wanted to be happy in a healthy marriage. This goes back to the point of this book. Don't allow one thing to make you make a lifelong decision. Get your data so that you can make an informed decision. Be wise as serpents and harmless as doves in dating.

Mr. Big Girl Lover: The thinking that big girls won't get any love is a myth. Many guys love and prefer big girls. I know someone who would have married me in a heartbeat! But there's only one issue: He loves big women. I am of average weight, and I am mindful about my weight. Every time Mr. Big Girl Lover saw me, he would say, "You know, I love you, but when are you going to gain another 200 pounds?" Lol! NEVER! Not if I can help it! Praise God! So princesses, don't think that you must look like a toothpick for your Boaz to find you. Sure, I believe in being our best self, and if that's losing some weight, then do that. We have all heard or read the studies that show that losing even a few pounds will help our health.

However, I know many of my sisters who struggle with weight, and that doesn't mean you are unlovable. You need to choose a husband who loves all of you. You still need to be mindful, vigilant, and prayerful! Just because some men love big girls doesn't mean they want to profess their love for you, provide for you, and protect you. Remember, ladies, vetting men to make sure they want to protect and provide is vital to your data collection.

And no, I'm not saying for women not to try to become healthier by exercising, eating healthy, and adhering to medical advice. Again, I'm of average weight, and the moment I pick up a few extra pounds, my doctor is on me. And I'm good with her because she's been my doctor for over twenty years. So lose the weight, ladies, get you a few supportive girlfriends, and most importantly, become healthier for you!

Mr. Extravagant: Opposite of Mr. Cheapo is Mr. Extravagant. This is the man who tries to live a life he cannot afford. He spends every penny he gets. He likes to buy women gifts or give them money. Whatever a woman wants, he willingly buys because he is trying to buy her love or attention. He will offer to buy you gifts by sending you pictures of what he thinks would look good on you. He spends extravagantly on dates and so on. Of course, there's nothing wrong with this if he can afford it. And as I have said, dates do not have to be expensive. Dates could be a simple walk in a public, busy, and safe park, meeting at a coffee shop, or by the boardwalk.

However, some men spend to impress women, running up thousands of dollars on expensive dates. Influenced by how much he spends on dates, you might get into a relationship with this man and even marry him, only to find out later that he has thousands of dollars in credit card debt. As you can see, these are two extremes; we all need to be in the middle, having a balanced and healthy relationship with money. Again, there is nothing wrong with a man showering his lady with gifts or expensive dates if he can afford them. So princesses, be mindful as you DATE, aka gather DATA on Mr. Cheapo or Mr. Extravagant. Finally, pay close attention to their relationship with money.

Mr. White Boy Who Loves Black Women: I love this mister. Many women of color are open to dating men of different ethnicities. At the same time, other women of color only date white men. And that's quite okay; however, don't overlook obvious red flags because this man meets just one of your criteria.

As with all the men you meet, have your checklist, and allow him to go through the process. Scoring a one on your list of ten things is not enough for you to turn your life over to him.

Mr. Red Carpet: Oo la, la! We all want a man who can give us the red-carpet treatment. Well, at least I do. Ladies, beware. Guys know what we want. They know we want to be treated like the Queen of England. Many will come in first pulling out all the stops and giving you the red-carpet treatment. Oh, the horror stories I have heard about Mr. Red Carpet. My heart breaks for my sisters because I know that many desire to be loved, protected, and provided for.

And then, when they meet a man that, on the surface, seems to do that, they jump headfirst. But babies, honey chile, please don't do that. Get the data before you jump in. Because the Mr. Red Carpet could be his bait to get your attention, heart, and mind. Next thing you know, you're footing the bill for Mr. Red Carpet so that y'all can keep up appearances. That is not wise!

Mr. Pilot: Lol!! There's a new scheme going on in our dating world? Well, the word on the streets is that there are men who are telling women that they are pilots. Oh goody! That sounds like a possible decent guy to take home to mommy and daddy, right? But remember, princesses, you need information about not only Mr. Pilot but every man you meet and date.

It's crucial that you do not choose a man because he meets one of the criteria on your list. That is the whole purpose of this book to show you how various men use different baits to catch us. So, yes, Mr. Pilot says he is a pilot, and we are thankful for all our pilots. However, the thing Mr. Pilot forgot to mention is that he is a drone pilot! I'll give you a second to think about that.

This man is passing himself off as a pilot, but he has never even been in the cockpit of a plane. Princesses, we all need to be careful, get data, and stop jumping headfirst because he sounds good on the surface. Investigate, ask questions, talk to people, Google, search them on social media, and so on. How many times have we seen

on the news people pretending to be doctors and so on? You need proof, princesses!

Mr. Fatten You Up: Have you heard the saying, "Men love a woman with a little meat on her bones"? Lol. Well, imagine meeting a guy who has that mentality. He is different from Mr. Big Girl Lover in that he needs you to gain more weight. I met Mr. Fatten You Up in my mid-twenties. I was fresh out of college, and I probably weighed about 135.

Mr. Fatten You Up, and I went out for dinner, and he took food off his plate and put it on mine. He claimed I needed to gain a few more pounds. Guess what? That was the last time I went out with him. As I thought on Mr. Fatten You Up, I realized that he was dropping little hints about various things that I ignored or didn't realize that's what he was saying at that time.

Ladies, we need to be what the Bible calls sharp in the Spirit. Be alert, ears perked up, eyes wide open, so that we can pick up on the subtle hints men drop. We can't afford to miss those subtle hints. Remember, we need to be wise as serpents and harmless as doves. Most importantly, be mindful that the men we marry will determine our future.

Mr. Uniform: Who doesn't love a man in a uniform? (Raising my hand.) LOL! Yes, I am one of those ladies who doesn't care for a man in uniform. Well, except for a firefighter! Lol! Many women love a man in uniform, and that's great if Mr. Uniform floats your boat.

However, ladies, beware. Just because he is a man in uniform doesn't mean his intentions towards you are right. Some men will use whatever bait they can to get your attention and get you. Yes, there are many good men in uniform. However, women need to vet men, whether he is in a uniform or not.

Oh, I could write a book on the horror stories I have heard. Seeing a man in uniform and thinking that he is a good catch for a husband is not a safe assessment. No, a man is a man. The only thing that makes a difference in a man's life is the Lord Jesus Christ. As women, we badly desire to be married and have the covering of a husband. At times, we think because a man shows interest in us that he automatically wants to profess, protect, and provide.

No, they don't, ladies! Please keep your guard up and beware of the wolves in sheep's clothing. Again, I am not saying every man is this way. However, I want to get in your head that, no matter the type of man you meet, you must vet him. Don't think because he looks and sounds good that he's a good man. Neither does it mean he wants to profess his love for you, protect you, and provide for you. Remember, princesses: I am not promoting toughness, aggressiveness, hardness, and callousness. Instead, I want to encourage a spirit of grace, softness, kindness, graciousness, wisdom, and femininity. Additionally, because I'm from the Islands, add a dash of spiciness in there too.

Mr. Virgin: This guy is like Mr. Nerd and Mr. Shy. He is so shy that he doesn't know how to approach a woman, which has prevented him from meeting someone. He is so shy of sex that, at forty years old, he is still a virgin and has never had an orgasm.

Now, in all fairness, God desires us to remain virgins or celibate until marriage, so be mindful of that.

Mr. Virgin also could be a Christian who claims he is waiting for God to send his wife so that they can enjoy blessed sex. However, many women fall for this trick, thinking he wants to wait to have sex only to find out otherwise. He was using his "virginity" to reel her in, and in the twinkle of an eye, they are at his place losing his "virginity." Why? Because Mr. Virgin uses his virginity as a ploy for women to "turn him out" and show him the "ropes" in the sheets.

Interestingly, I have recently learned that some men like Mr. Virgin use this trick because they like to be dominated in the bedroom, preferring a woman who has had more sexual experience and can teach him. But remember, ladies, this could be a trick. If he claims he is waiting until marriage to have sex, he won't put you in a compromising position.

Watch his actions because they speak louder than words. Also, a man who is ready to get married will not lead with "I'm a virgin." He won't be advertising his virginity to the highest bidder. And ladies, if you're a virgin, you don't need to announce it. That's no one's business. Stop advertising your virginity all over social media. Remember, use wisdom, ladies, in all that you do.

Mr. Well-Groomed: Ladies, please tell me that I am not the only woman who loves a well-groomed man from head to toe, haircut, and beard neatly trimmed, if he has one. Or if it's a goatee, nicely shaped up and clean, along with beautiful teeth and fresh breath.

Clean and cut nails, no snot sticking out of his nose, or wax sticking out of his ears.

Mr. Well-Groomed wears clean clothes, pants at his waist with a belt or suspenders, not below his buttocks with his underwear showing. I never understood how a grown adult male could walk around with his behind sticking out and his underwear showing. What's more, puzzling are the grown women who are with these males. I find it shocking but to each his own.

And do you know what's worse? You go to a grand event, where real men have a suit or tux on, but here comes this adult male with his pants sagging! I don't understand it. I don't know how any woman can trust her life with a man who can't even keep his pants at his waist. Lol! Now, let's use wisdom, ladies. I'm not saying a man can't be in a relaxed atmosphere, where he's comfortable and chilling.

At the writing of this book, my son is three years old, and he must wear uniforms to daycare. There's a father with a son who attends the same daycare, and one morning, the director said to the father for him to pull up his son's pants or get him a belt or adjustable waist pants. She called my son over to show him the pants that he wears with the adjustable waistline as an example.

The sad thing is, the poor little toddler had his pants below his butt just like his father. His father had his whole butt out with his underwear showing. My thought was, *"How can he be an example when he is wearing his pants below his butt?"* Ladies, I don't know about you, but I pay attention to things like that. If he can't keep his pants at his waistline or get a belt, why should I turn my life over to him? But once again, I always had a specific type of guy that I like.

Anyway, let's get back to Mr. Well-Groomed. I love a well-groomed, put together man. No, that is not proof that he will treat you right, I can hear a cynical person saying. But I can say this: if I am approached by Mr. Well-groomed and Mr. Butt Out, the latter doesn't stand a chance with me. He won't even get my phone number. But beware, princesses, some men who are well-groomed use it as bait to get women to jump into their inbox. I know plenty of well-groomed males with doggish tendencies. Again, don't allow one thing to get you to sign your name on the dotted line. Remember my cake example?

Mr. Looking for A Mother for My Kids: I had an experience with this mister. I was fresh out of high school and attending my local community college. I don't remember where we met, but he had a daughter the same age as mine. I thought, how sweet! He has a child, and I have a child around the same age. We're a perfect match. See that? The ONE thing.

Well, the next thing I know, the little girl was at my apartment every weekend he had her. At that time, I had a studio apartment that was one room with one bed that my daughter and I shared. One weekend, he dropped her off, and I couldn't reach him at all. When he finally came to pick her up Sunday evening after church, he claimed he'd slept all weekend. You know that gut feeling, that intuition God gave us, ladies?

Well, that was it for me! I cut him off, blocked his number, and even went away for a few weekends. After a while, I guess he got the message and stopped coming by or calling. This is another reason I preferred a man without kids, even though I was flexible.

Many single fathers will often post that they are looking for a mother for their kids because he and his baby's mama broke up. He talks bad about her or calls her names, such as a witch or "garden tool" and so on. Some women get busy taking care of his kids, trying to prove to him that she is not only mother material but wife material too.

Next thing you know, he's dropping the kids off at your house on the weekends that he has them. Now, you're the babysitter while he lives like a man without a care in the world, hanging with his boys and even entertaining other women. Another way to look at this is, if you marry this man, it's evident that you will be the one taking care of your children and his. Being a blended family is not easy, and both parents need to do their part. Actions speak louder than words. Accordingly, be alert, ladies, pay attention, and remember to be wise as serpents and harmless as doves.

Mr. Nerd: This mister could be classified as a Mr. Bait or a Mr. Build a Male. He could be using his nerdiness to bait women. But it could be he is hoping that you would help him to become manlier. Thus, Mr. Nerd could be classified as a build a male also because he needs a woman's help him to become manlier. I don't know about you, but it sounds as if he needs to go back home to his mom, but okay?

In this instance, he's a nerd, but he has a dash of sexiness, smarts, and seems vulnerable. He is a nerd but has enough desire for women to want them to "help him" become a man's man. Even though he doesn't necessarily carry himself like a nerd, he acts like he is. Mr. Nerd is the guy who is looking for a woman to help him become like Stephen from the T.V. show and help him come out of his shell.

He acts naïve to draw women in to give him a makeover. Only, if she "helps" Mr. Nerd out of his nerdiness, she falls into his plan; he gets the cookie and leaves her for his next victim. Beware, ladies, I have yet to understand how a woman can be attracted to a man who she needs to "help become a man." But to each her own.

Mr. Shoot Your Shot: Ladies, any man that tells you to shoot your shot is one you need to block right away! Mr. Shoot Your Shot is often the same guy who wants you to pay half the bills or go dutch on your date. Mr. Shoot Your Shot is lazy and doesn't respect or value you. A man who respects women will value and adore you and know that you're worth pursuing.

Mr. Shoot Your Shot wants to protect his feelings. He knows that if you jump in his inbox and pursue him, then most likely you won't reject him because you're doing the chasing. You're saying you want him, and you will do what you need to do to have him, including "shooting your shot."

Mr. Shoot Your Shot is extremely feminine, and his masculinity hangs in the balance. He is the same guy who says he wants a woman to propose to him. Mr. Shoot Your Shot is the guy who will have his wife working two or three jobs while he "contributes" to the household expenses. In the meantime, he sits at home all day, waiting for his wife to come home to wash, cook, clean, serve, and feed him, then bathe him, sex him, and put him to bed. If you happen to meet a Mr. Shoot Your Shot, please do us all a favor and RUN!

Mr. Tattoos: I don't get it, but some women love men with tattoos. I know some women who couldn't date a man who didn't have any tattoos. Not my cup of tea, but some guys love to show their tats because they know that many women like them, and it's a conversation starter.

Here again, ladies, it needs to take more than tattoos for you to allow a man in your life. Vet him, get the data. Will he be getting more? What if he wants you to get some? Is that okay with you? And ladies, the dumbest thing, recently, I've seen women tattooing between their legs with the saying, "Mr. Tattoo's Cookie." Guess what? Mr. Tattoo hasn't even married them yet, but these foolish women have his name on their bodies and between their legs? Ugh, how stupid!

Mr. Fraternity: Many ladies love a man who is in a fraternity and only date men who are in fraternities. My husband is an Alpha, and while I have many friends of various fraternities, some men use it to get women. I was never interested in pledging or searching out fraternity men when I was in school. I was too busy working and taking care of my baby girl. It wasn't until I met my husband that my knowledge of Greek associations broadened.

Now, I love the men of various Greek associations. Most are great, committed to servitude, community building, brotherhood, and family. If that floats your boat, so be it. But, here again, be mindful and keep an eye on any man that you date. My husband, his pastor, and other businessmen that he is associated with are

Alphas. Also, I have met many of my husband's fraternity brothers, and I can say they are men of standards. They are all great husbands, fathers, and great providers.

5-Mr. Character, aka Mr. Personality

Mr. Nice Guy: I must be the only woman who loves a Mr. Nice Guy. Unfortunately, he gets a bad rap. But I like a nice, sweet guy who respects women and loves his momma. A man who is educated, speaks well, is a great provider, and has the potential to be the president is my ideal. I love the nice guy who has thought out his life, built himself up. A man who has prepared himself to be a husband and an example to others around him. I love a nice guy who's a gentleman and who knows how to treat a woman like a queen.

Unfortunately, some women don't like nice guys. I have heard them say things like, "He's too nice" or "He isn't thuggish enough." But do you know what the sad thing is? These same women will waste their lives with thugs and then get into their forties and fifties still single, wishing they had given Mr. Nice Guy a chance. They spent their whole life with thugs, and now the sun is getting ready to set, and they have regrets.

Now princesses, beware. Just because a guy is nice doesn't mean he has your best interests at heart. Some guys pretend to be nice and use it as bait. Here again, be wise as serpents and harmless as doves. Get the 'DATA' and see if Mr. Nice Guy is "nice" or is just pretending to be nice. Finally, beautiful, remember that it's not enough for a man to be "nice." I remember as a young single, people both in and out of the church were forcing guys on me simply because he was "nice."

Mr. Selfie: Who doesn't like to take selfies? I love to take a good selfie, and I take my fair share of them. I love taking selfies with my kids, my friends, my garden, and oh, my beautiful lawn! I think it's a good thing to feel good about yourself and to want to share it with the world. Mr. Selfie, however, loves to take pictures of himself all day, every day, and every minute. Everywhere he goes, he's taking a selfie. In the bathroom, getting in his car, getting a coffee, or even pooping. Yuck! When you take time to look through Mr. Selfie's page on social media, it is full of guess what? Selfies!

Mr. Selfie is the selfie king because he is looking for compliments. He wants you to affirm that he is "all that." Mr. Selfie wants you to tell him how good he looks in his car, clothes, or getting a coffee. And when no one comments on his pictures, he'll post asking why no one commented on his selfies. Gathering data is important, ladies! And you can get data by merely looking at someone's social media pages. Is he full of himself? Is his ego too big for him and you? And be mindful, ladies. There might be guys checking out your profile and pictures to gather data on you.

Mr. Make Me Want to Stay Single: Have you ever met a guy who makes you want to stay single, boil your eggs, and eat them? He is a total jerk, turn off, a sorry excuse for the male species, and not a gentleman. He's rude, nasty, and full of himself, thinks the sun rises and sets on him. Mr. Make Me Want to Stay Single is easy to spot. Please don't think you can "deal" with him. I get tired of hearing wives say their husbands are such mean, inconsiderate jerks.

The truth is, he was always a jerk, but many women overlook that, thinking that they can change him. Newsflash! The only male you are to change is a baby who is in a diaper! Leave rude, condescending little boys in grown men's bodies alone. Your life will be a miserable hell if you think you can make him treat you right.

Mr. I Want You: Also known as Mr. Action, his name says it all. Princesses, let me tell you if you ever meet a man who you have a mutual interest with, and he wants you, trust me; you will never have to wonder if he wants you because he will do everything to show you.

There's no guessing game, priming, or asking him and begging him to marry you, or anything like that! You might be overwhelmed by his desires and actions planned for you. If you are wondering, then he doesn't want you. Please, understand this, ladies! However, remember ladies, data is fundamental. It doesn't matter who it is, remember to be wise as serpents, harmless as doves in dating.

Mr. Thinks He's Black: This mister is somewhat like Mr. White Boy That Loves Black Women. Every time I see a man who pretends to be black, I just holla. Often, this guy will say something like, "I'm white on the outside but black on the inside." This could be because Mr. Thinks He's Black grew up mostly with people of color and has adopted the culture, thus identifying more with people of color.

Ladies, beware of Mr. Thinks He's Black because some use it as bait so that he can fit in. He speaks the lingo and Ebonics like the next guy. This mister needs to be himself instead of trying to be someone else. Here again, ladies, be sure to investigate the man behind the melting pot. Remember though, not every man is using it as a bait. The main thing, as I have said several times, is that you need to vet every man properly.

Mr. Comedian: Also known as Mr. Funny Guy. Have you met a guy, either online or in real life, who is extremely funny? I love a man with a great sense of humor. This goes back to the question of what do you want in a husband? Do you want a man with a sense of humor? Or do you want a man who's always serious, or a balance of both?

Mr. Comedian speaks about his personality. But ladies, while a sense of humor is good, be sure to get the information that you need. Some guys will use their humor so that you don't dig deeper. But try to see who he is without the comedy. Does he measure up to your list? Does he meet your standards? Do you like his humor? Ask yourself several questions about Mr. Comedian or any man you will date. Does he use it as a ploy? Can you get beyond his comedy and get deeper into learning who he is?

Mr. Smarts: If you didn't know, I love a smart man. I love to sit and talk to a man who is versed in various topics, be it politics, education, history, religion, or the latest news. When Mr. Smart posts on social media, it causes you to pause and think, *"This man is so smart."*

You comment on his posts, and you have great dialogue. He seems to be a great guy. You might begin to start having feelings for him, and you're tempted to jump into his inbox. STOP. Don't do it! First, I don't think, as women, we should be "shooting our shot." If you are commenting on his posts, and he is aware of you, there is no need to jump in his inbox. If he finds you intriguing, he will message you.

But you want to jump in his inbox regardless! However, what information do you have other than you think he is "smart?" Sit back, relax, watch, and pray. Mr. Smart is no different from any other man. We need to pay closer attention to him because he could be using his smarts to deceive or bait you. I've seen it happen many times with women on social media.

Mr. Thug or Hoodlum: Sigh. I will never understand why or how women turn their lives over to thugs, but okay? And then many thugs have issues with "good girls" not wanting them, even though the saying goes, "Good girls like bad boys." That's a lie for me! And how about, "Oh, don't judge a book by the cover"? My issue with this is that Mr. Thug doesn't want you to judge, aka decide about him, based on him being a thug. He wants you to believe that he is a nice guy, and you need to overlook his thuggish ways!

My answer? I don't date thugs. So I will not waste time with a thug to try to find out if he is a nice guy. If you're a nice guy, then what are you doing on the streets all day, hanging verses, becoming a productive man to build your community? For the life of me, I don't understand why or how women get with thugs. What is it about a thug that is attractive? He sells drugs, stands on the corner all day, and doesn't have a legal job. He goes back and forth, to and from jail. Women are attracted to this guy and refuse to date the "nice guy."

Princesses, this is the thing about thugs: The life a person lives usually follows them and their children. Do you think about any repercussions on their part? What happens if the careless life they live catches up to them, to you and your children? Can you completely turn your life over to him?

Recently, a young man in my community was killed coming out of his job. As a teen and young adult, he lived a careless life, selling drugs, shooting people, and so on. He went away for some time and then moved back to his city. He had turned his life around and had a good job. But guess what? His past caught up to him. And they killed him right in the doors of his job. So ladies, think before you sign on that dotted line. Think about the safety and life of you and your children. Is that the life you want to live and raise your children in?

Mr. Heart Breaker: He is merely a heartbreaker. His goal is to break as many hearts as he can. He was hurt in the past by a woman he loved and now has flipped the script and has become who and what was done to him. He works his magic and treats you like a queen to get you to fall in love with him. Then Bam! He builds you up to drop you like a hot potato.

Ladies, it is imperative not to fall in love with a strange man who you don't know. A man who has not gone through the process to protect you has no business holding your heart in his hands. Get the information first! And another thing! How do you fall in love with a man you don't know? What information did you use to decide to fall in love with him?

Mr. Gentleman: Like Mr. Nice Guy, these two guys could get my number any day. I find them intriguing, engaging, and mysterious. I want to talk to them and pick their brains. These guys open the doors for women, pull out our chairs, send flowers and candy. Often, he is a hopeless romantic, thoughtful, and kind.

My husband is a Mr. Nice Guy and a Mr. Gentleman. Once he got my attention, I knew I wanted to talk to him outside of the event where we met. He was kind, pulled out chairs for my girlfriend and me when we got up, stood when we came back to sit, and even offered to buy us something to drink. (I said no initially; I don't trust people with my drinks.) However, when the waiter came over, he offered again, and the waiter took our orders.

He asked for my number after hours of talking and offered to take me out. When it was time to leave, he walked us to the security desk to make sure we got in our cars safely. I left thinking to myself, "Oh, I want to talk to him again." And of course, we got married after about a year and a half. But I also think it was my time and my season.

When you meet Mr. Gentleman or Mr. Nice Guy, you might be tempted to make a move and lean forward. But trust me on this one. Fall back, lean back, and allow him to take charge and control. If he wants you, he will pursue you. If he is aware of you, and he is interested, he will make a move. However, remember, you need to get the data to make sure he is indeed a Mr. Nice Guy.

Now ladies, here again, please be aware. Just because a man is nice doesn't mean he has good intentions towards you. I want to press this issue because many women jump into a relationship with various men without getting to know them or getting the DATA. Getting to know someone is vital to understanding if you can trust him with all of you. Please don't marry a guy just because he is nice allegedly, but he has no fruits to back up his "niceness."

Remember the old saying, "You can't judge a book by its cover"? Keep that in mind. You need to flip it over, read about it, read the description, look at the table of contents, and flip through it. Unlike Mr. Thug, Mr. Gentleman will make you at least want to flip through the pages of his book. My issue with Mr. Thug is that we are supposed to be our best and make our lives and ourselves attractive. Mr. Thug is not appealing to me at all.

Mr. Rescue Ranger: This is a trap. This guy is the one who comes in and rescues you, even if you aren't broken. However, Mr. Ranger mostly goes after broken women who are in need. Mr. Rescue Ranger will save you from your bad relationship and move you in with him so that you can become his woman. This seems like a good set up. But truthfully, have you ever wondered why any man wouldn't allow a woman to become healed and whole before he gets into a relationship with her?

Here are a few questions to ask yourself about Mr. Rescue Ranger. Does he feel sorry for you? Can he truly love you the way God intended for you to be loved? Do you love him, or were you looking for someone to rescue you from a bad relationship? Every woman I know who got with a Mr. Ranger has regretted it. It never works out because you are with him because you were broken. But once you become healed, and your eyes are open, you quickly realize that Mr. Ranger is not what you need in your life.

Mr. Fisher Man: This guy must be paid close attention to. He is the type of guy who might want to play but isn't ready to settle down yet. Some Fisher Men have a catch and release policy if he considers you a "good girl." Mr. Fisher Man will release you so not to damage you for a future man. The only issue is, even though Mr. Fisher Man might release you, will you go in peace or will you force him to choose you?

However, if you have un-ladylike tendencies, then he might want to play with you for a minute. You might think he's ready, even though he has told you he isn't. Also, the timing for him might be off. You might be the right girl at the wrong time. Assumptions should not be made. He is not necessarily a bad guy, but he is simply not ready to settle down. However, he wants to play in the meantime.

Choose wisely ladies; you are too precious to be played with. You are also valuable. Do not allow anyone to play with you. As parents, I think it's important to teach our sons that they need to prepare themselves to be husbands. Teach our sons that a woman is precious and shouldn't be used just for sex. I think many young men play with women because they were taught to do so. I pray that our generation will be the one to restore the sanctity of marriage to our young men and women.

Mr. Serial Baby Maker: Ladies, I know meeting a nice man is hard, but how do you settle for a serial baby maker? You know, that guy who's thirty years old, but he has eleven kids? When you were thinking about what kind of husband you desired, what did you say about how many kids were okay for you? For me, I preferred a man that didn't have any kids, but I was open because I had a child. So if I met a guy who had a child and he was a nice guy, I could marry him.

Earlier, I shared that there was a father of five who asked my dad about me. I refused even to meet him because I didn't care how sweet and kind he was or if he made a high income or not. For me, I was not open to marrying a man with five kids. Plus, I had one, and I wanted to have another two.

Princesses, people might say you're shallow for not wanting a man with fifty kids. Please tell them to mind their business! You're the one who's going to take care of them, not the nosey people who want to run your life. And if anything happens to the moms, you do understand that those children will be coming to live with you and their father, right?

Plus, I don't like men who spread their seed all over the place. I understand you might have one or two kids out of wedlock and even with two different women, but when we start to get to four and five baby mamas? Sorry, no can do! But that's just me; you might be different.

Mr. Follower: Have you ever heard the old saying, "For you to be a good leader, you need to be a good follower"? Have you ever known a man who is a follower of the mess? He doesn't have a mind of his own. He doesn't know who he is. As a result, he goes with the crowd. Oh, I can't stand a man like that! **Matthew 15:14** talks about "**the blind leading the blind.**" Keep this verse in mind if you meet a Mr. Follower. However, ladies, please do not confuse this with a man who needs to respect and honor his leader, such as a pastor, boss, etc.

Another reason you shouldn't just marry any man is that he must lead you. He is the one behind the wheel, the ship, or the 18-wheeler truck. Can you imagine one of those enormous cruise ships and the captain is a man who has never been behind the steering wheel or doesn't know how to navigate the choppy seas? How can you turn your life over to a man who goes with the crowd versus one who has sought the Lord for a vision, thus following His leading?

See princesses, I believe, because many of us marry men who are not leaders, we end up taking control of the family and becoming the leader. How about you choose a man who is capable of being the head of your home and family? Remember, princesses, the man you choose will determine the rest of your life.

Mr. Teddy Bear: Many women love a teddy bear type of man. I'm just not one of them. Lol! Unless it's a toy that I can pick up, and it looks cute on my bed, I am not interested in a Mr. Teddy Bear type of man. Never did and never will cause I'm happy with what I got. Lol!

Remember, princesses: this is all about what you like. If you love Mr. Teddy Bear, great. But don't allow his teddy bear-ness to distract you from getting the data you need to make an informed decision. I have heard so many women say, "I married him because he was so sweet." That's it? You turned your life over to him only because he was sweet? Be mindful princesses: a man needs to have substance! There must be more to him than "oh, he's so sweet." Can "sweet" put a roof over your head and protect you? Any man that needs a woman to take care of him can be sweeter than pie.

Mr. Title: I have known many women to fall for Mr. Title. He is the guy with the title but no character, integrity, or discipline to back up the title he carries. Think about it. How many pastors, senators, congressmen, and even presidents have done unbelievable things? Who would have thought that a man in a leadership position could do such ungodliness?

Please, do not allow the title to fool you. No matter who he is, what he has, or where he's been, you still need to gather data on every man you decide to date. Remember, never get emotions involved because they will mess you up every time. Emotions change frequently! I am reminded of the story in the Bible about the young and old prophet. The Lord gave instructions to the young prophet to deliver the word and then for him to return home without eating. The old prophet told the young prophet that the Lord gave him permission to come home and dine with him.

Well, as soon as the young prophet finished eating, the older prophet revealed that he had lied and that the young prophet should not have listened to him. Additionally, the old prophet said, because of the young prophet's disobedience to God, he would be killed. So princesses, don't allow a man with a title to fool you. A title without character or integrity means nothing!

Mr. Open Book: Admittedly, this was something I foolishly did as a young dating single lady. I would meet a guy, exchange numbers, get on the phone, and talk all night. Next thing you know, you start to have fuzzy feelings and become emotional. But after about a week, when he doesn't call, then you're thinking, well why hasn't he called me?

I was in my mid-twenties when I realized the damage this was doing and stopped participating in that foolery. I mentioned a young man who didn't call for a few days. I think I had started to wise up then. The next time he called, he asked why I hadn't called. I asked him why he didn't call me. I'm not 100% regretful about this experience because I learned about extracting information and picked up on red flags. However, looking back now, I feel that I wasted a lot of time.

Additionally, princesses, remember we are to gather data on several men at once. Sure, at times, there might be one man who you're gathering data on at a period in your life. We all go through droughts. Lol. Therefore, if you meet this one guy and you're on the phone talking morning, noon, and night, when exactly do you have time to gather data on other men?

Even if you are going through a dry spell, it is still not wise to spend all your time talking to a man you just met. No man deserves all your undying time and attention except the man who puts a ring on it. Balance is necessary. Remember the old saying, "Time makes the heart grow fonder"? Stop giving all your time to a man who you are gathering data on.

And guess what? By the time I met my husband, I was an expert and was satisfied with a little information, one drip at a time. At the same time, he was also unraveling me and the necessary information he needed to decide about me. But another thing: my husband was a forty-something businessman. He didn't have time to spend hours on the phone talking and texting me all day. And by the time he got home late at night, he didn't have time to speak to me for two and three hours. We talked the most when we were out on our dates.

The most significant benefit for me when I made this change was discipline and patience. I met my husband a whole month before he made any contact with me or took me out. However, he liked my posts on Facebook every morning. I didn't call, text, or message him, and I was not all up in his inbox. Thankfully, I had already gotten to the place where I felt that if he wanted to get to know me, he would make all the arrangements.

A guy being an open book can be a double-edged sword. He can be an open book because he is insecure about who he is or overly confident in himself. He could be a person who has a messed-up past, and if he tells you everything up front, you might take pity on him and choose to be his crutch or leave him alone. It also says you want to get all the information, be it good or bad, all at once so that your potential date can decide to choose you or not. Therefore, ladies, be mindful.

Mr. Real: He is a man that I can respect. Could I date him? Well, it depends. Mr. Real is the type of man who tells you the reality about him. He isn't perfect, might have made some bad choices, trying to get back on his feet but isn't entirely there yet. I met a Mr. Real while I was in college, and we attended the same Bible

Studies Group weekly. Mr. Real, who was older, expressed his interest in me and how he was working on himself.

Additionally, Mr. Real stated that he had done things he wasn't proud of but found Jesus while in jail and was getting on his feet. Ladies, as beautiful as that sounded, and I was thrilled he found the Lord, I had no interest in him. He was not the man for me at all! Now, some women might say, Oh, that's nice that he is real with you, so why not date him? He ain't ready to be anyone's husband. He needs to take the necessary time and steps to build himself up and become established. Another critical factor for me was that I didn't date men with a criminal history. Nope, just not the type of man for me.

Ladies, please be mindful that Mr. Real could be a divorced man or father who took a beating in a divorce. Now he is stuck paying alimony and child support or just child support. Here again, he needs to get himself together. He is not ready to date for marriage. Plus, it's not my responsibility to help a man get beyond his past. I'm not his momma! These men are not in the place to get married. They might not say it, but they are often looking for a cheerleader. And remember ladies, I have always wanted to get married. Hence, I was dating for marriage. So, if I met a man who was not in the place to get married, I didn't waste my time with him.

Be reminded though, dearies, that we need to date men who have prepared themselves to be husbands. Remember the Psalm 23 Husband. He is a prepared man. We have no time to be any man's contractor or cheerleader while he tries to get himself together. Most of the time, you're just preparing him for the next woman. In my follow up a book to this, I will show you that, based on scriptures, any man can find you. However, just because any man finds you, means you must choose him.

Mr. Culture: We all have preferences, right? Many women prefer not to date men of other cultures. Now, I'm sure you're saying, with the "shortage" of especially good black men, why would culture matter? I have always loved African American men. I am from Jamaica, immigrated here when I was twelve, and my first crush was African American. Maybe that's why? My childhood sweetheart was Jamaican, of course, but we were little children in grade school, so I don't know if that counts.

In my younger and learning days, listening to church folks, I tried to date men of various nationalities. What I learned is that I didn't like them. But I LOVED African American men. And as I write this and think back, I wasted a lot of time dating men I knew I didn't like, mainly because of church folks. Because of this, ladies, you know I am all for being "open" to dating various cultures if you like them.

However, if there is a culture of men that you can't stand to date, much less marry, please don't waste your time. Some people think that if you love each other, then it can work. And that's true to some extent, but are you both willing to do the work? Many cultural differences can't be overcome. And the way some men think, their wives need to learn everything about their culture and do it their way. Sadly, many of these men refuse to adjust a little bit to learn about their wife's culture or even relax about their lifestyle. "Chile, I ain't got time for it!" Lol!

Now, the exciting thing about this is that my husband is an African American, and he LOVES and adores Jamaican women, so it's a win-win for me! Yah! It is so important to know yourself and talk about everything. Ladies, if Mr. Culture is a man who is willing to give and take, learn new things, then why not? However, it's not in words only but in actions that you can see that he is willing to work at adjusting to you. But if he thinks you need to cook his food every day, learn his language, set his table the way they do back home, and all of that? No, ma'am!

I know many women in this predicament, and they are miserable. You see, marriage is give and take, and it takes two people working at it to make it work. I am all for trying and doing things the way your mate likes it. However, some men have ridiculously unrealistic expectations. Additionally, I encourage my sistas to be careful. Numerous men only pretend to be interested in us, but they want to "play with us." while in the meantime intending to marry a woman from their culture. Please don't be a toy. If you want to be a wife, do not settle for anything less than being a wife.

Mr. Tender Roni Lover: Have you ever heard the term "tender roni"? This is a term a lot of older men from the Islands use. Other terms are often used too by other men, but it means the same thing. It is used by an older man to describe a younger, perhaps innocent and virgin-like woman. It's almost pedophilia. Mr. Tender Roni Lover loves younger women. His whole purpose is to "hit that," hoping to "turn her out."

Tender ronies, aka younger women, seem innocent and chaste, and these men love to have sex with them, get into a "situationship" with them, use and then leave them. That is why I think it's almost pedophilia because once he's used up one, he drops her and moves on to the next innocent and unsuspecting victim.

How do you identify Mr. Tender Roni Lover? Well, he will come right out and say it. He will say something like, "You're gonna be my tender roni," or "You're such a tender roni." Also, if you have talked with him about the women he has dated, they will often be way younger than he is. For example, there was a twenty-five-year-old woman who was dating a forty-year-old man, and he had recently broken up with his nineteen-year-old girlfriend. C'mon, a forty-year-old man and a nineteen-year-old almost child? She can't even drink legally!

Then he told her that he often doesn't date women as old as she is. Are you kidding me? He is forty, and she is twenty-five, and he is calling her old? Princesses pay attention to everything a man says. Smile and take it all in and gather your data. But if I were this twenty-five-year-old woman, I would have blocked him after that! No need to waste my time. I'm sure it won't be long before he leaves her and moves on to an even younger tender ronie!

Mr. Browning: This was a song that was popular when I was coming up in Jamaica. It goes (I will write it in proper English) "I love my car, I love my house, I love my money and things, but most of all I love my browning." Lol! Browning is a girl who has a brown complexion.

To be clear, it's a woman who has brown skin. Not dark, light or high yellow, but brown. So the men would sing it when they see a brown skinned woman, and of course, that would put a smile on her face. Even today, when I go to some Jamaican establishment, the guys will sing that song. And yes, I get the smiling, grinning from ear to ear. Lol!

In this instance, Mr. Browning is a man who loves a particular skin tone. Often, they prefer women of lighter skin pigmentation. I will not fault Mr. Browning. I think we all have preferences, and it's okay. However, ladies, be mindful. If he likes light-skinned women and you're a dark-skinned woman, beware. He could say he loves and accepts your chocolate or brown skin, but pay attention to little things he says like, "Oh, you would look so much prettier if you lighten your skin." Or, "Use this cream; it will help to fade your skin." He might even mention that you have "dark spots," and you need to fade them.

This too can go for your hair. He might like blond hair, but you have black hair. In other words, he doesn't love you for you. He wants you to change who you are to become someone else that he can love. Now, I am all for fixing up ourselves and looking and being our best. But if I need to become someone else? No, ma'am!

6-Mr. Representatives

The Apostle Paul states in **2 Corinthians 5:20,** that **we are ambassadors for Christ.** In other words, we are not Christ, but we represent him. And as representatives of Christ, we need to bring good news. Additionally, **Romans 10:15** states **that beautiful are the feet of those who preach the gospel of peace.** While Christ wants us to be like him, many pretend to be someone they're not.

On the contrary, **Matthew 7:15,** warns us **to beware of false prophets who come to us in sheep's clothing but inwardly are ravenous wolves.** Also, remember that Satan took on the body and voice of the serpent to deceive Eve. In effect, Mr. Representative is someone who pretends to be someone he's not. He represents something, but not who he is. You're talking to him, but it's not the real him. You think you knew him only to find out later that you never knew who he was. How many Mr. Representatives have you entertained princesses?

Mr. Representative: Ladies, beware of this guy. He is like Dr. Jekyll and Mr. Hyde. He is one person when you talk to him and another person when you meet him. This mister can be a narcissist or a sociopath or just a guy who's trying to pretend to be someone he's not. I'm going to write more extensively about this guy in an upcoming book, so please stay tuned.

Pay attention, ladies. When things are not adding up, and he has to give you an outlandish explanation, I think it's time to walk away. Don't ever allow your emotions to get involved and attached. Remember that emotions change and are unstable. Therefore we need the heart and mind of Christ. If you do get your feelings involved, you will stay longer than you need to and get all tied up, tangled up, and messed up with a man who you don't even know who he is.

Mr. Fake It 'til He Makes It: This mister gets faking it 'til you make it mixed up with faith. **Faith is the substance of things hoped for, the evidence of things not seen,** according to **Hebrews 11:1.** One might say, well, isn't that faking it 'til you make it? Living by faith is not faking it. When it comes to faith, we believe that we already have what we have prayed for. However, we are only waiting for the manifestation of our healing or blessings, for example.

Faking it 'til you make it is buying the fake watch, shoes, and so on but trying to pass them off as being real. Also, it's living on credit cards and getting in debt to maintain a lifestyle that one really can't afford. Mr. Fake It 'til He Makes It will buy the fake alligator shoes and fake Rolex. He will post someone else's apartment, pretending it's his. He wants to be flashy to show off, only for the woman to find out that he's spending every penny trying to keep up with the Joneses.

Additionally, Mr. Fake It 'til He Makes It will monitor you if he has interest in you. Based on what you say, your hopes and dreams, he will try to become that to impress you. So, by the time you talk to him, it's as if ya'll have known each other for years! It's as if he can complete your sentences, and the next thing you know, you're walking around talking about "He's my soul mate." Girl, bye!

Don't forget, princesses; you need to pay attention to everything. See if all those sweet lies match up to some actions. Talk about finances early in the data collecting stage. Not when you first meet him, please! Lol! Please remember to use wisdom, ladies!

It shocks me when I talk to wives, and they don't know how much their husbands make or if he's in debt. How could you marry someone without checking their financial health? (See my blog post on this on www.janicehyltonblog.com.)

Red flags of someone faking it 'til they make it are all around you. You need to open your eyes and go with your intuition. Also, has he asked to borrow money from you? Has he come up with some sad story about some strange incident? Can he not afford his rent this month and need your help or else he'll be homeless? Now you tell me, ladies. Is this a man you want to continue gathering data on? Some women go as far as marrying this man. But why, though?

Mr. Status: This guy is full of himself. He always posts that he's 6 feet, 5 inches tall, 250 pounds. Then he asks, what's yours? That's so that he can pick and choose who he wants to play with for the moment. Remember, ladies, a man who is serious about finding a wife, is not going to advertise it. He uses wisdom to search so that he can find his helpmate.

Mr. Status posts his status so that his inbox could be full of desperate "pick me" women telling him their statuses. Some even send pictures to try to convince him to choose them. Ladies, do you think you're the only one messaging him? Do you think he's not going to entertain all those other women because you're so perfect?

Please do not jump in the cesspool of pick me, women. Learn to stand out from everyone else. If Mr. Status drops in your inbox asking you what's your status, sound the alarm, sisters. A serpent has found his way into your inbox. #BLOCKED!!

Mr. Season: What is your favorite season? Mine is winter! I could have winter all year round. I love the snow, sleet, cold, and ice. Additionally, I love sweaters, hot chocolate, soup, and a huge cup of dunkaccino. Ladies, men are like seasons. Some will be in your life for a moment, a few days or months, seasons, or a lifetime.

Have you ever seen someone in the middle of summer wearing a winter coat, hat, scarf, and gloves? Likewise, have you ever seen someone walking outside in shorts, tee shirt, and flip flops with snow on the ground in the heart of winter? What's the first thing that comes to your mind if you see this? You think that something is wrong with them.

So, what do you think you looked like when a man was in your life for a moment, but you're holding on to him for a lifetime? Yeah! Something is wrong somewhere, my deary! Therefore, it is essential to make sure you are not trying to hold on to someone you're not supposed to be holding on to. Why? Because his time might be up, and you need to walk away.

Properly vetting the guys, you meet on social media or as you go out and about takes skills, intuition, a whole lot of wisdom and grace. Consequently, it is imperative that you know what you need and want. Knowing what you need and want will keep you from making a seasonal man into a lifetime pain. Ladies, if Mr. Season is only for a moment, please don't make the mistake of making him a lifetime decision. Let him go and walk away so that you can meet your Mr. Forever!

In an upcoming book, I will write about how some men see us as the mommy type. In the meantime, others see us as the moment or minute chick. But when our Boaz finds us, we become his mission and ministry. That's what you want, princesses, a man to choose you for a lifetime because you are what he needs.

Mr. Drunk: This mister is a perfect example of Mr. Representative, but in time, the real him always comes out. Often drunk, he takes pictures of himself drinking with several drinks showing. This one is easy to spot because he shows that he loves to drink and is always drinking. The mistake many women make is trying to get a drunk to be sober. Ladies, if he is a drunk, there is nothing you can do to make him want to be sober. That is a decision he must make by himself.

The best thing you can do for Mr. Drunk is to refer him to AA. Ladies, I'm all for a glass of wine or two or whatever his favorite drink is. I am not one of those who thinks you're going to go to hell for drinking a glass of wine. However, every person who drinks knows when they're getting tipsy, which is the gateway to being drunk. Why would a responsible adult allow themselves to get drunk, talk a lot of crap, and look crazy?

Mr. Party: This mister is like Mr. Drunk. Here again, this mister is easy to spot; you need to accept what you see and not try to change him. I have seen so many wives complain about their husbands staying out until 4 a.m., partying and drinking. My issue with that is many of these women knew that's how he was before. We need to stop playing the victim card for God's sake and take responsibility for the fools that we choose!

Those things need to be discussed before you get married. If the man you're about to marry is still a party animal, don't expect him to change after the wedding. Many women think because they marry a man, he will stop cheating, abusing her, or being a party animal. No, he is who he is. So, ladies, pay attention to the man who pursues you and you decide to date. A man who is ready to be a husband will conduct himself as such.

Here again, I'm not saying we can't enjoy a night on the town. Neither am I saying there aren't special occasions when he can hang out. When my husband hangs out with his frat brothers, I go to sleep. I'm not up waiting for him, texting, calling, and worrying what time he's going to come home. Those boundaries were set while we were dating and courting. Additionally, my husband's frat brothers are all married men, and birds of a feather flock together.

Mr. Netflix and Chill: Every time I see a grown thirty, forty, or even a fifty-year-old woman say that she met a guy and their first date was at his place watching Netflix, I want to scream! Ladies, we have got to value ourselves just a little bit more. First, you are going to a STRANGER-DANGER house on a first date. Are you that desperate? Do you know this man? Do you know what his intentions are for you?

How do you know that it's not a trap to rape, kill, or rob you? How many times have we heard on the news of a woman going to a strange man's house, and she was raped, killed, or robbed? Princesses, please use wisdom! Remember to be wise as serpents and harmless as doves in dating. If he wants you to watch a movie at his home, then nicely let him know that you would appreciate watching the movie with him at the movie theater. You don't have to go off, or be nasty, or say anything unladylike.

But also think about what he feels about you. What kind of woman comes to a stranger's house on the first date to watch a movie? Many of these are booty calls. You come over, and he dims the lights, gives you some stale chips and flat soda, turns on the music, and next thing you know, your legs are wide open and your drows on the floor, as he hits it from behind as he asks "Is this what you came for?"

Come on, ladies. Let's do better. As mentioned earlier, a first date doesn't have to be expensive or extravagant. A first date can be simple and romantic. We have an event here in NJ called Music in the Park in the summer months. Also, there are tons of cute little restaurants, and again, a first date doesn't have to be typical. Hopefully, your Mr. First Date guy will think outside of the box and plan something thoughtful.

Mr. Dominant: Unless you are into a BDSM lifestyle, I don't know how everyday women fall for this guy. He jumps in your inbox, complimenting you and making suggestions for little things.

You think, how sweet and kind of him. The next thing you know, he's dropping sexual comments, like he wants to choke you, tie you up, spank you, and be your master.

Mr. Dominant demands complete submission and trust. He tells you that he will contact you, and you should not contact him first. He comes right out and tells you all the things he wants to do to you and that you would like it. Here again, ladies, a man going directly to talk about sex and what he wants to do to you should be a huge red flag.

Don't allow him to connect into your spirit, ladies. Sex is spiritual just as it's physical. The Bible talks about having itching ears. Learn to set your ears, heart, and mind on the things of God and what you desire. Ladies drop this guy like a hot potato and block him! What I find when I talk to women who fall for Mr. Dominant is that, as women, we have a need and desire to be protected, cared for, and provided for. We have a desire to submit and be spoken for. As accurate as that is, you don't want to submit to the wrong man. Now, many women are in this type of lifestyle. Hey! I'm for all your desire with wisdom. You don't want the wrong man dominating you! Leave that for your husband, honey!

Mr. Horoscope: This is the man who lives, breathes, sleeps, dates, and does everything by his horoscope. He often posts that his sign goes well with other signs or that his horoscope says this week says he should go out with this one sign so hit up his inbox. Here again, thirsty women fill his inbox, hoping to be his next victim.

Eager women jump in his inbox, hoping that their stars will align in marriage. Sadly, many women get used while trying to prove that they are the right ones for Mr. Horoscope. Remember, ladies: you want a husband and not a seasonal fling!

Mr. Marketable: This is my type of man, considering other things are in order. When I say I wouldn't marry a man who makes minimum wage, people think I'm shallow. But these are the same women who struggle to make ends meet, work two or three jobs, but because I wouldn't choose a minimum wage man, I'm shallow? Okay, whatever! Lol!

Ladies, Mr. Marketable, go back to Mr. Rap Sheet, Mr. Minimum Wage, and others. Mr. Marketable needs to have the characteristics that any man you choose to marry must have. Remember, a husband is to profess, provide, and protect. Specifically, a husband needs to carry himself in a way that he can walk into any place of business and walk out with a job.

If the guy you're dating or plan to marry is not marketable, I beg of you to think about this before you sign on the dotted line. Her again, your list is essential. Ask the guys that you date the following question: "If you lose your job, what will you do? If you get sick, how will you be able to provide? What is the plan? What's your five-year and ten-year plan?" Now, are you comfortable with his plans and answers?

While dating my husband, I asked those questions. And I was comfortable with his answers, not only what he said, but I saw the actions behind what he said. God forbid anything happened to my husband, but I know what the plan is. If he loses his job, we won't be pulling our hair out, wondering what we're going to do.

Data gathering, aka dating, is not all about fuzzy feelings. It's about gathering the information you need to make an informed decision. Collecting data is about getting down to the nitty gritty beyond all the cute little butterflies and plan your life out. When the stuff hits the fan, you don't want to be caught off guard. Remember the Shepard in Psalm 23, also known as The Psalm 23 Husband? He is always prepared.

Mr. Cheepo: There is nothing worse than a cheap man who claims he is looking for a wife. A cheap man and a wife should not be in the same sentence. Have you ever met a man who is so cheap that it's sad? I could never date or marry a cheap man. As soon as I find out that he is cheap, I ghosted him.

Being cheap has nothing to do with expensive clothes, shoes, hair, or so on. It has to do with being selfish, stingy, and mean. In my book *The Naked Wife*, there's a story of a wife who wanted to buy her daughter a training bra for Christmas. However, her husband was so cheap and thought it was a waste to spend $9.99 on a training bra for his daughter. That's beyond cheap, in my opinion!

Ladies, please don't marry a cheap man because you think he will change. Remember that it's the man in front of you that you should marry, not the man you want him to be. If you marry a cheap man, you and your children will suffer. Spotting Mr. Cheapo is easy. Just listen and pay attention to what he says and does.

Does a man think giving flowers is a waste? Does he only live to feed himself but not you? Does he give to others willingly? Here's a dead giveaway. Does he tithe and give offerings, or does he think the pastor is using his money to buy alligator shoes? Does he think that giving to the work of the Lord is a waste? Lol! Get your list ready, ladies! When you date, you need your list to go off. That's how you vet and ask the questions you need to make an informed decision.

Mr. Long Distance: One of the beautiful things about social media is that it makes it possible to connect with people all over the world. In my world of publishing, I've been able to communicate with editors and book cover designers from all over, like Germany, Australia, England, France, and so on.

Social media has opened the floodgates to the number of people we can connect with and date. I tried my hardest when I was single, connecting with people in my state or at the farthest my surrounding states, like New York, Delaware, Maryland, and Pennsylvania.

I figured, those states are close enough, if those guys wanted to move to NJ since I had no intention of relocating until my daughter was finished with school. Lol! However, my first option was NJ, and the closer to my city, the better. I can hear someone ask, "Aren't there schools everywhere?" If you don't have a child with special needs, it's hard to understand that, once you find something that works for her, you don't interrupt it.

And look at how God rewarded me because I was faithful to him and my baby girl? I met my husband right here in this city, who lives here, had a beautiful home here, and we purchased our home here. Won't the Lord do it?

Some women are open to dating whoever, which means someone must move. Mr. Long Distance is the guy who is so far away that you can only see him once or twice a year. Here's the trick, though. He wants you to do all the traveling, pay for the flight, hotel, rental car, and meals. And to top it off, he expects you to drop the drows while you're there visiting him! Surprisingly, I have known quite a few women who fall for this trick.

Here again, ladies, it's critical to know what you need and want. Remember that a man is to pursue you, and if he wants you, he will make the necessary sacrifices. I've had guys from different states come to NJ to meet me. No matches were made, but I am still friends with a few of them on social media today. I learned a lot from them, and I was able to be rooted and grounded in what I wanted in a husband.

Mr. Ghost: Dealing with social media, where we can block, unfriend, and unfollow people, I am sure we have all been ghosted at some point. Mr. Ghost will ignore you when you refuse to give in to his demands. Also, he might ghost you because he thinks you're too aggressive by pursuing him or coming on too strong.

But most of the time, a guy will ghost you because he's already got what he wanted, and he no longer wants you. Or it could be because you refuse to send naked pictures or even money. But if you were talking to someone and he suddenly ghosts you without an explanation, it could speak of his maturity level. I say, praise Jesus. Be sure to learn from it and move on. Stop trying to figure out what happened! If he wants you, he will pursue you. And for God's sake, please stop demanding closure! Therefore you don't get emotionally involved and attached. Stick to your list and stop trying to make a not into a knot. Do you know the knot is a three-strand knot that is representative of Christ, the husband, and wife?

Mr. Crush: Aww, how sweet. I have had quite a few Mr. Crushes in my day. I'm 50/50 on this one. I shared earlier about a brother I met on Facebook, who called me his crush. The issue was, he claimed he was shy, but he didn't make any effort to come and see me. When he saw that I wasn't going to fall for his game, he moved across the country in the middle of nowhere and married a girl he met on Facebook. Reportedly, the marriage was over in less than ninety days. You see, ladies, you must let Mr. Crush pursue you.

The thing about crushes, they are crushing on you for a specific reason, but they don't know the real you. However, I have heard many testimonies of people marrying their crushes. Same rules apply: be wise and vet him even if he is shy. Allow him to do the work to have you. Just because it's flattering that he has a crush on you, and you think he is cute does not mean he gets a free pass.

7-Mr. Faiths

I know we like to apply scriptures based on our situations. However, the Bible is clear about born again believers not marrying unbelievers, according to **2 Corinthians 6:14: "Be not unequally yoked together with unbelievers."** Furthermore, I do believe that believers can be unequally yoked with other believers. For example, remember earlier, I mentioned the husband I choose must be a tither?

Well, there are some born again believers who do not believe in tithing. Me believing in tithing marrying a man who does not believe in tithing, in my opinion, we would be unequally yoked. Many women marry men they are unequally yoked with and try to change their minds, creating various tensions, resentment, and bitterness in their marriages. I will write more about being unequally yoked extensively, but for now, let's see what Mr. Faiths has to say.

Mr. Intend to Get Saved: I saw this often and had a few run-ins with this guy in my single days. He is not saved but tells you he intends to become saved. Some of my single sisters are so desperate and gullible that they fall for this old trick. Ladies, first, I never understood why women who are saved, sanctified, and filled with the Holy Spirit are attracted to a man who is not born again.

Instead, they decide to do what is called an Evangelistic Marriage. Another term for these relationships is missionary marriages. You know, marry a sinner and then try to get him saved. Or what many women do is get him to "confess Jesus," so they can get married. But before the wedding is over, she finds out he's a devil in disguise. Sisters, I beg of you: it's better to be unmarried than to marry a demon!

Sure, some women married men of other religions, and they have been married for twenty or thirty years. That doesn't make it right for you! The Bible is clear about not marrying unbelievers. Here's something else I don't understand. As women, we are told that we cannot raise a male child to be a man because he needs another man to teach him how to be one. We have never been a man, so we can't teach our sons how to be a man. I am one of those women and moms who believe this wholeheartedly.

Here's the dilemma: If a mother who birthed, loved, and tried her best with her male child can't raise him to be a man, how then do some women get with males who are not men and try to teach them how to be men? This makes no sense to me! Therefore, ladies, it is to our benefit, if we meet a male who has not become a man, to allow him to become the man that he needs to be. It is not your responsibility to take him under your wing to teach him how to be a man.

Neither is it your responsibility to teach him to get a job and keep it, open doors for you and so on. No, you will end up becoming *The Naked Wife*. A husband must be invested. His heart, mind, and soul should be about pleasing his wife and taking care of his family! You cannot force a grown man to do something he doesn't want to do. It's best to leave Mr. Intend to Get Saved alone and choose a saved man!

Mr. Saved Long Enough: I have known many sisters who fell for this guy. Mr. Saved Long Enough is the guy who comes to the church and is straddling the fence. He has one foot in the church and one foot out. He catches your eye, and he has convinced you that he is saved and sold out for Jesus.

You, taking his word, believe him, and marry him. But about a month later, he is done with the church because he's not a churchman. I know someone who is going through a divorce with Mr. Saved Long Enough. He got saved long enough to marry her. She wants him to go to church like he was when they were dating and just got married.

On the other hand, he wants her to accept him as he is because he is not a church guy. He has changed his mind, and he doesn't want to be a Christian anymore. Princesses be mindful when vetting guys. If he progresses past dating to a possible marriage prospect, more info is needed.

Saved Girls, please do not choose Mr. Saved Long Enough! Why get with a man who's straddling the fence, thinking you can change him? Choose a sure-enough saved man who has prepared himself to be a godly husband.

Mr. Lead Me to Jesus: He leads with, "I'm looking for a woman to lead me to Jesus so that I can get on the straight and narrow." Ladies, I cannot say this enough: if you are a born-again woman, then please do not entertain a man who isn't. Mr. Lead Me to Jesus is a trap!

When did he know that he needed to be led to Jesus? If he knew he needed to be saved, why hasn't he gone to Jesus? Why hasn't he fallen on his knees and asked Jesus to come into his heart and save him? If a man approaches you and he is not saved but wants you to lead him to Jesus, please refer him to your pastor or the church down the street.

Please do not get into the evangelistic or missionary mode, trying to save a man so that he can marry you! When I was coming up in the church, my father in the faith often said, "If a man is new to the Lord, he is a baby in Christ, and we need to give him time to grow up!" You do not need to get a man saved so that he can marry you. Also, the Bible states in **1 Peter 3:7 "... husbands are to dwell with their wives according to knowledge..."**

Make up in your mind that you will only marry a man who is saved and has fruits to show that he is a born-again believer. Sure, when you meet someone, you don't know what his faith is. That's fine. That's where gathering data comes into play. Have your list of questions, use wisdom, be wise as serpents and harmless as doves. Then skillfully and gracefully extract the data you need to make an informed decision. Say no to evangelistic and missionary marriages!

Mr. I Need A Prayer Partner: This mister is like Mr. Preacher. He knows that men desire a "praying woman." Taking advantage of this, he will announce that he is looking for a prayer partner. Women who are thirsty and trying to prove that they can pray will blow his inbox up with prayers or offer to pray for him. Little do they know that he is using it as a ploy to get them to get on their knees so that he can "prey" on them.

See princesses; even if you are a church girl, there are men out there who will prey on you under the disguise of wanting you to pray with them and for them. It's only baiting so that you can be caught up in their web of deception. Don't be deceived, ladies. Not everyone who names the name of Christ is about the business of Christ. There are many wolves in sheep's clothing trying to get all your cookies without having to pay the price.

Mr. Preacha: This mister could be a wolf in sheep's clothing. This is the man who's the preacher, deacon, pastor, or elder who's always quoting scriptures. He loves to pray and read the Bible when you're on the phone. So, princesses, you start to thank your lucky stars that you finally met a man who loves the Lord, loves to pray, and knows the Bible.

Yeah, until he starts asking about what kind of sex positions you like. Or he offers to take you away for the weekend under the disguise of spending some "alone time" to get to know you and "prey." Excuse me; I meant to say, "pray." Yeah ok? You foolishly oblige and go to spend a weekend in a hotel room alone with brother preacha and one bed. Girl Bye! You've just become his prey.

I know you feel safe because he comes off as a man of God. But sweetie, don't let your guard down for anyone! I don't care what package he comes wrapped in. Remember to be wise as serpents and harmless as doves. And like my father told me, beware of men who want to take you away for weekend trips and getaways. Nope! Let's spend time right here in town, out in public so that everyone can see us. You go to your house at the end of the day, and I'll go to mine. Lol!

Mr. Prophet: Princesses? I could write a whole book about Mr. Prophet. I had my share of them pursuing me and claiming they have a word from the Lord for me. And for me to come back to their offices, call them, and come back to church tomorrow for them to give me a word from the Lord. I thank "GWOD" for my father, who taught me how to hear from God for myself.

Additionally, he warned me constantly of the traps that men set to catch the unsuspecting and innocent young lady. Ladies beware of Mr. Prophet prophesying his way into your inbox. The next thing you know, he's at your house, and you're giving it up to him on your couch as he spills his seed on your living room floor! Oh, the horror stories I have heard! This is probably another reason I didn't care to date preachers or men of the cloth.

Mr. Evangelist & Mr. Missionary: This brother could be either. He is often saved, attends church, quotes scriptures, and is always offering to pray for you or give you a word from the Lord. Now, on the surface, this seems innocent, right? However, as time progresses, you will come to learn that this was a ploy.

Like Mr. Ranger, he is always looking for someone to save or rescue. Though seemingly innocent, his heart might not be in the right place. Time will reveal if he is genuinely looking for a wife or his next victim. Ask questions; see if he invites you to church to meet the saints. Patience is a virtue, ladies. Be wise as serpents and harmless as doves.

Mr. Wolf in Sheep's Clothing: I think we've all had a run-in with this guy. He is pretending to be a sheep but is a wolf who will kill and devour. Here again, ladies, this is a perfect example of the need to get to know someone before turning your life over to him. He is easy to stop, especially if you are praying and seeking the face of the Lord.

His actions don't exactly match up to the words that proceed out of his mouth. Observe him, and you will undoubtedly begin to see his claws slowly pierce through his fake fur. One thing about fakes: if you give them enough time, they will tell on themselves. It's always good to take your time and be skillful in extracting information; it is life and destiny saving.

Think about the many women who have met a man and plastered him all over their social media platforms. They claim they are in love; this guy is so wonderful and is the best thing since sliced bread. About two to three months down the road, you notice that things are different, and her language is different.

She drops vague messages about wolves in sheep clothing. What happened? His claws began to show, and now she's like, "Oh, he's a wolf in sheep clothing." No, sister dearie, he was always a wolf, but you were so desperate that you didn't take the time to vet him and gather data. See, this is another reason why dating several guys at once is necessary!

Meeting a new man doesn't mean you are automatically in a relationship with him. And it doesn't mean that he's the one for you. I have seen countless women say, "He sent a dingaling picture, and I told him I'm not like that. I haven't heard from him since, but

I hope he calls or texts." Lol! What? Why? He already showed you who he is. What other proof do you need that he doesn't respect you?

But you know the truth? She probably allowed that man to get all down in her spirit, got emotionally attached, perhaps thinking about how that dingaling would be. Lol! Ladies, ladies, please don't do that. Once you realize that he's not it, do the "hot potato." Drop him and move on!

Mr. Brother: My heart is for this guy. He is a brother in the Lord, who might be pursuing you. He genuinely is looking for a wife. He truly loves the Lord and is living his faith. He is faithful in church attendance, Sunday school, Bible studies. He brings his tithes and offering to the Lord, and he is committed to the work and service of the Lord.

If you sense that he is interested, please allow him to pursue you. If he wants you, you will not need to do anything other than be faithful to the Lord, and He will enable this brother to chase after you. This has always been the desire of my heart. To meet a brother in the Lord who is saved loves the Lord, and desires to walk in the ways of the Lord.

Take time to get to know him, ask questions, watch him, see what he posts on his page and so on. Be honest with yourself. Are you comfortable with him? Does he make you feel safe? Is he willing to answer questions? Most of all, do his actions line up with his words? Please note that these questions are ones you are to ask yourself of any guy you meet as things progress.

Mr. Saved But...: Women fall for this guy, even though his name is Mr. Saved But.... He is saved, but you can't see any fruit. He is saved but doesn't attend church, Sunday school, or Bible studies. He doesn't read his Bible, pray, or fast. Mean as a rattlesnake and cusses like a sailor. You keep looking, hoping, and praying you will see even a li'l seed or a fruit of the spirit.

Listen, it's either he is saved or not! There is no in-between. But many women are so desperate that they will take this man with the intentions of getting him right and saved, only to be caught in a web of lies and deception. This is the guy who comes to church only on Easter and Christmas. And don't you dare think of giving to the work of the Lord because he believes the pastor is taking his li'l $2.50. Ladies, please leave Mr. Saved But... alone.

Mr. Spiritual: What in the name of Jesus does this mean? Ladies, if your faith is important to you, please don't waste your time with Mr. Spiritual. He dibbles and dabbles in all religions. He will say something about not believing in organized religion like Christianity. Or that he reads, accepts, and applies all spiritual books.

Mr. Spiritual can also be categorized as Mr. Believe in A Higher Power or Mr. New Age. Personally, any man who is not born again gets none of my time. But if you feel the need to dig deeper, ask him what the name of the higher power is? Now, let me be clear. I believe people are free to believe and live as they choose. That is the beautiful thing about God. He created us and gave us the gift of free choice.

But princesses, if you are a born-again believer and you desire a born-again husband, then choose a man who believes that Jesus Christ is the son of God and he is Lord. I have known so many women who marry Mr. Spiritual, Mr. Saved But... and Mr. New Age and lived in hell on earth. A husband is a choice, ladies, so please choose wisely. Again, if your faith is important to you, then marry a man who believes as you do.

I cannot stress enough how important it is for you to know exactly what you want in a husband. Write it down, memorize it, meditate, and apply it to your dating life. One of the most baiting questions that I was asked is, "But what if you met a very spiritual man who had all the qualities that you 'need,' but he doesn't follow a 'manmade book' such as the Bible?" Ladies, I don't know about you, but why would you want to marry someone who thinks this about the Holy Bible? If he is not born again, then he doesn't have what I need.

The most critical characteristic for my husband is that he is born-again. A man who lives his life according to the scriptures in context. That is number one on my list and the most important thing I need. So, princesses, what do you mean he has everything else you need, but he's not a disciple of Christ?

Answer this for me! How did this man make it all the way to number ten on your list, when he didn't have number one? Your number one on your list, the man you will choose to marry, must have! If he doesn't have your number one, he cannot move on to number two. Therefore, do not get emotionally invested with some man you just met who is "nice." Talking about, "He ain't saved, but he is sweet and kind." Yeah, he can be sweet and kind to someone else! That's if your faith is important to you, of course.

Think about everything that is involved in having a Bible-believing husband. First, a husband is to love his wife like Christ loves the church. Okay, but he doesn't love Christ, so how can he love you the way Christ loves the church? And how did Christ love the church? He died for her!

Second, if he doesn't believe in Christ, will he "allow" you to tithe and give offerings? A lot of women get caught up in this because he says, "Sure, you can tithe." That's until you get married, and he says, "Don't you dare take my money down there to that church." My philosophy is, if he weren't doing it before he met you, he would say enough to get you because he baited you by saying what he knew you wanted to hear.

Third, will y'all wake up every Sunday morning and go to church? Sunday school and Bible studies? How about dedicating your children to Jesus? Understand this lady: there are already so many other issues which many marriages face that you don't want to add anything else to it.

My husband and I have never argued about going to church, tithing, giving offerings, supporting ministries, dedicating our children to the Lord, or anything like this. Our most prominent discussion is, "What service do you want to go to? 7 am, 9 am, or 11 am?" Lol! Choose a husband who you have as many things in common with as possible. Princesses, I cannot tell you the peace I have been with a man who is saved and filled with the spirit of the Lord.

Mr. New Baby in Christ: The Bible declares that husbands are to dwell with their wives according to knowledge. Also, husbands are to love their wives like Christ loves the Church. Additionally, our beloved Apostle Paul encouraged us not to be unequally yoked with unbelievers. Because of this, many believe that we can only be unequally yoked with those who are not saved. However, I do believe that we can be unequally yoked with a newborn believer and even a believer who is "mature" in the Lord. I will write about this more in another book coming soon.

Ladies remember that we are to submit to our husbands, and I believe that our husbands are to submit to us, too. The church often teaches about wives submitting to our husbands, but you never hear about husbands and wives submitting to each other. The truth is, before the command was given to the wife to submit to her husband, the command was given to brothers and sisters in the Lord to submit to each other. A wife is a sister in the Lord before she is his wife and vice versa.

Both husband and wife need to submit to each other and consider each other. There have been some situations where I have suggested to my husband to do B instead of A, and it was the right thing to do. Now, what if he jumped up and said, "Woman, the Bible says you need to submit to me and do what I say"? There have been many instances where he listened to me. And ladies, I am a praying wife. I have never suggested that he do something, and it was the wrong thing.

Sadly, what I see most is the wife sacrificing to please the husband. Paul said for the husband to love his wife like Christ loves the Church. And again, how did Christ love the Church? He sacrificed for her. So, when you have a husband who always wants his wife to sacrifice for him, but he never makes a sacrifice for her, you have got to wonder which Bible he is reading. You can read more about this hypocrisy in my book coming soon on marriage.

Accordingly, I believe it takes both the husband and wife working together at their marriage to make it work. And, like my dad often says, ladies, when a man is a newborn babe in Christ, give him time to mature. Our issue is, we see a new man come to Christ, and we automatically claim that he is our husband. Even on social media, I have seen sisters claiming certain men as their husbands; the second he comes to Christ.

Mr. Newborn Babe in Christ is just that. A baby. As women, most of us have had children. What are some things your newborn babies can do for themselves? How about when your baby begins to walk? He is like the new student who sits behind the wheel of the car for the first time.

Mr. Newborn Babe is like the first-time swimming students who need to learn to navigate the water. If a man has just come to Christ, please don't bomb rush him, claiming God told you that he's your husband. Leave him alone and allow him to grow up. If he is your husband, in time, he will pursue you. In the meantime, leave that man alone!

Mr. Saved Thug: This is the guy who is saved, but he is still a thug. The attire, the language, the hat to the side, several chains around his neck, and of course the thug walk, with the pants below his behind. Oh, and what about his vocabulary, "What's up, mama?" Lol! Now, I'm not talking about when you're chilling with your friends, and you all get comfortable code-switching, speaking Ebonics. I'm talking about this is how he talks all the time!

I've had several run-ins with Mr. Saved Thug. I don't know if it's just something about me that the thugs, both saved and unsaved, think that I would be interested in being a ride or die chick. Perhaps it's my church girl and good girl persona. And you know the saying, "Good girls love bad boys"? Nothing could be further from the truth for me. I don't like bad boys, never did, never will. For as long as I have known myself, I have always loved the clean-cut, walk the straight and narrow path, good choir boy type who speaks well and has the potential to be president.

Here's an example of one brother that I am still friends with on social media all these years later. Here again, is another brother I met via another friend's post. He jumped in my inbox because he was impressed with my comments. "Any who," we talked, and I learned that he was divorced with one child. As we got acquainted, I learned that he was divorced because he married a church girl and she wanted to—wait for it—change him from a saved thug to a choir boy. To her surprise, he was not about that life!

He liked his thugishness; she didn't care for it, and it was a constant battle between them. Ladies, please listen to me. Never try to change a man! Marry the man in front of you. If he is a saved thug and you don't like that, move on. If he is obese and you don't want an obese man, move on.

If he is a cheater and you think you can change him, please don't try; move on. Because as much as we desire for men to accept us for who and what we are, they also wish we would accept them for who they are. Too many women are busy being their husbands' mothers instead of their wives. If you want a man to mother, then I suggest you have a son. But if you marry a man, please marry the man in front of you and not who you want him to be.

If you don't like Mr. Saved Thug, please don't marry him with the intention of trying to change him. Leave him for someone who doesn't mind being with Mr. Saved Thug. And that's what I did. I knew I didn't like thuggish guys, so we remained only friends some ten years later on Facebook. And as you know, I got my clean-cut, choir boy type husband. However, Mr. Saved Thug is still single to my knowledge.

Mr. Submission: I shake my head in disgust every time I read that a girlfriend is submitting to her boyfriend. Or a woman is asking how to submit to her man! Girl Bye! Read this carefully: SUBMISSION IS FOR HUSBANDS ONLY! Ladies, please stop submitting to these males who haven't gone through the sacrifice to make you their wife! What are you submitting to? Shacking up and making babies, while you pay 50% of the bills or more? In the meantime, he lives the "single: drinking and partying 'til 4 A.M while you stay home and 'submit' to him!" Please stop it!

Let's get something out of the way. First, he is living the single life because he is single. If a man is not your husband, why are you submitting to him? But you know, you're so thirsty that you'll accept anything. And how foolish are you to submit to a man who hasn't gone through the process for you to submit to him? What are you trying to prove to him that you can be a submissive wife? Submission is about a husband protecting his wife. If he hasn't made you his wife, how can he protect you? And for God's sake, why would you seek to submit to him?

Mr. Sinner: Can we call a spirit a spirit? This man is a sinner in every definition of the word. But for some reason, you find yourself attracted to him. It's just something about him that sends chills up your spine. Remember, the Bible warns us to guard our hearts with all diligence. Don't allow anyone or anything to get into your heart and spirit. If a man is not a born-again believer, do yourself a favor and walk away if he wants to get to know you. Ladies, remember, we are on a mission, so there's no time to waste with men who don't meet your STANDARDS!

Mr. Sinner is who he is. He doesn't believe in your God. He ain't coming down to your church; he doesn't even go to church on Easter or Christmas. And we know that everybody, including the devil, attends church on those two days. Again, ladies, what do you want? Lol!

Mr. Anointed: One word: "oxygen." Princesses, how many of you love an anointed man? Raising my hand! I love a man who knows his way around the ministry of the Lord. In my younger days, I thought I would make a good pastor's wife. As I got older, I realized I didn't want to marry a preacher. And there was not one preacher that I was ever attracted to.

Princesses beware of an anointed man. Why? Because the anointing will make the devil look good. LOL! Oh, I know many anointed preachers who treated their wives like crap. Don't let his anointing fool you. Vet him, ask questions, study his fruit, and pay attention to his actions.

Mr. Bible Scholar: I love me a smart and well-versed man who can discuss all topics. Oh, and if he is a man of the Bible? I love a man who knows his way around the Bible so that we can discuss the scripture in its entirety. But guess what? I did not necessarily desire a Mr. Bible Scholar. From my experience, the men who were Bible scholars were often arrogant, full of themselves, and were know-it-alls, except my father, an anointed man of God and Bible scholar.

But that's why getting data is essential. Mr. Bible Scholar might be good at one thing, but overall, what is he like? Will he listen to you as you talk? Will he cut you off and make you think that your thoughts and ideas are not important? Is it his way or no way at all? Data, data, data—get it, princesses.

Mr. So Heavenly Bound, He's No Earthly Good: Oh, don't you hate people like this? These are the brothers who walk around with a Bible in their hand all day. They claim they don't do anything "carnal" like go to movies, listen to music, and so on. You know women like that who wear stockings in 100-degree weather, don't perm their hair or wear makeup, lipstick, or even a little skin toner.

When I was in school, I remember a guy who refused to wear deodorant because he said God was against it. Can you imagine being in a room with him on a hot summer day? Ladies, please be careful of Mr. So Heavenly Bound, He's No Earthly Good. If you marry him, trust me on this one, you will be miserable unless you are just like him.

Mr. Let Us Pray: I chuckle every time a sister tells me, "Oh, and every time before we talk, he says, let us pray." Honestly, who does that? Yes, I am all for praying, but no one prays every time before you talk to a person. Sure, perhaps sometimes, but every time? No, ma'am! Ladies, I want you to realize that people use smoke screens to pull you in and then bam!

When I was single and dating, I would tell my dad some of the things men said; he would laugh until he cried. Lol! A lot of that stuff is just crap and smoke screens they put up for the unsuspecting victim. Don't fall headfirst before you have all the data to make sure he is who he says he is. I am big on character and integrity. It takes time to get to know a person.

You should not allow Mr. Let Us Pray or any man to make you choose him because he does one thing right. If you are not able to answer the following question, then if I were you, I would pause. How does he act in other areas? Does he have character? Integrity? Does he bring his tithes and offerings to the Lord? How does he handle anger? Hard situations? When he is stuck between a rock and a hard place, what will he do?

Mr. Converter: I have known quite a few women to fall for this brother. As a Christian woman, it baffles me that many of my sisters in the Lord fall for Mr. Converter. Often, he is of another religious belief. I will not speak of any one religion by name. However, there's one that states that the men can date Christian women, but their women are not allowed to date men of any other religion.

This same faith believes that Jesus was a good man, but they do not believe that Jesus Christ is the son of God. The belief that Jesus is the son of God is what separates Christianity from any other religion. If a man doesn't believe that Jesus is the son of God, my Christian sisters, why would you marry him?

Let me share one example from a friend. We met at our job, and we became friends quickly, as we were both raised in the church. We both desired to be married, and we often prayed and talked about meeting our Boaz. She met Mr. Converter, and I must say he was incredibly handsome. She kept him a secret for a while but then broke down and told another friend and me about how she had been going on secret dates with him.

The first thing our other friend and I said was, "C'mon, sister, you know we are not to date men who do not believe Jesus Christ is the son of God." She insisted they were "just friends." However, we knew differently, especially when she decided to fly overseas to meet his family. But the Lord always has a ram in the bush! This young man's mother was a Christian girl, like my friend, when she met her son's father. He convinced her that they could get married and that she did not have to convert to his religion.

Well, the mom pulled her aside and told her not to marry her son if she loves the Lord Jesus Christ. His mom explained to my friend that she was just like her as a young single lady. She believed the lie they told her that she didn't have to convert. However, once she was married, it was only a matter of time before her new husband and his family were pressuring her to convert. To God be the glory, our friend came back to the U.S., told us what the young man's mom said, and in no time, she broke it off with Mr. Converter.

Princesses do not be deceived. The Bible is very clear about not marrying unbelievers. Apostle Paul states in **2 Corinthians 6:14, "Be ye not unequally yoked together with unbelievers: for what fellowship hath righteousness with unrighteousness? And what communion hath light with darkness?"** I love the way the Message Version puts it. It states, **"Don't become partners with those who reject God. How can you make a partnership out of right and wrong? That's not partnership; that's war. Is light best friends with dark? Does Christ go strolling with the Devil? Do trust and mistrust hold hands? Who would think of setting up pagan idols in God's holy Temple? But that is exactly what we are, each of us a temple in whom God lives."**

God himself put it this way: **"I'll live in them, move into them; I'll be their God and they'll be my people. So leave the corruption and compromise; leave it for good," says God. "Don't link up with those who will pollute you. I want you all for myself. I'll be a Father to you; you'll be sons and daughters to me." The Word of the Master, God.** Can you say Wow? The Message Version makes it extremely clear, doesn't it?

I have known many women who would meet a guy and convert to his religion overnight. Then, when the relationship doesn't work out, they take off their religious garb and run back to Jesus and the church. I feel so sorry for these women because, consequently, they are as the scripture states in **James 1:8, A double-minded and unstable in all his ways.**

For this reason, it is vital for us to be rooted and grounded in the word of the Lord, establishing our faith and word upon him so that we shall not be moved. It is crucial for us, as the King's Daughters to be stable in who we are and what we desire. My number one on my list of things I wanted in a husband was: "He must be born again."

Therefore, if a man who was not born again approached me, we had absolutely nothing to talk about. They would try to con me into going out with them by saying, "oh, but you could tell me about Jesus." For that Princesses, my dad told me to give them his number so he could talk to them about Jesus. Lol! Sadly, I see many of my sister princesses get involved with unbelievers and pray that they would become saved. Wrong as two left shoes! Princesses, please don't do it!

Mr. Polygamist: It is unfortunate to see women willingly fall for this guy. He sometimes comes right out and lets it be known that he is looking for "another" wife. But even if he doesn't say it, if you listen to him carefully, you can pick up that he is into the lifestyle.

Now, I know some folks are into this lifestyle, and that is their right. However, princesses, if you want your own husband, then pray to meet your husband. And the crazy thing is, many of these men can't even afford to provide for one family, much less two. So basically, you're signing up for some part-time dingaling?

8-Mr. Build A Males

*D*on't ever try to build a man or teach him how to be a man. The best thing you can do for a man who needs you to build him is to refer him to another man who can help him to become a man. Most importantly, it's a man's responsibility to go before God and find out what God has said to and about him.

Additionally, he needs to know God's will for his family. Then you can reinforce what God has told him once he chooses you to profess, provide for, and protect you. Please reserve the teaching ONLY for your son, not the man you are gathering data on.

Daily, I remind my husband of what a great man, husband, and father he is. I thank him for being my professor of love, protector, and provider, how he provides so well for the kids and me, and how much he makes us feel safe. My son, I speak greatness into him that he is a godly child, a good child; he brings us joy and peace, how he is respectful and obedient and how one day he will be President of the United States or whatever God created him to become and fulfill.

And as the King's daughter, I understand that I have creative power and delegating authority. I can speak, and it will, but God knows I didn't have time, energy, and strength to be speaking greatness in every man's life that I met. Because my greatness, delegating authority, and my creative gifts are reserved for my husband. So, I didn't have time to build any and every man I met in hopes that he would become the man I wanted to marry.

Many women spend years building up men who aren't theirs. I know many women who have built a man for herself, but then he skips off to marry a woman who can appreciate him for the man that she built him up to be. Build A Males are men who are looking for women to build them. The knockback I get from this is, "But we're supposed to build up our man." No, ladies, stop using that as an excuse. We are to build up our husbands, not every man you meet and date.

How do you build up your husband? You build him up in prayer, honor, and respect. You build your husband up by nurturing him so that he can become an even greater husband, father, and man of God. The keyword here is husband, ladies! Not some man who isn't adult enough to marry you.

Mr. Fixer Upper: I have a blog post about this, so please be sure to read it on www.janicehyltonblog.com. I hate that, as women, we are pushed to fix men up so that they can become husbands for us. I wanted to go off when church mothers would tell me to get a man and fix him up. Feed him, buy him some clothes and cologne, give him a lovely home cooked meal, and put some money in his pocket! My issues with that were, no one fixed me up! I struggled as a teen mom to make a life for my daughter and myself. I made the necessary sacrifices so that we could have a decent life.

Some males are looking for women to fix them up and build them up! Ladies, please leave Mr. Fixer Upper alone! Like Mr. Build a Male, once you are finished fixing him up, he often leaves and goes to find a woman who can appreciate him for the fixed-up man you have made him. Because in your eyes, he will always be the man you fixed up.

Mr. Build Me: He's like Mr. Fixer upper, except you're building this man from scratch. He leads with he's looking for a woman to build him up so that he can get on the straight and narrow. He's just a shell, and he needs you to tell him who he is, give him a vision for his life, give him masculinity, and tell him who God created him to be. I'm sorry, but you are not his momma!

But many women do this with the hopes that he will turn around and marry them. Listen, I can't say it enough! Sisters, a husband is to profess his love for you, provide for you, and protect you. The only male you need to be building and fixing up is your son, not a grown man who requires you to be your leader and protector!

How many women have you heard say they took some man in, fixed him up, and told him who he was then when he was good, he left her and married another woman? Do you know why? Because those women were playing his momma. And what do sons do once their moms are finished raising them? Once Mom is finished grooming and training, they leave Momma and find them a wife to profess their love to, provide for, and protect.

Ladies, you are not a contractor, counselor, or a maintenance woman. Many women get frustrated because they are trying to build up every man they meet. No, choose an already built man because you are a built woman who wants to get married. Then you can spend the rest of your life building and supporting each other.

I've even heard grown men whining about women only wanting ready-made men! Heck yes, we want a ready-made man! Again, we are not contractors. I don't know about anyone else, but I do not like to put furniture together. I don't even want to try to figure out how to put my baby's toy together, much less a grown man!

Mr. Struggle: Oh, gosh, this guy! He comes right out and lets the world know that he is looking for a woman to "struggle with him" and build him up. For some reason, some men think it's attractive, which translates to the fact that he has not prepared himself or is not ready to provide for and protect a wife. Some women think this is an opportunity to show a struggling man that they are ride or die chicks. For the life of me, I don't understand why any woman would sign up for the struggle male and life. Apparently, many women and men think that signing up for the struggle life proves love and faithfulness.

Males should be ashamed to ask a woman to sign up for the struggle life. Males who do this don't believe it is their responsibility to provide for and take care of their wives. And often they do not value women or understand that wives are a gift that needs to be treated with love, honor, and grace.

On the other hand, as women, we need to know our worth and refuse to sign up for the struggle life. Ladies, if you meet a man who wants you to struggle with him and take care of him, run please! A husband is to complement your life, add value, and make your life easier. A husband is not to make your life harder or cause you to struggle more than you're already struggling, perhaps as a single woman or single mom.

A husband is to multiply many blessings to you. If you are struggling to feed yourself and your children, why would you choose a man who will cause you to struggle more? Why do you want to struggle? Do you know that struggling is a curse? Please don't rush into a relationship to have a man. You would need to pray every month for the Lord to work a miracle for you and your children to eat and pay rent. That is no way to live!

Mr. Can't Keep A Job: Ladies, this is where your data collecting must be on point! Here again, is another perfect example of why you don't commit yourself to a man you don't know before getting the data you need. How do you find out after you are married that your new husband can't keep a job? How do you marry him without knowing that he can provide for you? If a man has had ten jobs in two years, ladies, he cannot keep a job.

Another critical factor to understand is that after a certain age, there's a difference between a man's job and career. A man who's at least thirty years or older needs to have a career. This is one reason I am not a fan of couples getting married too young. Often, the man is not established in a career to provide for and protect his wife and profess his love. Of course, use wisdom for those who have to study for years.

Sure, many couples got married young, but oh man, the stories they tell! When I was twenty-four, I decided to stop dating for a period because I realized that I was not meeting the prepared man

I wanted in my age range. And when I was in my twenties, marrying a man in his late thirties or forties was a no for me.

The guys in my age range or a ten-year age max were struggling the same way I was. Fresh out of college, trying to establish themselves the same way I was. Also, I took some well-needed time to pen my first book, *Praying for Our Children*. Yes, if someone asked me out, I would go out, but I decided to step back and take inventory of myself.

Also, right around that period, I went into a depression because I just knew by then I would be married and finishing having my children. I was going to the doctor, having all kinds of tests because I felt sick all the time. I remember my doctor grabbing my shoulders and saying, "Janice, you are fine. You're healthy. Live and enjoy your life." I decided then to focus on my book, and it was during those days I wrote more passionately than ever. So, ladies, please think before you leap.

Some women foolishly think they can make Mr. Can't Keep A Job get and keep a job as if she is his mom, and she is going to put her stilettoes on his neck to wake him up every morning, drop him off at the job, and watch him to make sure he's doing right. Princesses, you need a leader who is an example, not a toddler, you must make eat his vegetables.

Mr. If: I believe most women mess up with Mr. If more than any other man. I am amazed at the number of women who say, "You know, I knew he wasn't the one for me." Or, "I just thought if I helped him and encouraged him to become XY& Z, then maybe he would become AB& C." Ladies, I cannot say it enough! If he is not what you want, please don't marry him. If he must become something so that you can marry him, please leave him alone.

What do I mean by becoming and being a Mr. If? Often women would say to me after they wasted years on Mr. If that they thought some of the following:

1. If he could get a job, then I could be with him.
2. If he could keep a job.
3. If he would stop drinking.
4. If he would stop sleeping around.
5. If he could stop abusing me.
6. If he would stop partying and acting like a teen.
7. If he would marry me.
8. Etc.

Ladies, if you think you can marry Mr. If on the hopes that he can become who you need him to be, you are making a big mistake. Mr. If will always come back to kick you in the heart, and you will shed many tears because you build your foundation on the uncertainty of "If."

One crucial factor to remember about Mr. If is that he must prove himself. Remember when the devil was testing Jesus, and Satan said to Jesus, "If you are the son of God, then command that these stones be made bread"? Satan wanted Jesus to prove to him that he was, in fact, the son of God. But Jesus knew he was the son of God, so he didn't have to prove himself to Satan. Because Jesus was the son of God, he didn't need to perform. Jesus just walked in his anointing. A prepared man is just that, prepared to be a husband! Leave Mr. If alone, please!

Mr. Beast: I love fairy tales just like the next lady. However, have you ever realized that, in fairy tales, it's often a young beautiful virgin girl and a beast of a man who she needs to fix up and get right so that she can marry him? Why are we, as women, so brainwashed into fixing up men? Think about it! As women, we are soft, gentle, kind, and in need of protection. Why should we try to tame a beast? An animal that rips our delicate parts to shreds? They tell us to tame the beast and turn him into a prince so that he can marry us. No thanks!

Additionally, ladies, men are hunters! Remember that every man is hunting for something! Many men are hunting for a woman to mold, build, tame, and fix them up. I'm going to write about this more extensively in my follow up book because we seriously need to have a come to Jesus moment.

Mr. Frog: I'm so tired of hearing my sisters in the Lawd crying about how many frogs they've kissed! Here's an idea: As of this moment, you need to develop a severe case of germaphobia and stop kissing frogs to see if one will turn into your prince!

If a prince is what you want, then wait for your prince. Leave those dirty, germy, slimy frogs alone! Yuck! A husband is a choice; you don't have to choose a frog or a beast. You can choose a prepared man.

Mr. Goin' Be: This was another guy folks tried to stick me with when I was younger. Again, I ask, if I fixed myself up, went to school, and struggled to make a life for myself and my daughter, why should I get with a man and make him into someone? "Oh, he works at a fast food restaurant, but you know girl, he might own it one day." Okay, question: What is he doing now to work towards owning it? Is he just hoping and a wishing with no plans?

Sorry, no thank you! And what if ten years later, still nothing? Then what? I have known many women who married Mr. Goin' Be, and years later, still nothing. This creates issues in their marriages, such as anger, regret, resentment, and bitterness.

Ladies, I believe in marrying the man who is in front of me. If he works at a fast food restaurant, marry him based on that, not on "Oh, one day in the sweet by and by, he might own it." If you can't love him and accept him for who he is today, then don't marry him. Because if he never becomes that, then what? Your husband is a choice, so please choose wisely!

Mr. Potential: This mister requires a careful eye. He could be like Mr. Goin' Be, but you need information on his potential. Here again, I say marry the man in front of you, not a Mr. Potential or what he's going to be. But it's up to you to look at him carefully. I remember some church folks used to say, "Sister Janice, Brother John has potential. You need to work with him."

Here again, I refused. If I needed to do anything to help him become who I needed him to be, to profess, provide for, and protect my baby girl and me, I was not interested. Why? A husband is a calling and a title. A wife is to reap all the benefits of the title "husband." The same way the church is to reap the benefits the title of "Christ." So, I wanted a man who was anointed to be a husband for me because God prepared him.

But here's where Mr. Potential needs a careful eye. Let's say there is a guy who has been saying for years he's going back to school, yet twenty years later he is still talking about going back to school. What has he been doing for the last twenty years? On the other hand, there's another guy who says, "I'm taking a class to get certified so that I can make a better income and be able to provide more."

The first guy, even though he might be full of potential, is doing nothing about it. The second guy has already taken a step, independent of you, to become better. So, when you hear a guy saying he's going to do this and that, then you need to pay close attention. If the actions don't line up, it's time for you to say #NEXT!

Mr. Shy: This mister is like Mr. Nerd in that he could be bait or a build a male. Like Mr. Nerd, Mr. Shy knows that many women will baby him and help him "break out" of his shell so that he would be shy "no mo!" And sure, there are some genuinely shy guys out there, but there are some who use that to get women under the disguise that he needs her to help him.

Ladies, it is not your responsibility to get Mr. Shy to be shy "no mo." A man who has prepared himself to be a husband will do the work he needs to do to be the man he needs to be. Also, I heard a sermon once by one of my favorite Evangelists, Andrew Womack, preaching that being shy stems from being selfish. People who are shy need to spend time in the word, reading and seeking the face of the Lord.

So princesses, beware of a shy man who wants you to help him be shy no more, who needs you to help him become a social butterfly. That is not your place as a woman who desires a husband who can profess, protect, and provide. Women who take it upon their bosoms to be the anchor for such men often end up with a lot of regrets. He never becomes the husband she desires.

Mr. Rap Sheet: I don't understand how any woman can marry a man with a rap sheet from here to Timbuktu! I do not date, nor would I marry, a man with a criminal history. I have often said I wanted a husband who could be the President of the United States. Granted, none of us are perfect. But I also said if he stole a car when he was twelve and has lived on the straight and narrow path since, then perhaps, I could at least investigate and learn more.

Some men without criminal records can't always get a good job anywhere. So, it's probably harder for men with a criminal history. Sure, many men have overcome their past, have jobs, or have created their own. Congratulations, but no thanks! I am also aware that many of our men have been incorrectly incarcerated but have gotten their record cleared. I am not talking about those brothers. I'm talking about a revolving door criminal who goes back and forth to jail and has not cleaned up his life to be a productive member of society, looking for a woman to get with so she can be his ride or die chick.

So, ladies, if you don't mind a man with a criminal past, the rules still apply. You need to think things through. The Bible says to count the cost ahead of time. I'm not a woman who believes in making a man do anything he doesn't want to do. Therefore, I will not be the one pushing him to go back to school, get a job, and so on.

I have had women try to push off their sons on me because "He needs a good woman to get him on the straight a narrow." Wait, wasn't that his mother's responsibility? Please don't fall for this trap. You will spend your life trying to get Mr. Rap Sheet to be a decent and upstanding citizen. Again, yes, many men have done time and turned their lives around. If you're okay with that, then great. However, the rules still apply.

Mr. Trying: He is like Mr. Help A Brotha Out and Mr. Excuse. He is the guy who's looking for someone to baby him and take him on as her son under the disguise that he wants to be her "man." Why? Because he is "trying." Trying to do and be right. Trying to get a job, go back to school, get on his feet, get out of his momma's basement, leave his wife, etc.

Pay attention, ladies, because Mr. Trying has done absolutely nothing about "trying." You don't need a husband who is trying to be a husband or a man. You need a husband who is doing the business and is ready to be a husband! Just think about it this way. Can you try to have a shelter over your head, try to eat, or try to wear clothes? Remember that a husband is to profess, provide, and protect you. If a man has not prepared to take on the responsibility of a husband when he "finds" you, do yourself a favor and run far away.

When the mortgage comes in the mail, you can't try to pay it. When you go to the supermarket, you can't try to pay for the food. Unless you are ready to take care of a grown man who's looking for a mother to take care of him, please leave Mr. Trying alone!

Mr. 1 Want to Start My Own Business: Starting one's own business is an excellent venture, and I believe everyone should, even if it's on the side. However, this mister has been starting his own business for fifty years. He comes off as if he needs someone to help him start his business. He throws this out, often to get the attention of a woman who is willing to invest her time, efforts, and even finances to help him to start his own business.

Internally, as women, we want to help him become who he wants because, in helping him, we think he will see what a suitable "helpmate" we can be. Only for her to get it all done for him, so he can move on to the next woman who can do more favors for him. Listen, if he wants to start his own business, then allow him to do it. Women often want to come in like Mrs. Fix Him, acting like his momma and pushing him. I am so against forcing a man to do what God created him to do. I am all for supporting and encouraging, but as far as making a man do what he is supposed to do? No, ma'am!

I am also against wasting good time waiting on a man to get himself and his stuff together. You don't just meet a man and settle on him because he might not be ready to be the husband you need. Unfortunately, this is the mistake many women make, meeting a man who is not prepared to be a husband but forcing him to become a husband.

Becoming a husband is a journey, and each man needs to take time to prepare himself for this sacred service. So if you meet a man who can't even take care of himself, but you decide that he is the man for you, you are setting up yourself for disappointment.

Mr. Thinking and Planning: This guy is always thinking and planning to do something, but no one can see the manifestations. Mr. Thinking and Planning has been talking about going back to school for twenty-five years. He has also been planning to get a job, a car, to get on his feet, and so on.

If you listen to him, it sounds good and promising, and he sparks your interest like a man who has a plan. However, beware ladies. Don't fall for a man who has no manifestation of what he has been thinking and planning to do for twenty years. It doesn't take rocket science to go down to the community college and register.

Mr. Limp: Mr. Limp is like Mr. Help a Brother out. Have you read the story in Genesis about Jacob? Jacob wrestled all night with the angel of the Lord. When morning came, Jacob held on so tight to the angel that he had to touch Jacob's hip. Thus, Jacob had a limp.

Interestingly though, Jacob had an internal limp his whole life that he never addressed. It began with conspiring with his mother, Rebecca, to steal his brother Esau's birthright and continued to lie to his father. Like Jacob, some men have had things happened in their lives that they never addressed. Therefore, they never healed from it.

Mr. Limp is the guy who fell off his bike when he was three, and at forty-three, he is still crying about how he scratched his knees. It's a trick, ladies! He is just looking for someone to baby him and be his momma instead of seeking professional help. Now, let's be honest. Many of us have had some things happen from abuse to struggling to make a living. However, as adults, we need to be mature enough to fix our mess and not bring the baggage into a new relationship.

The women who fall for Mr. Limp say that, at first, they thought it was cute how needy he was and that he would mature. They end up marrying him, and they must spend so much time stroking his fragile ego and his bruised knee that they get burned out. If a man has unresolved issues that he hasn't worked out so that he can be healthy, how can he be a healthy and prepared husband? Leave Mr. Limp alone, ladies!

Mr. Video Games: I don't understand for the life of me how a man who has a wife and kids to take care of can spend all day and night playing video games. Does he work? Does he help with the kids, dishes, or groceries? My heart breaks when I hear many wives crying that their husbands play video games 24/7 and don't help around the house. Or worse yet, don't work!

This was an instant turn off for me. If I met a guy who played video games, I would friend zone him. There was no need for me to go any further in gathering information about him being a possible husband! So, princesses, be sure you think these things out. That's why it's important to know what you want. Now, does every man who plays video games not help around the home or with kids or not work? I'm not trying to find out. LOL!

Mr. Minimum Wage: People might think I'm shallow, but I wouldn't date or marry a man who makes minimum wage. I often said, when I graduated from college, I was making over $12 per hour as a work-study student. I think minimum wage was $5 something, maybe $6? I haven't lived on minimum wage since my first year at Essex County College. My first job out of college was paying me less than $18,000 per year. Then I got another position paying a bit more, and all this time I was working as a secret shopper to earn extra money.

Finally, in my late twenties, I got the job I have presently, doubling what I was earning with all my jobs added together. Since then, I have worked hard to provide a home for Lexi and me. So no, I will not date or marry a man making minimum wage. I believe a husband is to provide for his wife and kids. Minimum wage cannot provide for my daughter and me. And ladies, it's okay to come to that conclusion, so please do not allow anyone to talk you into putting your 50 cents with his 25 cents to make 75 cents.

I struggled as a single mom, and I refuse to marry into the struggle. My preference is a man who has a good job, who can provide comfortably for me. Additionally, he is to be a man with a plan in the event he loses his job or gets sick. Princesses, ask questions, and be sure you are comfortable with his answers. God forbid, if my husband comes home and tells me that he lost his job, I'm not going to freak out, get nervous, or even ask what he's going to do. Why? I already know what the plan is!

Finally, do you know what the crazy thing is? All the women who defend the struggle life and call women like me shallow are struggling! Lol! That makes no sense. They work two and three jobs, missing out on time with their kids, but they are defending the struggle life with a grown man who can't even take care of himself, much less a wife and kids. Something is not clicking somewhere.

Mr. Momma's Boy: This mister loves his momma so much that, at forty, he still lives at home and is currently looking for another momma, except with more benefits. He's looking for someone who can cook like his momma, fold his drows, and starch them the way his momma does. The only difference is, he wants someone he can have sex with. He doesn't even mind if she would give him money.

Now, in defense of "healthy" momma's boys, they are not all like the guy above. There is nothing wrong with loving one's mother. However, at some point in a boy's life, he must leave the apron strings and go out in this big world and make a life for himself and find him a woman he can respect and protect like his mom.

A healthy momma's boy, like my husband, understands that, while he will always be his momma's baby, if he desires a wife, it is not because he wants her to treat him like his momma does. A healthy momma's boy makes sure his wife is taken care of and that she comes before his momma.

Many women love a momma's boy because they think he will love them like he does his momma. But I have heard many horror stories about the momma's boy. In my book *The Naked Wife*, there is one story of a wife in the hospital giving birth. Her husband's mom didn't like his wife. His mom needed someone to take her to her bingo. Guess what he did? He left his wife while she was in labor to take his momma to her bingo game. I don't know about you, but that would have been it for me!

Mr. Businessman: This Mr. comes off as a man who has his stuff together. Could be like Mr. White Collar, but as you investigate more, you will find out that it's only a trick. In all fairness, he could be a businessman, but I'm talking about the man who tries to pass himself off as one. He has a business idea, but he's just looking for the right woman to help him get it off the ground.

Question: Why is he waiting for someone to help him, instead of doing the work himself? Many women will jump on this opportunity because they think they are showing these men that they can be a suitable "helpmate." But ladies, why would a man who is seeking a wife not figure out how to get all of this done? Why sit around and wait for a woman to do it for him? Finally, why would you use your credit to take out a loan for a man you're not married to?

Mr. Hygiene: Have you met a man who was just dirty? He smells, and he has dirty fingernails, hair that needs to be cut, a face that needs shaving, etc. When he takes pictures to post online, you can see a lot of junk in the background. Or maybe you've been to his apartment, and it's just a mess? Dirty dishes all over the place, clothes on the floor, and he's merely a slob.

Many women make a mistake with Mr. Hygiene because they think they can get him to take a bath daily and groom himself. Oh,

I have known many women who have married Mr. Hygiene. The stories I hear make me want to throw up! One church sister of mine said her husband would drop his underclothes and wouldn't even put them in the hamper in front of him. Another one fights with her husband to flush the toilet. How disgusting! The only woman Mr. Hygiene need is his momma, not a wife!

9-Mr. Hobosexual

I am not sure who coined this term, but oh my do I love it! This scammer is like Mr. Roommate. He is like the revolving door criminal who commits a crime in the wintertime, so he can go to jail, where he will have heat, shelter, three full meals, and access to medical care while it's cold.

Mr. Hobosexual: Princesses, be mindful of males who want to move in with you. I'm sorry to tell you that he might be using you for shelter. Therefore, Mr. Hobosexual gets with you for housing purposes. He will say and do all the right things to get into your home. He is homeless and needs shelter, so he will wash, cook a meal or two, and yes, he will even help with the children. He will offer to watch and babysit your kids while you go to work to put a roof over his head! Why any mom would trust a man she just met with her most precious gifts, I don't understand for the life of me!

Also, I call Mr. Hobosexual, Mr. Humping, for a Home. I am often amazed when I talk to women about men who have been shacking up and living rent-free. Why do they tolerate it for so long? One of the top reasons is that sex is good, and they couldn't let go of that dingaling. Princesses, don't you think you deserve more than a warm body? Write down what you desire in a husband.

If the man who approaches you doesn't match up to your prayers and desires, please don't waste your time with him. Read the Bible. One of the first things a man must have had before he could marry a woman was a house for her, provided entirely by him! Why should you settle for less?

Mr. Roommate: I can't stand this guy! It bugs me that women fall for this fool! This guy is looking for someone to pay his bills or help to take care of him. He is not able to take care of himself, so he finds the perfect woman to move in with. He might say something like, "Baby, you know my lease is getting ready to be up, and I want us to move in together. I mean, I love you and all, and you know, we're gonna be getting married, so let's move in together."

You're so desperate and "thirsty" for him to move in that you missed the sign. You see, ladies, he gives offers of marriage, and you think that, by washing, cooking, cleaning, and sexing, even having his babies, eventually he will marry you. Some of these guys will move in with the woman, and a month later cry, "Oh, I lost my job." Some women trying to prove that they are wife material assure him that she can hold it down until he gets back on his feet. Oh, and what about the famous "helpmate"?

Ten years and five babies later, he is still trying to get on his feet while she holds it down, begs him to marry her while at the same time plays wifey without the paperwork. I can't say it enough, and I will repeat it. Princesses know who he is before you join your life with him. Husbands are to profess, provide, and protect. If a man is not able to do that, why are you wasting your time with him?

Why play wifey when he hasn't even made you his wife? Why be a roommate when God created you to be showered with adoration, protection, and provision of your husband? Don't you know your worth? And you know the sad thing about Mr. Roommate? You will give this fool all your young and vibrant years; you will spend time, energy, money, and have ten babies for him. But then he will get up, leave you and all your kids, and marry a woman he has only known for three months.

I have seen it so many times. I know someone right now going through this. She shacked up with this man for eight years, stayed with him during no jobs, lost jobs, and even homelessness. Three babies later, he is on his feet and doing ok. Guess what? He has given her three months for her and HIS KIDS to move out because they are "not compatible anymore." Think about that for a second.

Remember, princesses: some men are looking for a roommate and a playmate. However, it's up to you to know that God created you to be a helpmate which comes at a very expensive cost. And a helpmate has nothing to do with you helping him to become a man and get on his feet, while you work three jobs to take care of a grown, able-bodied male. You work several jobs if necessary, to take care of your children, not a grown man!

And for God sake, please stop putting yourself on clearance! Don't sell yourself cheap! Remember the following, ladies: every man wants a virtuous woman. But guess what? A virtuous woman is not cheap. Therefore, not every man can afford rubies, much less far above rubies! I will be writing extensively about being a helpmate soon and how not every man can afford rubies. But I am sure a Prepared Husband can afford you!

Mr. Tester: Many of us, as women, have been taught the lie that the way to a man's heart is through his belly. We have also been brainwashed into thinking we need to show men that we are wife material by washing, cooking, cleaning, and dropping it like it's hot on a silver platter, even for the men who are not our husbands. Unfortunately, many men also have the mindset that women are to do wife duties to prove their worth to them.

This is where Mr. Tester comes in. You've been going out and talking. Finally, he invites you over, and his place is a mess. Instinctively, you will want to clean up for him. Why? Because you want to show him that you are wifey material. However, you have read this book, and you know the game, so the new you don't clean up, wash, and cook for him. Most importantly, you won't be laying up in his dirty apartment and sex him!

You leave his place the same way you found it, and a few days later, he'll say something like, "That was a test, and you failed it!" But that's okay because you were already hip to the game. He decides he doesn't want to see you anymore, and you should happily say, "Thank you!" Ladies, please keep this in mind. We are gathering data on guys, and so are they on us. They test us with their kids, their money, and their dirty homes.

Some ask, "So how do we prove to him that we are wife material?" First, you need to know whether he is looking for a wife or not. Remember, not every man is looking for a wife. Second, does he want you to be his wife? If he is, you need to be yourself.

Who are you? What are your gifts? Be kind, feminine, say "thank you" when he does anything for you. Be gracious, encouraging, and inspiring with your words. There's a lot you can do other than sexing, washing, cooking, and cleaning to show him that you are wife material.

When I was dating my now husband, I never washed, cooked, cleaned for him, or sexed him. But he proposed to me in less than a year. I was different from any other woman he has ever dated. I wasn't trying to jump his bone to try and get him to ask me to marry him. I wasn't pursuing and running him down. It took him a month to ask me out, but I never once jumped in his inbox asking him when he was going to take me out. I never called or texted him or do anything to show him that I was interested.

As far as I was concerned, he was a very nice and intriguing man that I met that I would have loved to talk to, but he never called to take me out. Additionally, I was busy going out, living my life, and dating other guys, so he was a non-factor. But princesses, when he finally called and took me out, he asked for a second date halfway through dinner, and we've been happily married almost six years as of the publication of this book.

Mr. 50/50: This mister is all over social media advertising himself. He is not afraid to let it be known that he believes a woman should pay 50% of the bills. Ladies, please do not argue or try to convince him otherwise. This goes back to what you want in a husband. Do you want a 50/50 husband, or do you want a husband who is a provider?

What many women do is marry this guy and then fight with him every month because he has his hands out for her 50% of the bills. He goes on and on about what a woman's money is doing and if it's all for her to go shopping or to do hair and nails. Ladies, I have stressed for you to pay attention to what a man says. You can know his heart just from the things he says.

This is another reason I would not marry a man who made less than me or a man who is struggling. As mentioned before, I struggled to provide a life for Lexi and me from the age of sixteen. I refused to attach my life to and turn my life over to a man who was struggling. My father always told us, "The least a man can do for his wife is put a roof over her head." Many women marry men who can't even pay rent, much less a mortgage.

Ladies, you must think things through. The Bible says for us to count the cost before we build. Please know that marrying a man who is struggling will only cause you to struggle. And this thing about marrying for love ONLY is foolishness. Because every month when our mortgage is due, my husband goes to the bank and writes a check of money, not a check of love!

Mr. Trying to Get A Record Deal: This is the fifty-year-old who's been trying to get a record deal since he was five. When you ask him if he works, he says he doesn't have time because he has been pursuing his rapping career. Then ask how he provides for himself; he says he stays with his mom, and he has "friends" who help him out. Ladies are so gullible that they fall for this guy. They move him into their home, take care of him, and work two or three jobs so he can work on getting a record deal.

Ladies, I can't say it enough. The only man you need to work to take care of is your son. Let me be clear that I am not talking about a husband who has lost his job through no fault of his own, and you need to help until he gets back on his feet. But keep in mind that a husband needs to have a plan for if he loses his job or gets sick and can't work.

However, I am talking about a grown adult male who is looking for women to take care of him. I don't know about you, but I don't have any friends who would fund my whole life while I work on being an author. I wrote my first book when I was nineteen, sitting on top of my toilet. I had a studio apartment, and while my baby girl slept, I would sit in the bathroom and write. I couldn't fit a chair in the bathroom, so I would sit on my toilet to write and study.

In the meantime, I was going to school, working, and perfecting my craft of being an author. And before I met my husband, I was taking care of my daughter and myself, and I provided a good life for us. Now that I am married, my husband is our sole provider. So, I didn't just sit, hoping and a wishing. Over twenty years later, I'm still working my writing gift. And that was one of the things my husband said he loves about me.

Mr. Trying to Get a Record Deal is looking for women to sponsor him, and in return, he promises to take care of them when he gets his "record deal." Now, I am all for people pursuing their dreams and visions. However, ladies, in the meantime, you need to eat, have a roof and healthcare and so on. Remember that husbands are to provide. He can work on his craft, but in the meantime, he needs to be able to provide a comfortable life for you. Please leave the adult little boys who are looking for moms and sponsors.

Mr. Help A Brotha Out: He makes me sick and disgusted all at the same time. This mister is always looking for a handout. He always has an excuse for why he needs help. And he needs help with everything. He's always borrowing money and needs you to do his resume for him. And yes, go and fill out the job application, drive him to the job, and work it for him!

Mr. Help A Brotha Out is a sorry excuse for a "man." He is showing you ladies that he is going to be that man who is always looking for a handout. He will be the guy that who sits on the couch eating bonbons and playing video games all day while you work three jobs to take care of yourself, your children, and your adult male child.

Mr. Help a Brotha Out is always talking about how he needs a break and that "the man is against him." Ladies pay close attention to needy men! There is nothing sexy, safe, or secure about a needy man. You need a man who is doing his "thang," handling his business, and always on point! The only thing a man must need is a wife who he wants to profess his love, provide for and protect. No, Mr. Help a Brotha Out needs more of a mommy than a wife. Leave that needy man alone!

Mr. Taking Care of Mom: This man lives with his mom because he says his mom is elderly, sickly, and needs him to help her out. You think that's sweet and admirable of him. So you allow yourself to foolishly fall for him without investigating and getting all the information. You then find out that he is living with his mom 'cause his mom is taking care of him. He is not able to provide for or take care of himself, so he's been mooching off his elderly mom.

Princesses don't just take a man's word at face value. Ask questions and investigate before you "fall in love." However, this mister might be taking care of his mother, who requires someone always to be home to take care of her. If you get married, "Mom" might need to live with you, and you will become her caretaker. Don't allow your emotions to get you into something your heart's not feeling. I know many women who are trying to impress a man by taking care of his mom and agreeing that she can live with them, and it has ended up destroying their marriage. Both of you need to come up with a fair way to take care of your sick or elderly.

Mr. Waiting for A Settlement: Like Mr. Waiting for a Record Deal, he's been waiting for a settlement for twenty years. The issue is, he's just waiting. He isn't doing anything to try to better his life, go back to school, or anything like that. His full-time job is looking for a sponsor to subsidize his life while he waits for his settlement.

Some women are so gullible that they fall for this and move him into their homes with their kids. Listen, princesses, I believe that a man is to provide for his family. I don't believe in marrying potential but instead marrying the man who is in front of you. You've already struggled to take care of yourself and your babies. Why add another person that you must take care of?

10-Mr. Situationship

Have you ever heard someone say, "Gosh, how did I just myself in this situation?" I have always wondered about that because it says that someone has not planned their steps and life out to the best of their ability. Cheating husbands say they accidentally cheated. As if his penis fell out of his pants and rolled to find the woman at the hotel and jumped in her kitty. Lol!

Or it could be a man who wants to move from place A to destination B, but situations are keeping him from moving on. Ladies, as you date, beware of men who have themselves in "situations."

Mr. Complicated: This is the guy with a complicated life. He has six baby mommas, a wife, girlfriend, and a side chick. His life is such a complicated mess that he can't afford to take care of himself or his kids, which causes him to be living with his mother or is shacked up with a "friend" across town. His life is a tangled web, and after child support, he can't even afford a hamburger. Mr. Complicated claims he is looking for a wife because all the other women who have been in his life were crazies and gold diggers.

The problem is, Mr. Complicated has no gold to dig. He states that he is looking for someone to build a life with and needs a ride or die chick who will sign up to be a part of his complicated mess of a life. Ladies, please tell me why you would even continue to talk to this guy with his complicated life. Do you know that being with a complicated man will end up causing your life to be full of complications?

Mr. Separated: This guy needs to go sit down and try to save his marriage if possible. But he presents himself as the victim (and he could be) and uses it as a crutch and as bait. He promises women marriage as soon as his wife gives him a divorce. Ladies need to beware because he already messed one woman's life up, and he is looking for another life to mess up.

A man who is married but seeking another relationship doesn't respect himself, you, or his wife. He wants to use you for sex and sex only. But many women are so desperate to have some male attention that they believe the lies. Next thing you know, you are washing, cooking, cleaning, and sexing him. And he shacks up with you when he doesn't go home to his wife. Ladies? Don't you think you deserve better than a piece of a man?

Now, I know there will be some women raising their hands to say that this is not true because their now husband was separated when they met, and they eventually got married. And perhaps that's true; however, ladies, a separated man is still a married man. And honestly, I understand the struggle, ladies. I mean, he is not with her, living with her, and maybe the marriage is over. But he is still attached to her by not signing those papers.

Mr. Unhappily Married: This man is merely disrespectful and a user who is looking for sex. He is married, isn't ashamed to say he is married, but prefaces it by saying he isn't happy. He is telling you that all he wants to do is to use you for sex. He doesn't respect or value you, which is why he thinks you will gladly sign up for him to use your body like a toilet.

However, there are a few women who confess that their now husbands were married when they began to date and that it can work out. My response is that dating a married man is committing adultery no matter how you cut it, slice it, or dice it. A married man is a married man. Don't fall for the game, ladies. And you know the saying, "The way you get him is the way you will lose him."

Many women got involved with a married man and are still single. After they have wasted years waiting for him to leave his wife, he decided to try and work it out with HIS WIFE. In the meantime, you are left trying to pick up the pieces because you foolishly fell for his lies.

If you meet this guy, please run and block him on all platforms. A married man pursuing a woman other than his wife is after one thing and one thing only, and that's sex. Don't be fooled by game. Stop being so gullible and desperate that any man with a dingaling will do. Know your worth, princesses!

Mr. Divorced: Princesses, pay close attention to this guy. Sure, many men are divorced. But many say they are divorced, papers are signed, and the judge has issued the divorce, but they still act married. He might live in another state or a few hours away. He's never available on holidays because he claims he's spending time with his kids, the kids who you have never met, even though you've been in a relationship with him for years. So the question is, is he divorced?

For many men who are divorced, usually, they are not quick to jump back in a relationship. If they are, they are probably on the rebound, looking for someone to help them get over their wives. Some women make the mistake of getting with a divorced man and expecting him to ask them to marry them right away. Ladies, going through a divorce for whatever reason is exceptionally life-altering. A divorce is like pulling one's limb from your body. It is a traumatic experience. So, getting with a man who just came through a divorce might not yield the desired result.

This is where your list is crucial! And you need to ask honest questions so that you can get an accurate response. Additionally, if a man tells you that he doesn't want to get married again or isn't ready, please believe him. Sometimes, it's just best to walk away so that man can be healed and recover from the trauma of a divorce. And ladies, honestly sometimes he might not want to marry you, but that part is silent like the "L" in salmon. Something sure is fishy!

Mr. My Baby Momma is a Witch: This jerk disgusts me. Think about this, ladies! The mother of his child was a woman he once courted, dated, took care of, and might have been married to her. Now that the relationship is over, she is a #itch? He trash-talks the mother of his child/ren, yet he expects to attract other women.

Princesses, do you understand that, if he calls or refers to the mother of his children as a #itch, it will only be a matter of time before he begins to call you one, also? Please do not entertain any man that would call a woman out of her name and demean her.

Mr. I'm In A Relationship, But...: This mister is like Mr. Married and Mr. Separated. I'm not mad at him, because what he is saying is that he is in a relationship, but he is still searching.

However, it takes a man of character and integrity to be "single" until he finds his "ONE." I also understand that there are times when men have told women that they are not looking for a relationship right now. However, some women insist on being in a relationship with the man who plainly stated that he doesn't want one right now. As a result, some women get used because they force men to be in a relationship with them, even when the men have plainly stated they were not ready.

Additionally, some men need to find the courage and let the women know that they are not the one for them. These men should not get involved with women, even though some women think that because a man "sex" them, that means they are in a relationship.

Therefore, princesses, beware of this man. He could be using his "I'm In A Relationship, But..." status as a bait. The purpose of his status is to make you think he's not happy and he's looking for something else. Some women will get into the mindset of trying to be what he wants, so they get busy washing, cooking, cleaning, sexing, and even take care of this man just trying to be the ONE. In other words, she is trying to prove that she can be wife material to a man who is already in a relationship but claims that something is missing.

Mr. Mostly Single: Unbelievably, women fall for this guy. Mr. Mostly Single is single when he wants to be. He could be married, separated, in a relationship, or even engaged. He will be mostly single, so he can get his wants met. He will post that he is single this weekend, and who wants to hang out? Now, I do believe that we are all single until we are married.

C'mon, ladies! Don't you think this is a red flag? What is he when he isn't mostly single? Honestly, if I were you, I wouldn't even waste my time with this trapper. I prefer a man, to be honest, and give me the right to choose. But when a man says he's mostly single, ladies, please take pause. We need husbands, not boyfriend, playa, or anything like that! Husbands only!

11-Mr. Professional

Mr. Suit: Ooh, la, la! Ladies, I love a man in a suit! I like a man who can wear one, without the suit wearing him! See, that's why I knew I had to marry a man who wears a suit to work. Not every man can wear a suit! There's a difference between President Barack Obama in a suit and President Donald Trump. Now you got the picture?

There's even a difference between President George W. Bush and President Donald Trump wearing a suit. Because it's all in how you wear it. Have you ever seen President Bush in a pair of slacks and a business shirt with the sleeves rolled up? Well, you probably wouldn't notice if suits aren't your thing. Lol! I love a man in a suit or dress shirt and slacks! A suit is to a man like heels are to a woman. And not every woman can wear heels. Some women's heels wear them versus them wearing the heels. Likewise, some men's suits wear them, while others wear their suit.

Mr. Suit knows that many ladies love a man in a suit; they know that's a conversation starter. They take lots of pictures in their suits, flexing those sexy muscles. Mr. Suit knows that it's only a matter of time before the women are in his inbox complimenting him on how handsome he looks in his suit. Don't fall for it ladies; it's a trick! Now, remember ladies, I am not saying that every man who wears a suit and posts pictures is doing so for the sole purpose of getting women to flood their inbox. However, you should recognize the ones who do.

Mr. Profession: This man is often married and uses his profession to pick up women. I've had a run-in with this guy recently. I wasn't feeling well on a Sunday and had to go to urgent care. Well, there was a male doctor, and he was flirting with me! I was disgusted because I had on my wedding band, while my baby was going back and forth between my husband and me in the waiting area.

I kept telling my baby to see Daddy and to stay with Daddy. So this doctor knew that I was married. He was still flirting and even gave me his business card with his cell phone number for me to call him anytime. Later, while talking to someone else about the situation, I learned that he is married but that he is a flirt. And ladies, this is not to boast, but who can miss the "bling" my husband has adorned my finger with? This goes to show you, ladies, that even if you are married, some men don't care. They will still try to get you!

Here's another example. There's a popular restaurant in my city. The owner said to me, "Wow, I can see that fancy ring you have on, and I can tell you aren't going anywhere."

"Excuse me?" I asked.

He said, "Your ring tells me that, even if I want you to be my girlfriend, you aren't going anywhere." He went on to say, "Some women come to my business, and I can get them to take their rings off. I can also tell if they are going to stay with their husbands or not just by conversation. You, you're different. I can tell that you're not going to leave your husband."

To say I was shocked was an understatement. But ladies, this is what I am talking about. Some men take notice of you and try to figure out how to bait you, how they can get you to become what they want you to be. Therefore, ladies, it is vital for you to remember that not every man has your best interest at heart.

At the same time, not every man you meet wants to devour you like a roaring lion. There are some good, great, and godly guys out there. However, you must be wise as serpents and harmless as doves, so you can know the intentions of a man before you let him in. Remember, getting "DATA" is necessary.

Another experience I had was when I was in my early twenties. Here again, it was another doctor. For years, my daughter and I were patients at this dental office that had multiple dentists. Lexi, my daughter, was about eight, and she'd been going since she was one.

Over the years, I've had various dentists, but at this appointment, I had a particular male dentist for the first time. He examined my mouth, and everything was great. Well, sort of! He asked if I had ever thought about getting braces. "Braces?" I asked. "No, I haven't thought about it." I kept looking at my teeth in the mirror and began to wonder if I needed braces. In the meantime, I was asking him if he thought I needed them. This was back in my naïve days; I was still learning the tricks and baits of the enemy.

Then he gave me his cell phone number and told me that if I wanted to talk more about it, to call him. He would take me out to dinner so that we could discuss it over some of his delicious cultural food. Suddenly, I started thinking that I needed braces. In all honesty, two of my front teeth could use some braces for about a month. LOL!

But do you see how men can get into your head? I'd been going to the dentist office for years, and none of them had ever said I needed braces. We knew that my daughter would eventually need braces because she sucked her thumb, but none of our dentists had ever said I needed braces.

Again, ladies, I am not saying every man has bad intentions. You need to be smart, alert, and listening for the little hints, they throw out. However, for you to recognize the bait, you must know what it can be. This book is full of examples.

So princesses, beware of men who use their profession to try to bait you. That was the last time I went to that dental office. I thought it was best to avoid conflict. Presently, I am forty years old, and none of my dentists since him have said that I need braces.

I have tons of other examples, too many to share. But ladies, stay focused. Don't allow counterfeits to get you out of the will of God. Oh, and did I mention that the dentist had on a wedding band?

Mr. White Collar: He is like Mr. Suit. He is the type of guy that I would fall for because I love a man in a suit who is also a white-collar guy. He knows that many women don't want to struggle with the jack of all trades guy. Sure, many of them make good money, and women love stability. However, be mindful that because a man is a jack of all trades, it probably means he doesn't have a stable income. I am not a woman who could marry a man without a steady income. Ladies, it is crucial for you to know the type of woman you are.

Mr. White Collar knows that, even though many women claim they don't care about how much a man earns, women desire a man who can provide an excellent life for them. Mr. White Collar is often marketable; he has a great job with great benefits plus dental and about two or three back up plans. If he wants to "play," he knows that all he must do is let it be known, and the women will come running.

Remember, ladies: this does not apply to every man. The point is to be alert and pay attention. A man who is serious about settling down and getting married will pursue who he wants. And he will not use what he has or who he is to take advantage of women.

Mr. Doctor: Who doesn't want a doctor as a husband? This mister is like Mr. Uniform, so be aware and look out. Mr. Doctor knows that many women dream of marrying a doctor. He knows that many young women have been told by their parents to bring home a doctor or a lawyer. Some use this to their advantage to bait women. I am amazed at the stories I hear of women crying about how "He told me he was a doctor." Come to find out, he is married and lives in another state or is the hospital janitor. LOL!

Princesses don't be so gullible! Conduct your research. Sure, doctors make a good salary and can provide for a family. In my book *The Naked Wife*, there's a story of a young woman who "trapped" a doctor and got pregnant by him. She begged and pleaded for him to marry her, and eventually, he did, less than a month before their first child was born.

In the few short months after the first child was born, she was pregnant again, and again after the second child was born. She believed that he would eventually fall in love with her, but to this day, he resents her. And even though she intentionally "trapped" him, now she is the one who feels trapped because he is going about and living his life and sexing everything that has a hole.

She said he told her that the only reason he stays under the same roof as she is that his mom was a single parent, and he doesn't want that for their children. And she knew that about him and used it to trap him. Ladies, that is no way to live. You don't want a man who doesn't want you. A husband is to love, cherish, and honor his wife. Not to despise, resent, and disrespect her. She chose him, but did he pursue her? And who is paying for that today?

12-Mr. Sexuality

Sexuality is a huge topic today. I believe God has given each of us our lives as a gift, and we are to live it to the best and fullest.

Everyone has a right to live their lives as they choose because it is their lives to live. The same way, it is my right to live my life as I want because it is mine to live. However, we all need to be mindful that we need to live our lives honestly! Do not take away a person's right to choose. Be true to you and who you are as you live your truth.

Mr. DL: Yes, princesses, DL brothas are still alive and well. These are men who have not made peace with their sexuality and sleep with men on the down low. Many of them date women during the day but sleep with men at night. These men think that just because they sleep with other men, that doesn't mean they are gay.

Be mindful ladies: these men do not classify themselves as bisexual. They will swear on their mommas that they are not into men. Just be careful and ask questions, and I am a believer that the Holy Spirit will let you know when something's not right. I have heard so many horror stories. And I believe there's a story of a downlow husband in *The Naked Wife.*

Mr. Bisexual: This man has made peace with his sexuality and considers himself bisexual, which means he has sex and like with both men and women. Now, that might be okay for some women, but ladies, it is crucial for you to ask these questions. This way, if you find out something later, he can't say you didn't ask him. That was one valuable lesson I remember learning when I attended a woman's conference. The speaker encouraged us to ask the man who we are going to marry if he has had sex with other men. Some women might not feel comfortable, but your life depends on it.

Also, please be sure to go to pre-marital counseling. If you don't feel comfortable asking your potential husband alone, you can ask in marital counseling. Again, I have heard the horror stories from broken women who found out their husband cheated on them with a man. Ladies, if you desire a heterosexual man as I believe most women do, it is essential that you choose one.

Mr. Transgendered: This Mr. has made peace with his sexuality also. He was born female but feels as if he is a male. He has made the transition and is now living his life as a male. However, he might not be comfortable with letting women know that he was born female and has transitioned. While I believe it is vital for every person to make peace with who they think they are, I think it is deceptive to make another person think you are "A" but biologically was or is "B." The same thing goes for males who transition to being female.

It is not fair for a man to choose what he believes is a biological female, only to find out later that she was biologically male. Give people the right to choose you. Additionally, I heard a story of a transgender woman who lived and married as a female, but never told her husband that she was biologically male. As the marriage progressed, her husband was ready to have children. However, she could not have children because she was biologically male. Now honestly, do you think that was fair for her husband, who believed he married a biological female?

Remember that a mate is a choice, and we all have a right to choose the person we want. So, choose wisely and don't be afraid to ask questions. Again, be mindful that the husband you choose will determine the rest of your life. Pray, seek the face of the Lord, pray in the Holy Ghost, and obey His leading.

Mr. Beard: Ok, remember earlier, I mentioned that I would discuss this Mr. Beard, also. This is a man who is "in the closet." He has not made peace with his sexuality and is not honest about sexually loving men. Therefore, he chooses a woman who will go along with it, and she becomes his beard. Allegedly, some celebrities have their wives as beards. I have not known anyone in this position, so I don't know much about it. But I just wanted to mention it. Again, know what you want and choose according to your desires. The Bible says in Proverbs 12:4 that a wife is a husband's crown, so please remember to choose wisely.

13-Mr. Crown Myself

Princesses be careful who you turn your life over to. You might not think that's what you're doing, but dear, that's precisely what marriage is about. Submit means to come up under! That's why many women have issues submitting to their husbands: he doesn't have anything for them to come up under. And you know what I always say, you should have thought about that before you turn your life over to him. Also, I think of King Saul. He did not have the heart of God. Choose wisely, who you make a king over your life.

Mr. I Am the King: This guy frustrates me! He is a self-proclaimed king and requires that you treat him as such. However, he doesn't even have a kingdom or ability to provide for one. He is looking for a queen, so she can take care of and provide for him.

This is puzzling to me because I don't understand how a fool of a man can convince women to crown him king of their lives when he doesn't even have a pot to pee in or a window to throw it through. Ladies, I know you desire a husband, but please don't be fooled by a fool!

Sure, we all desire our king, but how can we crown a male king when he isn't able to be a king at all? In other words, why make a man your husband when he can't profess, provide, and protect?

Mr. 1 Am God: His name says it all. He thinks he is God's gift to women, and he can fix all your troubles. Mr. 1 Am God has the answers to everything. There's only one issue you need to pay close attention to. He will require your undying affection, focus, and your worship of him.

He is all about him and requires that you serve him as God Almighty. Many women are attracted to Mr. 1 Am God because he comes off as a safe and secure man. But as you peel back the layers of his pride and ego, you will find that he is a scared little boy. Ladies, little boys belong with their moms. Don't confuse little boys with grown men. Please send him home to his momma and don't waste your time!

Mr. That's a Woman's Job: Misogyny is alive and well! This guy is such a hypocrite. He says housework is a woman's job, and he shouldn't have to do anything around the house because he works. Here's where the issue comes in. He is not able to provide for his wife and family, so most likely, the woman he gets will have to work to help him provide for them. He doesn't want to help his wife care for their home and kids. This guy wouldn't even get a conversation from me.

When 1 was dating, one of my non-negotiables was a man that would help around the house. With all the older couples 1 knew who seemed to be happy, the husbands willingly helped around the home. Also, 1 remember one of my favorite Bible teachers stating there was a study that was done that found that the happiest couples were those who shared household responsibilities.

The happiest couples were the ones that helped each other. If she's folding the towels while they're sitting on the couch watching T.V., it doesn't hurt for him to help her. Many wives say it turns them on when their husbands willingly help them around the home. I can say amen to this.

I walked away from a childhood boyfriend who said he wouldn't help around the house and that housework was a woman's job. And that included not helping with the kids. I am not of the school of thought that a husband should "only" work and do nothing in the home. I know many people who don't believe a man should do anything in the house, even if he offers. Well, that's where you need to talk and ask questions and be honest with yourself. Remember that a husband is a choice.

If you desire a husband who would help around the house, it's probably not a good idea to marry a man who doesn't believe as you do. You will have to convince him that he needs to help you around the home. Just choose a husband who doesn't mind helping around the house. Oh, I know many couples where this is a huge issue. It's unfortunate and breeds a lot of tension, resentment, and bitterness, primarily when the wife works outside the home to help her husband provide for them. Then the whole household is left up to her. I knew one husband who wouldn't even bathe his son or dress him or change his diaper. Now, c'mon!

Thankfully, I married a man who thinks the same way I do. He loves to cook and helps me with whatever he can do around the home, which includes giving the baby baths and changing diapers. I love that about him, and it turns me on when he does anything in our home. Interestingly enough, though, when I asked him if his father helped out around the house when he was growing up, he said no.

I remember when Mr. Wonderful and I were engaged, and I was at his home. I offered to help clean up, and he said to me, "No, I don't need you for that. I've been washing, cooking, and cleaning for myself for years." He went on to say, "I want a wife, a life partner to help me raise a godly family. I don't mind cleaning up and helping around the home."

That turned on a light for me because, as women, we are taught mostly from other women that the way to a man's heart is through his belly, and that we need to show a man that we can wash, cook, and clean. My husband confirmed that he didn't believe that. And it wasn't that I was trying to win him over, because I had already done that. I had the most gorgeous ring on my finger that his frat brothers helped to choose and a wedding date set, but I just wanted to help. And even now, as a married couple, we have never had a fight or argument about what needs to be done in our home. If there's anything that he can help with, he willingly and lovingly does it. I am so grateful!

Mr. God's Gift to Women: Oh, this guy makes me want to vomit! Like Mr. I Am God, he thinks he is God's gift to women. He might have a good job, house, and car, and he seems to have his stuff together. But he is arrogant, full of himself, and is only looking to conquer as many women as possible.

Women need to understand that this guy is only looking for "cookie." He also uses his ability to fool women that he is looking for a wife. Women give up the cookie, thinking they are locking him down, only to find out that Mr. God's Gift to Women was a pawn in the devil's hand and an arrogant and deceptive snake.

You see, a good man is one who is humble, loves the Lord, and who is not full of himself because he is full of Christ. Many women fall for this guy, despite his arrogance, because they feel as if he can provide then they can deal with the other things that come with him. However, life is worth living. Remember, your husband will represent you, so choose wisely.

Mr. Scissor Hands: Lol! Ladies, have you ever met a guy that you like, and he says he likes you too? But there are just a few things about you that he would like to fix. Your boobs aren't big enough; your waistline needs to be smaller; you need to wear lots more makeup, and let's not forget to add a head full of weave.

I have experienced this a few times. Fresh out of high school, my prom date expressed interest in me. I was a bit skeptical because I didn't feel like he was right for me. Anyway, we started spending time together, and we lived near each other so that we would visit each other often. I am more of a laid-back type of girl when I'm home. I'm relaxed, no makeup, lipstick, etc. Well, Mr. Scissor Hands wanted me to dress up more, even when I was in the house, wear more makeup, and keep a head full of weave all the time. Guess what? I dropped him shortly after that.

And that was one of the questions I asked my husband while I was dating him. Did I have to dress up all the time? Can I throw on some sweats and lay around the house and relax? I had a funny story of how I knew I would marry my husband that involved me taking my ponytail weave out while sitting next to him. I will share later in an upcoming book I am working on about dating. Lol! Another time, I went out with a guy a few times, who asked me when I got married, and my husband wanted me to get breast implants if I would. I was so shocked that I choked on my food. Lol!

Of course, I told him no, I would not do surgery to make a man happy with my body and that he needed to find a woman who he is satisfied with or who would gladly oblige to his request. After some intense discussions, with him telling me that a wife is to submit to her husband and blah, blah, blah, I cut him off. And you know what the crazy thing is? I got married at thirty-five, and I have never had another guy ask or suggest any surgery to enhance my body. And that's another question I added to my interview questions when I was vetting guys because some of these men take submission to a whole other level. Ask your questions, ladies!

In my book *The Naked Wife*, there's a story entitled "Barbie doll." It's the story of a woman who one day looked in the mirror and didn't recognize herself because her husband had turned her into a Barbie doll. This was after he suggested that she remove a rib or two to make her waistline slimmer. Princess, beware of men who are not happy with your body and want you to have surgery. That is not the husband for you because he is telling you that he is not pleased with you and your body.

Furthermore, he has a picture in his head of what he wants you to look like. Could it be he is trying to turn you into someone else? Perhaps he wants you to look like someone from his past or his imagination?

Mr. Explanation: This mister needs to be charged with a crime. Have you ever met a guy who is interested in you, but you're not interested in him? You have expressed several times that you are not interested. However, he insists on you explaining, repeatedly, why you are not interested in him because he is such a great guy. I wish I could write this in my Jamaican dialect because I have had such an issue with men of various nationalities demanding an explanation as to why I was not interested in them. Why isn't, "Sir, thank you so much for your interest in me, but I am not interested," enough?

Ugh, I have felt so harassed by many men because they didn't understand why I didn't feel the same way about them as they did about me. Why can't they understand that, just because they are interested in me, doesn't mean I'm interested in them? Ladies, I encourage you to stand your ground when talking to a man who insists you give him an explanation about why you are not interested in him. You should not have to explain yourself or go point by point so that he can give a rebuttal. It is not your responsibility to stroke his ego about you not being interested. A simple, "Thank you, sir, I am not interested," should suffice. See princesses, this is how men feel when they have let you know they don't want you, but you insist on them choosing you. Let him go and walk away, please. Ladies should never have to beg!

Mr. I'm Your Man: This guy makes me giggle. Apparently, the Lord has downloaded a file on what you need because he jumps in your inbox with "Baby, I know what you want and need." Or, he sees you on social media and drops in your inbox offering himself up to you, insisting he is your man. Even when you have expressed that you are not interested, he will do everything in his power to make himself your man. Lol!

He sends nude pictures and even offers to send you money to help pay your bills and so on. Now, this is where some women get caught up. "Oh, he said he would send me money to help out, so he likes me." Ladies, you can't be so desperate, thirsty, or needy. Pay close attention to any man who wants you to drop your guard by trying to bribe you.

Ugh, the stories I read daily on social media have me cringing. I remember this one young lady who has three daughters, and this guy had taken a liking to her and her girls. He was always asking about them, what they did today, offering to send money for them to go to various events and for her to send him pictures of the girls. I don't like that at all, and all my predator sensors come alive.

14-Mr. Toxic

What is the first word that comes to mind when you hear the word Toxic? For me, it's the word poisonous. In other words, it will kill you immediately, or if you don't get the necessary help, it will eventually kill you. Have you ever been in a toxic relationship? Do know anyone who is currently in a toxic relationship? Do you know how to recognize if a guy you're dating is toxic? See if any of the following guys ring a bell for you.

Mr. Fool: There is no way on God's green earth; I would marry a fool. I love the book of Proverbs, and it talks a lot about the foolish man. I try to read a chapter per day, and I have even written a book on Proverbs, coming soon. So, I am very much aware of what the scripture has to say about "fools." The following is one of my favorite stories in the Bible about a fool.

Abigail was beautiful and wise. However, she was married to a foolish man named Nable. Oh, I feel so sorry for Abigail and the countless women who have married fools. In spite of Nable, Abigail was full of wisdom, and when King David was on his way to kill her whole family because of her husband's foolishness, she stepped up and saved her family. Some would say she should have stayed in her place. But at what cost?

You see, ladies, the reason you need to avoid binding your life to a fool is that you will never be safe with a foolish man. Recently, I read the sadness of a wife whose husband received a settlement for $30,000. She suggested they pay off some bills, save some, and put a down payment on a house. To the dismay of his wife, he told her that it's his money, and she can't tell him what to do with it. In less than six months, he blew every penny. He then blamed his wife and said to her that it was her fault that he only got $30,000.

You see, ladies, this man always a fool. He didn't become a fool when he got that money. He was always a foolish man, and I'm sure his wife knew that. Money doesn't define us, but it magnifies who we are. That's why the man you choose to cover and protect you is significant. Know what your man would do in situations before you bind your life to him. Remember that the decisions your husband makes will affect you and your children either positively or negatively.

Mr. I Am What I Am: This is for all the guys who need to look in the mirror and say they need to change. This includes the revolving door criminals, abusers, cheaters, and the like. I believe a man cheats because that's who he is. A man abuses a woman because that's who he is. A man is a revolving door criminal because that's just who he is. It is not your responsibility to get him to become who you think he can be.

Many women marry men who they know are cheaters, abusers, or criminals. Until they have a come to Jesus moment with themselves as Jacob did, you are wasting your time and maybe your life. STOP thinking you can fix a man! You cannot! If Jesus can't fix him up until he submits to being fixed by God, what makes you think you can override his will and fix him up? Why choose a man who is a known abuser or cheater, or who can't get his life together and then complain that he is a cheater, abuser, and irresponsible?

Let me be clear! No one deserves to be cheated on or abused. Recently in one of my sister churches, an elder killed his wife in front of their children. Did you notice I said, "elder?" Abusers come in all shapes, forms, and personalities. Please do not stay in a domestic violence situation. Your life is more precious, and you cannot change an abusive man into an adoring husband. Therefore, I am screaming from the mountaintop for you to vet the guys you date. Pay attention to red flags. If he was abusing you while dating, he could kill you when you're married. I had a saying when I was dating. "The next time he hits you, he could kill you!" Think about that, my sisters.

Mr. Arrogant: I cannot stand an arrogant man. Arrogance spews from every post, comment, and the picture he posts. Usually, he is full of himself and thinks that he is the best thing to women since sliced bread. See, I know I could never be with an arrogant man. I know what my grace can handle. And that's a humble man. Usually, an arrogant man is insecure, and he tries to prove to everyone that he is who he says he is.

Remember the example I shared earlier about Jesus? How the enemy wanted him to "prove himself" that he was the son of God? Mr. Arrogant is a know-it-all and must have the final word. He thinks he is all of that plus a bag of chips and dip on the side. Be mindful, ladies, and pay close attention to words and actions.

Mr. Ego: This thirsty male is like Mr. Arrogant. He needs you to stroke his ego. He doesn't even know you, but once he meets you, he feels that you need to spend your time stroking his ego. Mr. Ego acts like a baby that needs to nurse while his mother brushes his hair. Princesses, do you want a real man for a husband or a little boy who needs to be reminded every second that he is a man?

Now, I am all for stroking my husband's ego. I tell him how handsome he is, how I love it when he does things for me, how much I need him, and how he makes my life so much better. I tell him what an exceptional husband, father, leader, and man of God he is. Oh, honey, I fluff my husband's ego so much I'm sure his head gets so big it can hardly hold going through the door.

But the keyword is "husband." I am supposed to stroke my husband's ego. Some strange man who you just met on social media, who demands all your attention and your praise and adoration, needs to be dropped and blocked immediately! And think about this, ladies. You are like a fountain that flows over.

If you keep giving yourself, energy, and strength to all these strange men, you won't have much left for your husband when you finally meet him. Therefore, use lots of wisdom, dearies. I'm all for being nice, graceful, kind and feminine, but honey, my lovely words of wisdom and ego fluffing are reserved for my husband only.

Mr. Bad Communicator: Communication is a huge issue in many marriages, so it is imperative that you pay attention to how a man communicates early on as you date. This mister jumps in your inbox and gets you all interested in him. However, in a day or two, it seems as if he has ghosted you. And he could have, but give it a few more days, and he will hit you with, "Why you ain't message me?" You are being the lady that you are by allowing the man to pursue you, so you say something like, "I was waiting to hear from you."

He then asks you, "So if I don't call, text, or message you, you won't contact me?" This is the beginning of you trying to prove to him that you are interested. As a result, you start to do all the things he's not doing because you like him. You plan dates, text and call him all day, send him good morning texts and all. You figure he's a great guy, so you feel that you can deal with this "one little issue."

His text messages or answers are one or two words with no follow-up. He is comfortable with you doing all the communication and contacting. When you go out on a dinner date, you carry the conversation because he has no words. Mr. Non-Communicator prefers dates where he doesn't have to talk. Pay attention ladies: it takes both of you talking and planning to move on to a happy and fulfilling marriage. That's the reason I have a no movie policy for first dates. I need to sit in front of him and see how we communicate.

Some ladies overlook his communication issues and get married because they think they can "fix" him. That's until it's time to communicate with you, and he shuts down or says something like, "You knew I was like this before you married me." Ladies, this is what I mean when I say marry the man in front of you. Stop trying to make him into someone he's not. Communication in any relationship is critical, and you cannot survive without it. Although communication goes beyond verbal, it is the foundation. A man's actions communicate a lot about how he feels towards you and so on.

Mr. Red Flag: Sigh. How many of us ladies can honestly admit that we have overlooked Mr. Red Flag's red flags? Ladies, red flags are named because red stands out. Remember, it is vital for you to know what you desire in a husband. Mr. Red Flags has many signs, and all you must do is accept them. You must choose to see them and yield to the warning signs.

Don't try to defend him, twist him, or make excuses for him. Accept Mr. Red Flag for who he is. Remember that you are not his mom, and he is not a toddler, and you need to make excuses for him. It is what it is, and therefore I have stated several times for us not to get emotionally involved with a man that we are still vetting. Why? When you see the red flags, you want to be able to walk away instead of trying to "fix" him and turn those red flags the way you want them.

What are the red flags? He can't keep a job. He spends countless hours playing video games but isn't out trying to find a job. He is abusive, a cheater, extremely aggressive. He throws things when angry, gets violent at times. For women with kids, how does he act towards your children? Are your children comfortable around him? There are several red flags, but if you choose to ignore them, then those will be the things to haunt you for the rest of your relationship.

Mr. Insanity: What is insanity? Insanity is doing the same thing repeatedly while expecting a different result. Mr. Insanity is the same guy you continue to get into relationships with while expecting him to be different. You continue to choose the same guy, so you get the same result. Why? Because you have yet to renew your minds about men and what you desire in a husband.

Mr. Insanity is not about him, but it's about you. Because it is YOU who continues to choose the same crazy man. You continue to choose the jobless man, the thug on the street who lives by crimes and drugs. You continue to choose abusers and cheaters. You expect the same man you choose again and again to change and become the man that you want instead of choosing the right man that you need.

When it comes to Mr. Insanity, as women, we get caught up in him and other men to the point that we choose not to discern and accept what is in front of us. The truth is, God has given us wisdom about our lives, but he won't force it down our throats. We foolishly choose not to see what God is showing us regarding what we see and hear.

Sweetie, if you continue to choose the wrong guy, then your chooser is off. Please to stop, step back, and get into your prayer closet right now! Do not date another guy until you learn how to hear from God for yourself. Now that's wisdom, beloveds!

15-Mr. Purpose

Mr. Kill, Steal and Destroy: In John 10:10, Apostle John said **the enemy comes to kill, steal, and destroy.** This is one of those scriptures that I have kept dear to my heart because I believe the enemy is out to destroy the people of God. I believe he will use any tool or person to do it. As single women who desire marriage, we need to realize that the enemy has fakes and counterfeits, and they will pursue us with strict orders from the devil to destroy us. As soon as you understand this, your dating view will get 50% better by recognizing those the enemy has sent in your path.

As women, we are very trusting and often gullible. And because we desire to be married, if we are not careful, we can get desperate. We feel as if every man who approaches us wants to profess his love, provide for us, and protect us. But the truth is, most men do not want to do that for us. Most men who approach us want to get in our panties. Think about that in your own life: when you gave up the cookie thinking it will make him choose, love and marry you, only for you to find out after you dish your cookie on a silver platter that they weren't interested in anything serious "right now."

Notice I did not say "all." I said, "most." The enemy will use some men to get us off our destiny's path. I cannot tell you the number of young women I have seen this happen to. And it was also evident in my life as a single young woman when the enemy tried to distract and deceive me. Today, I still thank God for my father, that I listened to and applied his wisdom and guidance to my life and data collection strategies. Ladies, we need to be alert, vigilant, prayerful, and watchful! Trust no man with your heart or your cookies, except the man who has gone through the process to protect you.

Mr. Master Manipulator: I believe that people are who they are. A cheater cheats, an abuser abuses, a thief steals, and a liar lies. A good man manifests excellent characteristics, and a faithful husband is faithful, and so on. A Mr. Master Manipulator has the characteristics of the devil. He comes to steal, kill, and destroy. His only purpose is to get what he wants at any cost to you.

This mister is easy to spot if you are praying, seeking the Lord, and reading your Bible because the Holy Spirit will alert you. Mr. Master Manipulators are the guys you meet on social media, and they talk to you and sing you all that your soul desires. They pull on your heartstrings.

Next thing you know, Mr. Master Manipulators are asking you for money because they are in need. Or they want to see you, but they're not getting paid until sometime in the future. They promise to marry you, but only if you could help them by sending them money.

Mr. Master Manipulator can also be classified as Mr. Con Artist. This is the guy who says, "I'm going to deposit $5,000 in your bank account," but he needs you to send him $1,000 back. C'mon ladies, how gullible can you be? He could also be the guy that says, "Why don't you pack up and move down here to be with me?"

You foolishly resign from your job, give up your apartment, pack yourself and your kids, and move to be with a strange man in a new state. You get there to find out that the address he gave is an abandoned building, and the number is now disconnected. I don't understand how someone can be so foolish to do this!

Don't be deceived, ladies. Mr. Manipulator could also be the guy you met at your local diner. Next thing you know, he has moved into your house, is driving your car, and has all your bank information. Princesses remember to be wise as serpents and harmless as doves because no matter how deceptive a man is, there's still a God who sits high and looks low. And if you spend time praying in the Holy Ghost and seeking the face of the Lord, sweet Holy Spirit will never lead you wrong.

Mr. Deception: Yes, this man is a deceiver. He is faking being someone to get you, only to switch when he gets you right where he wants you. Please tell me how a Christian woman who is attending church, reading her Bible, praying, seeking the face of the Lord, and fasting ends up marrying a man who's an atheist without her knowing?

How does a sister who is in fellowship with the Father, marry a deceiver? How does one get so entwined that we need Matlock to get her out? Ladies, please stop with the desperation and vet these males properly. Stop turning your life over so quickly to a man who hasn't been through the process for you to turn your life over to him.

Beware of the oh-so-obvious bait and switch, when he tells you that he will attend church with you. Once he gets you right where he wants you, he stops, and you beg and plead for him to attend. To shut you up, he might make promises of marriage or even propose. You are so engulfed in the excitement that you don't realize this is a trap. Ladies, please do not accept a proposal from a man who you are not at least 95% sure of. Yes, no one is perfect.

Mr. Trap a Treat: Ugh, this guy is awful. Mr. Trap a Treat only looks for, entertains, pursues, and dates women who have money. He patiently scans social media for women who advertise what they have. The catch for many of these women is that they have everything, but there's only one thing that's missing: a man who will love, honor, treat her right, and marry her.

Mr. Trap a Treat will show up on the scene, passing himself off as an eligible bachelor. But the truth is, he is looking for a treat. Ladies, I know a few women who are with Mr. Trap a Treat. These women foot the bill for trips, vacations, cars, clothes, and money. So ladies, if you have everything going for you except a good man, make your list and make yourself available to be found. Please do not settle for a Mr. Trap a Treat. When I was about twenty-eight years old, I made up my mind that I would rather be single than settle for less than my heart's desire. Sometimes, we need to get to that place.

Mr. Seed Dropper: Initially, I termed this Mr. Seed Sower. The Lord spoke to me, so I changed it to Mr. Seed Dropper because there's a difference between a shower and a dropper. You see a sower is mindful of where he plants his seed because he wants the best harvest. A dropper doesn't care where his seed falls, doesn't look back to see how it's doing or come to check on it. So, princesses, please keep this in mind when you decide to date and lay with a man. Mr. Seed Dropper reminds me of the story of The Sower in **Matthew 13**. Notice the number of places his seed fell and the result?

I am sure you've heard some older males telling younger males to sow their seed or wild oats. What many fails to realize is that, when you plant seeds, they often will yield some harvest. Hence Mr. Seed Dropper has produced millions of fatherless children and single-mother households.

The seed of a man is in his sperm. Men need to get back to a place where they value their seeds. Timeout for males, having five and six babies with different women, mostly leaving the women to raise those precious children alone. So princesses, when a man approaches you or jumps in your inbox, please investigate if he is a seed dropper. A man with lots of kids from different women speaks of the man himself.

Another thing you need to know for sure is, is he taking care of those children? It puzzles me when women get with a man who's not taking care of all the children he has. Many foolishly allow themselves to get pregnant and then get mad because Mr. Seed Dropper is treating them the same way he treated all the other baby mamas he had before. While a man taking care of his children is a good thing, count the cost, ladies. Do you understand that the more he gives out, the less he has available to provide for you? If he takes care of all his children, that is less income that will be coming into your household if you marry him. So choose wisely! This is what I mean about planning your life out and thinking things through.

Now, I believe there's someone for everyone. All I'm saying, ladies, is to investigate before you turn your life over to Mr. Seed Dropper or any man. I cannot tell you how many women cry after marrying a man with several kids that he is taking care of as he should. However, his home with his wife is lacking, and she is expected to maintain the household financially. Let me be clear again a man is to take care of and provide for all his children!! I want you to think things through and count the cost before you marry Mr. Seed Dropper or any man.

This is another reason vetting a man is essential. I believe that what a man has done with his life up to when we meet speaks volumes. Please do not overlook a man's past, ladies; it will come back to haunt you. Vet, investigate, ask questions, talk to people who know him. Google him, search him on social media, and so on. Your life depends on it! I saw this one guy's paystub once. He had four orders of child support. If I remember correctly, his leftover was $46.00. I mean, what am I supposed to do with $46? My water bill for a good month is about $70.

Mr. Good Time: I'm still surprised that women fall for this guy. He is telling you that he is looking for a "good time." That means he isn't trying to date you, court you, or marry you. He is looking for someone to give him a good time for a moment and then, by tomorrow, he will be looking for another gullible woman to have a good time with.

Mr. Good Time is not ashamed of what he wants. He comes out and tells you that he's looking for a good time. Remember, ladies, because Mr. Good Time wants to have a good time with you doesn't mean you have to accept. It's up to you to participate or not.

However, be mindful of what you desire. Many women fall for Mr. Good Time, get into a pretend relationship, and then cry that he is always going out and never wants to stay home. Question: When did you know he just wanted to have a good time?

Mr. String Along: Tell the truth. How many women do you know who have been strung along for years, waiting for Mr. String Along to put a ring on it? Perhaps you've been strung along or are currently being strung along as you read this. Ladies, Mr. String Along is all around us. And because they are experts in making you think something is going to happen, they have no fear of jumping in your inbox, sweet talking you, and stringing you along.

Mr. String Along is easy to spot. He is the guy who's had steady "girlfriends" for years, shacked up with several women, or even have several baby mamas. He was probably engaged for years but never jumped the broom. Here again, ladies, is where your data collecting expertise comes into play. Please don't be delusional and think you can get him to put a ring on it. Women who feel like this usually end up getting used, abused, left, and strung along! The best thing to do is to leave Mr. String Along so that you can be knotted up with your husband.

Mr. Bozo: You've heard of Boaz and Ruth, my favorite love story in the Bible. Boaz is the example most Christian women use to describe the type of husband we desire to marry. Boaz is the man who "found" Ruth in the field while she was busy gathering grains for herself and Naomi. Boaz was a good and godly man. He was rich, and he showed Ruth favor. He took all the necessary steps to position himself to marry her. Boaz professed his love and admiration for Ruth. He protected her and provided not only for Ruth but her mother-in-law, Naomi.

Be encouraged, ladies because your Boaz is out there. Nevertheless, there are also fake ones known as Bozos. Yes, my dearies, Bozo, is the fake version of Boaz. Mr. Bozo pretends that he is looking for a wife. However, if you study him carefully, you will find that he's only acting like he's looking for a wife. You will discover that Mr. Bozo is faking because his actions don't line up with his words. A man who has prepared himself will not string along the woman he believes is his wife.

Princesses, it is vital to appropriately vet Mr. Bozo or any man that you are gathering data on. Remember to take your emotions out of the data collecting stage and look at the facts and make the best decision for yourself about any prospect. Dating is a process and is in stages. You might have to talk to Mr. Bozo for a few weeks before you figure out that he is a Bozo. Don't waste any more time; drop him and move on.

Mr. Get the Dog Out: My Spiritual Father told me about this mister when I was younger. There was a young lady who was head over heels in love with a young man. Well, four babies later, he still didn't marry her. In the meantime, he was "getting the dog out" with whoever would yield to his bark and had several other children. Finally, under pressure, he married her, but instead of him taking her on a honeymoon, he dropped her off at her apartment and went out to "get the dog out" with someone else.

While I don't agree with this concept, I do understand. According to the Bible, our bodies are the temple of God, and we are purchased possessions. Therefore, God's desire for us is not to have sex until we are married. Judging from the number of so many single mothers with children, church folks are having sex and lots of it!

So, princesses, beware when a man approaches you via your inbox or in the supermarket; get the data before you spread your legs. Even after you get the data, I encourage to maintain your sanctity until he puts a ring on it. Remember, ladies, men are hunting, and they are not all hunting for a wife. Some men are just trying to "get the dog out." And if you are willing to help him, then he will oblige.

Mr. Hunter: I know a few Mr. Hunters in name, so let me be clear. I am not talking about any man whose name is Mr. Hunter. Lol! My father often spoke about the "hunt" in a man. Men are born hunters. I do not believe that men are dogs. God did not create men to be dogs. God created men to hunt! It is something that God has put into men, to hunt, pursue, conquer, and subdue. If you have little boys, pay close attention to them, and you will see that they want to conquer everything. The living room couch, the steps, the toys, jumping off the bed, etc.

Recently, I had to rush my toddler to the hospital because he felt like conquering the couch when he tried to jump from one to the other. Our living room is 18 x 30. Can you imagine as an adult trying to jump 18 feet from one couch to the other? I can't, and I use to run track when I was younger. Additionally, the couches weren't even in front of each other. So, his jump wasn't directly across the room. Lol!! But that is something that God has placed in the male DNA, where they want to conquer everything they encounter. So, princesses, it is in men to conquer, overcome, subdue, and take control. And yes, that includes women they meet. Getting your cookie is a badge of honor and proof that they have conquered you! Therefore, I wrote in *The Naked Wife* to take the cookie off the table.

Therefore, the question becomes: If men are born hunters, what are they hunting? Not every male you meet is looking for a wife. As women, because it is in us to desire marriage and babies, we think every man we meet wants to marry us, protect us, and provide for us. This has gotten us in trouble, used, abused, and left. Some men are looking for women to take care of them. I know guys who only date women who can take care of them.

Sisters, it is imperative for us to understand and remember that men are born hunters, and they are always hunting for something. They desire to conquer and subdue. On the other hand, it will take a disciplined man to hunt protectively, find a wife, marry her because he has conquered her into his love, his ability to provide, for her and to protect her.

Now, wait for a second, Janice. Does a man need to conquer his wife? Yes, a husband is to conquer or overcome his wife with his declaration of love, protection, provision, adoration, and leadership. See, when a man who is not our husband conquers us, he is using us for his gain and selfish desires. When I think of a husband conquering or overtaking his wife, I think of the scripture in

Deuteronomy 28:2 that states; **all the blessings of the Lord will come upon us if we listen to the voice of the Lord.**

Mr. I Want to Be Your Best Friend: I find it extremely funny and scary that women fall for a guy they just met last week, and by the next week, they are best friends? Are you kidding me? The issue is, we romanticize everything! I remember when I was growing up, we would hear in church that we should marry our best friends. Well, my best friend was a girl, so I couldn't marry her. Lol.

Technically, I understand what they were trying to say. But honestly, the whole concept, in my opinion, is not a very smart one. Demanding to be a man's best friend has caused many disappointments. First, when we meet a man, we are encouraged not to date or be engaged too long, so we don't participate in sexual immorality. And to be a person's best friend could take years. Becoming someone's best friend doesn't happen overnight.

Do you want to know a secret? I did not marry my best friend. When I married my husband, he was not my best friend, and I was not his best friend. Why? I didn't want a best friend. I wanted a husband, and that's what I was praying for. A husband, not a best friend. We both had best friends at the time. His were his two friends he grew up with, went to school and college with, and pledged with. Mine was my girlfriend that I grew up with. However, over time, we are becoming each other's best friends.

So please don't fall victim to this marry your best friend idea. How do you know he wants a best friend? And I feel like a lot of women are friend zoned because they talk about wanting a best friend. Many women push their way into a man's life, demanding they become best friends. That is so intrusive!

Think about it, ladies. How many women do you know who said, "I was his best friend, and I thought he was gonna marry me"? But instead, he married a girl he met three months ago! Why? Because she wanted a husband and not a best friend. Likewise, he wanted a wife and not a best friend. And another thing. How many women do you know who became friends with a man, hoping he would marry them? Please stop the madness!

Stop bombarding a man in a corner, demanding to be his best friend so that you can marry your best friend. Remember that men and women are not the same. Most men don't marry the girl who's like "one of the boys." He doesn't need you to be his best friend during the dating stage; he wants a wife. And over time, that's when the best friend comes into play. Imagine every man you date, aka gather data on, you demand to be his best friend?

I believe this is a reason many women stick around, waiting for a man to marry her because they are "best friends." How many years, effort, and energy have you wasted trying to be his best friend when you wanted a husband, and he wanted a wife? If you believe in dating several men at once, how do you become all their best friends?

Remember, ladies: dating means to gather data, not becoming his heartstring, not getting emotionally involved, or any of that. Stop trying to be his best friend and find out if he wants you to be his wife. You can become best friends once he chooses to profess his love, provide for you, and protect you.

Have some women said they married their best friend? Yes, there have, but that's not the norm. If you went to school together, grew up together, lived in the same city, and have been friends for umpteen years, sure, you're best friends. But is the man you met last week that you're gathering data on your best friend? Nope!

Mr. Pressure Points: This "lovely" mister knows your pressure points. For example, I mentioned the car and the rent earlier. He comes in, and he is just filling that need and void that you have. If you're a single mom with a child who needs a father figure, he jumps right in. And this might not be a bad thing, but again, princesses, beware. Vet and question every man who shows interest in you.

How any women trust their babies with a man, they just met baffles me. Hello? Stranger danger, remember? I am all for meeting a good man who can do all that we desire and over and above. Princesses, I want you to be mindful, prayerful, and to ask questions. I know we get tired of being alone, and we need a man around the house to do all the manly things, but we still need to be wise about every man we gather data on. And there's nothing wrong with that. All I'm saying is, take your time with each man you meet. Refuse to be gullible and desperate. Don't take any man's word to heart. Instead, like the Apostle Paul says in **1 Thessalonians 5:21 "Test all things; hold fast to what is good."**

Mr. Full Package Pretender: This man is seemingly good, but time investigating him will reveal that he is dangerous. He is the man who pretends to profess his love, pretends to provide for and protect you. Because he has a form of professing, protecting, and providing, it seems as if he is the real deal. I am reminded of the scripture that talks about having a form of godliness but denying the power within.

Therefore, we can't be gullible, ladies, and think that every man that approaches us wants to love, provide for, and protect us. Mr. Full Package Pretender comes ready and willing to do so much for you: pay your cable bill, rent, alarm service, and all. Mr. Full Package Pretender will get your car fixed and anything else he needs to do to cloud your judgment. But the truth is, he is pretending to be the one, and this is where we all need to be prayerful and vigilant.

Thus, as a young woman, I didn't accept any gifts, money, or help from any man that I was not related to. Any man that I met who offered to help me in any way put me on alert. And I learned early on from my father that men want something in return for helping you. Think about it. What man is gonna pay your rent just because?

Why does he want to do all that for you? 'Cause you're a sweet and beautiful girl? 'Cause he has so much money he wants to give you some? Okay! At what price, though? I cringe when I read women post, "Oh, he wants to pay my rent for me." And they get all giddy and excited because a man offered to pay their rent. SMH! I remember my landlord offering to give me free rent and so on if I would just let him come by occasionally for a nice Jamaican meal. Or he could lower my rent! Nope, no thanks. I worked very hard to provide for my baby girl and me, and I can afford to pay my rent.

So, when I was single and moving from one apartment to another, I would pay the brothers from the church to move me. When I needed a car, I saved up my money, and my bio-father bought my first two cars. I got AAA, so I didn't have to depend on any mechanic to get me. Because here again, men will use any bait to get you. In my book *The Naked Wife*, there's a story of a wife who helped her husband start his mechanic business. You see, she was being his mom and fixing him up. In about two years, he had run the business in the ground because he was sleeping with the women as pay for him to fix their cars.

Any man who offered me anything didn't faze me or move me. And that's why money never influenced me as a single woman. You see, I had already disciplined myself not to accept anything from any man. And I believe that one must intentionally plan your life out. Wisdom is looking ahead, seeing the traps, and avoiding them at all cost.

Countless women get caught up with the pretender! Next thing you know, he's moving in, driving her car, has her bank account information, and all. I knew one young lady who was thrilled that a guy she had just met wanted her to get an alarm service with video. Little did she know, he was watching her and her teenage girls without her knowing. Think about it this way: unless a man has been through the process to protect you, what royalties does he have to protect you? Apparently, he convinced her to give her the code because he was paying for it. I mean just gullible!

Don't be so needy! Get everything you need, so you don't have to depend on anyone to do it for you. If you have a car, you need a trusted mechanic who isn't trying to get into your panties. Get

AAA, so you don't have to call Tyrone to come to pick you up. Save your money so that, if you lose your job, you don't have to move a man in to pay the rent. When I was single, I kept a one-bedroom apartment in a decent area for an affordable price. I was earning $50k per year and still had that one bedroom, where I gave my daughter the room, and I slept in the living room on a futon.

Why? I was planning my life out. I knew it was only temporary. I was saving up my money so that I could have an emergency fund. I was paying off student loans while saving to purchase my first home. I didn't get into credit card debt by buying expensive stuff to keep up with the Joneses.

My father bought my first two cars, and then I bought a used car from a private owner to save money. So, if I ever got into a situation where I was sick, couldn't work, lost my job, or got laid off, I knew my baby girl, and I would be good. And I didn't need to depend on any man who was not my husband or father for anything. And guess what, ladies? My husband has told me over the years that one of the reasons he married me was because he saw how I was with my money. He knew that I wouldn't waste his money when he married me.

Mr. Marriage Is a Piece of Paper: This one has puzzled me for years, not so much for the man but for the women who accept this foolishness, even though they want to get married. If you desire to get married, why would you sign up for and build a life with a man who doesn't believe in marriage or thinks marriage is a piece of paper?

And what I find it's not that they don't want to get married; they haven't met the one they want to get married to! So, they meet some foolish woman who thinks she can change Mr. Marriage Is A Piece of Paper into a man who will marry her. Here's an idea: Why not just choose a man who wants to get married? These women will foolishly shack up with these men, have babies, pay bills, and then years later, he moves on with his life, and guess what? He signs that piece of paper with another woman!

If you want to get married, please don't fall for this foolery. Mr. Marriage is a Piece of Paper will say things like, "A piece of paper doesn't prove that I love you." When it comes to paperwork and a man providing for and protecting his family, he will say something like, "We can do a living will or do power of attorney for stuff. I will make you my beneficiary on the life insurance, and you can add me to your deed for the house."

Many fall for this, and while some of this is true, why sign that piece of paper? Mr. Marriage is a Piece of Paper often says women look at marriage as getting her husband's social security, pensions, and so on. But why not? Why leave money out there on the table, when a wife can reap all the benefits of what her husband has left?

Mr. Marriage is a Piece of Paper also brings up the price of a divorce and how costly it can get for the man. While studies have shown that women initiate divorce more than men, women often get divorced because of something the man has done or is doing. To avoid this, Mr. Marriage Is Just A Piece of Paper believes it's cheaper and safer for men not to sign that government-sponsored marriage license.

But, is marriage government sponsored, or is this something that came straight from the Bible? How about, instead of the mindset it's cheaper to keep her, say it's cheaper to be faithful. It's cheaper to be a man of honor and respect and do the right thing for his wife and kids.

Isn't the government structured around the Bible? The funny thing is that those men who think like this don't believe in the Bible or the authority of it and the church. So, princesses, it's not just that he doesn't believe in marriage. He doesn't believe in your God, either. You see, marriage is a picture of the union between Christ and the church and is the example we follow as husbands and wives. Therefore, you can't accept anything less than marriage if this is what you want.

Princesses, let me express to you in the kindest way possible, "Please resist shacking up!" Don't believe the lies and deception of the devil that it's ok to live with a man without being married. If you are not married, that's shacking up. Many don't consider this, but if you are a believer, this is what the scripture teaches. Stop being a marriage bootlegger and choose a husband who will marry and cover you.

Mr. Scratch Your Itch: This mister goes hand in hand with Mr. Wrong and Mr. Right Now. This "pick me" man is not afraid to let you know that he wants to "scratch your itch." His sole purpose is as an itch scratcher or to fulfill your "sexual need." That's why, ladies, it is essential to have a list of talking points when you are getting to know someone. That goes back to my ten things you desire in a husband. Write them down, get to know them, and meditate on them.

Some guys you meet have no business knowing you are celibate, that you haven't had sex in a while, and all those private things. When you meet someone, you need to get to know him based on your top ten list. But in those top ten, you can develop lots of questions. Princesses remember that just because you are trying to get to know a guy, you desire as a husband doesn't necessarily mean he wants to get to know you as a wife.

Pay close attention to what everyone says, but most importantly, pay attention to their actions. If Mr. Scracth Your Itch, always wants to talk about sex or is sending enticing pictures of his dingaling, you already know what he is about.

Mr. Celibacy Breaker: For the life of me, I don't understand why any woman would announce all over social media that they are a virgin or celibate! Like Mr. Heart Breaker, he is determined to break your celibacy because it is only relevant to you and not to him. You tell him that you're celibate, and he'll say something like, "Oh, I'm gonna be the one to get you to give it to me." Or "Well, that's not for me because I want to test drive before I commit." You will then try to prove to him that you are wife material, but little do you know it's a trick.

Can you please tell me why a guy you don't know or not planning to marry needs to know that you are and have been celibate for years? A man you are planning on marrying is one who has gone through the process to get to that place. Make up your mind that the discussion of sex is only for the man with whom there's a progression towards courting for marriage. You nicely let everyone else know that you don't want to talk about that right now. Sex should not be discussed with some strange man you just met.

Sweetie beware of Mr. Celibacy Breaker! Ladies learn to pay attention to the signs. A man who always wants to talk about sex is only about sex! Let's say you told him that you are celibate. What is he talking about for the next few conversations? Does he want to know more about your celibacy? Is he trying to talk you into letting him "hit that?" Pay close attention, ladies, because this could be a sign that you need to let him go and move on to next.

The Cobweb Cleaner: He is like Mr. Celibacy Breaker, but the difference is with you, ladies. You are not celibate because of a vow or choice. You're celibate because you haven't met anyone you want to have sex with, and you know how I feel about having sex with whomever! You haven't had sex in so long that you have "cobwebs growing," as the saying goes. But you foolishly announce on social media that you've got cobwebs.

Suddenly your inbox is full of guys who want to clean out your cobwebs for you. Ladies, ladies, it is crucial for you to know what you want. Do you want a husband? Or do you want a sex buddy? Ain't nobody's business, but yours and Jesus's that you have cobwebs. And, please stop talking about your sexcapades all over social media. 'Cause if all you want is a cobweb cleaner, they are waiting in the wings for the job.

Mr. Woman of Childbearing Years: I met this man who was fifty-five years old. I was in my late twenties or early 30s. He was a brother who attended my Bible study group. He was overly friendly and thoughtful and never missed a class. I was a bit suspicious of him because anytime he hugged me, he would linger and seemingly pass his hand over my body. One evening, Mr. Woman of Childbearing Years said there was something he wanted to talk to me about, and he would like to take me out for dinner. Not thinking that this older man would be interested in me in a romantic way, I accepted the dinner invitation.

First, the way he drove and stopped, I wanted to vomit. At dinner, he told me that he wanted me to be his wife because he is looking for a woman of childbearing years. Lol! If I could have pooped on myself, I would. I almost bust out laughing because I don't know how this old man thought that I would want to marry him! Anyways, I did let him down easy and told him that I just saw him as a brother in the Lord and was not interested in him as a husband.

During this same time, I had another pastor who said he was forty-eight and wanted to marry me. I was disgusted because, even though he said he was forty-eight, he looked about sixty. I let him down easy, too because I had no interested in marrying a man that much older than me.

So, princesses, be mindful that there are old men who want your eggs. Lol. I wanted an older man but not that old. Plus, they just looked old, acted old, talked old; they were way too old for me to marry. This is not ageism. All I am saying is, as a twenty-eight to a thirty-year-old woman, I was not interested in men who were twice my age. I wanted a husband, not a sugar daddy. I always saw myself as a wife and not a sugar baby wife. Yuck!

Mr. Buttercup: Mr. Buttercup is for all the ladies who have all these male friends thinking they are going to marry them. Or he might be a friend that you had no interest in, but as you get older, you begin to have an open mind about him. Mr. Buttercup will spend ten years being your friend, buttering you up so that you can feel comfortable and gain his trust.

When you finally let your guard down and give Mr. Buttercup a chance to take you out, he offers to take you to a hotel! See right there: sense should tap you on the shoulder and whisper in your ear that Mr. Buttercup was only buttering you up to get you to give him the drows. Don't fall for it, ladies. Leave all the Mr. Buttercups alone.

Mr. Target: I have learned that I was the focus of this mister a few years back on my job. Mr. Target is the guy who thinks he is all that, so he can get any woman he wants. He targets you to get your cookies. If I were a single woman in this age of social media, I would not be as vocal as I am as a married woman about dating and choosing a husband. This is mainly because, by stating your views, there are men who will target you to get the cookie.

Therefore, be mindful, ladies! Remember that not every man wants to profess his love to you, provide for you, and protect you. It takes time to find that out about every man you meet and date. Sure, there are some men you will know in a short time that they're not for you.

Mr. Rebound: C'mon ladies! Who doesn't know about a guy who is on the rebound? I am amazed at the number of ladies who jump in a relationship while Mr. Rebound is ending a relationship, finalizing a divorce, or depressed merely from a broken heart.

For some reason, you think you are Wonder Woman, and you can heal him, fix him up, and get him to marry you. Sadly, many women who feel that they can get Mr. Rebound to settle down with them have been left with a broken heart and disappointed hopes and dreams. A healed, whole and prepared man is best, ladies! A husband is a choice, so choose wisely.

Mr. Cookie Scammer: Like Mr. Heart Breaker, his only intention is to get the cookie. Oh, I have had run-ins with this mister on many occasions: on the job, at church, at school, and in the streets. There have been guys whose only intention was to try to get my cookie. At my job a few years ago, I learned there was a bet going around about who could get my cookie first. That is funny to me because you see, princesses, my mind was already set that I didn't date or even go out with guys I work with. Therefore, I would never fall for any of their tricks.

The sad thing is that many women have fallen for guys they work with. And I know a few guys who have slept with many women, both single and married, on the job. Ladies, you must set your standards and stick to them. I beg you to use wisdom. If you know that the man who is pursuing you is a whore, he might not be the man you want to go out with. Maybe, just maybe, he is only about checking you off his list of "cookies" and broke him off a piece.

You see, the mistake a lot of women make is to think that they're going to be the one he chooses to settle down with because you're different and more special to him. Honey Chile, sweetie pie, please stop deceiving yourself! Mr. Cookie Scammer is all about scamming the cookie! And as soon as you let him taste it, he will be off to sampling somebody else's cookie. Remember now, what is your purpose in dating? Do you want to get married, or you want to get scammed out of your cookie? This is another reason I'm all about taking the cookie off the table.

However, while the guys on the job are not for me, I know many couples who met on the job and got married.

Mr. Control: This guy is so obvious that I'm shocked that many women fall for him. It puzzles me that women fall for this control freak! He wants to control everything about you. He tells you how you can be and who you can talk to. He forbids you to speak with your friends and family and even people you work with. He wants to control how you dress, when or if you wear panties or thongs.

How does this happen? He talks to you and gets all in your emotions. He is skilled at finding his victims to control, and these women always seem to fall for the same type of guy. You think he is such a nice, caring, and sweet guy. You open emotionally, and before you know it, he is in control of your life and decisions.

The next thing you know, he's in every group you're in on social media. He watches every post and comment to see what you are saying. And if you like other male's pictures, if he senses a hint of you showing interest in someone else, he becomes jealous and possessive. Question: You know all this; you sense that something is not right, so why are you planning on dating/marrying Mr. Control? Do you realize it will only get worse?

16-Mr. Gift of Gab

*P*roverbs 4:23 encourages us **to guard our hearts with all diligence because out of it are the issues of life.** So, if out of our heart flows the issues of life, I submit to you that issues can flow in your heart because of "words. Also, in **1 John 2:16,** Apostle John states that **all that is in this world is the lust of the flesh, and the lust of the eyes and the pride of life...**

Princesses be mindful of a man who has the gift of gab. He might be able to talk you out of the promise of God. Think about it. How many times of Mr. Gift of Gab talked you out of your panties? Therefore, we need to guard our hearts by protecting what goes in of it via our eyes and ears.

Mr. Gift of Gab: This mister needs to be closely watched. He has the gift of gab. He can talk a baby into giving him its lollipop. Nevertheless, I am amazed at the number of women who meet a man this week and are ready to drop the drows next week because he is saying all the right things. Or you'll hear a woman say, "Oh, he's so sweet. I want to give him some." I often come back with, "And what does that mean? Does that mean, because he's so sweet, his reward should be your kitty kat?"

This is a man you have met via social media, talked with in your inbox, maybe texted or had a few phone calls, yet you're ready to "drop yo' drows?" Think about that, ladies. And ask yourself the question, "How much does it cost to sleep with me?" Is it because he texts you good morning, gives a pocketbook, weekend getaway, or a free meal? How much will it cost a man to get between your legs, aka the holy of holies? What about those "WTD" text?

When you meet Mr. Gift of Gab, he is easy to recognize. Everything you say, he comes back with, "Oh baby, honey, sweetie pie," making empty promises because he knows you're gullible and desperate. So he can tell you anything, and you will sop it all up with a biscuit of desperation. Here again, ladies, I cannot say it enough!! Before you fall all the way in, get the data you need.

Mr. Have A Way with Words: This is the man who has a way with words. Be it the Bible, politics, sports, or the latest news, he is well-versed because some guys know that women like a man who knows how to use words.

This mister is all talk, and he is not using his ability for good but to lure women in, only for them to realize that he is all talk. I knew a young man like this in college. He was well-educated, versed in all topics, and all our friends thought he and I would make a good couple. They believed that, while he had some rough patches, he just needed a good woman like me to rein him in. See there? How do people continue to think that all these immature and undisciplined males need "good women" to rein them in? We need to stop!

Now, I don't know about you, but I do not want to have to rein a man in. I mean, how old is he? Is he my son? I refused even to go out with him. I just knew there were many character flaws, and

I was not interested in being with someone who was all talk. Also, princesses, remember that you want a prepared man as your husband, someone who has thought things through and who have, **count the cost as** mentioned in **Luke 14:28.** Remember also Mr. Psalm 23, aka Mr. Shepard. Husband; he is a prepared man who plans.

Almost twenty years later, I was once again faced with this man who was trying to con the system versus building a life of his own. All I thought about was *I was so glad that I picked up on who he was, and I was not interested in who he was.* Ladies, this is what I meant when I said write down what you want so that if a man approaches you who doesn't line up with what you prayed for, there is no need for you to waste your time with him.

Mr. Talk Only: Ladies, it's essential to pay attention to Mr. Have A Way with Words and Mr. Talk Only because they are different. The difference is that Mr. Talk Only talks a lot about all that he is and what he's going to do and be, but it is only talk. No action! Princesses, this is where getting the DATA comes in. You don't have to say or do much; give him a listening ear, and he will tell you everything.

Beware, however: don't give him too much of your time because his words will get down into your spirit. This is the guy who has been going back to college for the last thirty years and hasn't even looked up what the requirements are. He dreams a lot but does absolutely nothing other than talk a lot of "words." He is so skilled that he can get you to believe in his dreams without a plan. Next thing you know, you will be pushing him to accomplish his goals, but to your dismay, they are still only words.

Many women pay all the bills while waiting for him to accomplish his words. Nothing ever happens, and, ten years later, she is still waiting for him to manifest all that he's been saying he's going to do. Ladies, that old saying "Actions speaks louder than words" will save you lots of time and heartache.

Mr. No Action: Like the former two, he talks a lot but doesn't follow through. Oh, he's going to take you out, but a year later, he hasn't. He's going to call you, but four weeks later, you're still sitting by the phone, twiddling your fingers and waiting for him to call. You're wasting time for this stranger you just met, who you've put your hope in that he's going to call. Here's an idea. Why don't you get up, get out, and get dating other men who want to date you?

Ladies, this is another reason why we need to get DATA on several guys at once, if possible. Here you are waiting on Mr. No Action to call you when you could be getting DATA on someone else. This is another reason you are not to assume any male you meet is your husband until you get the DATA, and you agree that marriage is what you both want with each other.

Pay close attention to the words he speaks and, most importantly, his actions. So if he says he's going to take you out but weeks later still nothing, then you know he is not serious about taking you out. He might be a guy who wants you to plan the date, pick him up, and pay for it. I say, drop him and move on! I shared how my now husband didn't call to take me out for a whole month. Guess what? I was still going out, meeting new guys, gathering data on other guys. But when he finally called, he was about the business. He didn't miss a beat, and he got busy about making me his wife.

Mr. Serpent: He will talk you out of what God said if you don't know what God said and apply it to your life. The story of Eve and the serpent comes to mind. I plan to write a book extensively on Eve. In the meantime, ladies, it is vital to get rooted and grounded in the word of the Lord.

I have met a few Mr. Serpents in my single days. Several was trying to get me to sleep with them. One said that he would pray and ask God to place my punishment on him. Therefore, I should sleep with him. Lol! How foolish! He made promises of money, a house, and cars. But praise be to Jesus, I wasn't desperate, gullible, or needy. Be alert and exercise wisdom. Remember, be wise as serpents and harmless as doves.

17-Mr. Sensitivity

Mr. Heart on his Sleeve: Don't you love a man who is in touch with his feelings? Well, here you have him. He wears his heart on his sleeve; he cries, is compassionate, and gets emotional. When you read what he posts, you can't help but say, "Aww, how sweet!"

But before you thank the Lord, ladies, please beware. Don't get caught up because it could be a ploy. Dig a bit deeper to see how he deals with other emotions. How does he handle stressful situations? Can he hold it together or does he fall apart like a $2 suitcase?

How is he with anger? Does he know how to control himself, or does he break and throw things? Does he throw tantrums like my three-year-old son? Can you feel safe around him when situations arise that require him to man up? In those times when you need him to protect you, can he? Can he be strong when you are weak? Or will he turn and run and leave you in danger?

Mr. Give Me Your Heart: Ladies, your heart is like your cookie. No man should get it except the man who loves you enough to profess his love, provide for you, and protect you. The only man who you should be entrusting your heart to is the one who has gone through the process to become your husband. Please T H I N

K about that. Mr. Give Me Your Heart pulls at your heartstrings. He will claim that he doesn't want you sexually until you have given him your heart. He wants you to open the doors of your heart and let him in as if he is Jesus Christ. Be very careful of this guy, ladies!

As women, we shouldn't go around dishing out cookies to every Tom, Dick, and Harry in the same way we need to stop giving our hearts to men who haven't been through the process to have them. I don't understand for the life of me why women fall for this guy. How do you give your heart to a man you don't know? How can you trust a stranger with something as precious as your heart?

It's no wonder many women end up with broken, crumbled, and destroyed hearts because they have entrusted a stranger with their most precious treasure. Mr. Give Me Your Heart uses his sweet and twisted lies to get into women's hearts and heads. It sounds so promising and romantic, doesn't it?

Especially if a woman is vulnerable and was hurt in the past, he comes in like Mr. Fix it. He claims to be able to fix all your broken heart issues. He is so skilled in getting into your heart that you open and tell him all your deepest desires, secrets, hurt, and pain. Princesses, please remember to guard your heart and renew your minds. Guard your heart against the lies and deception of the enemy, who comes to get you outside the will of God. Renew your mind on the promises of God, so that you can be rooted and grounded in the Word.

Make up your mind and heart that your heart belongs only to the man who loves and honors you enough to go through the process to have your heart. Do not entrust your heart and life to a male who didn't go through the process to profess his love, provide for, and protect you. Ask yourself this question: Has he taken the necessary steps to ensure your safety and protection?

Finally, ladies, please stop telling strange men all of what you want and need! When you tell him everything, all he must do is become what you said by pretending. Before you know it, you will be like a lamb in the hands of a hunter. This is another reason a list is essential. Remember, be wise as serpents and harmless as doves. Learn to get the information you need without telling him all that's in your heart.

Something else to be mindful of is that, as women, we want to belong and feel protected and cared for. So, we think if we give our hearts and our bodies to someone, then he will care for us and protect us. However, that is the worst thing you can do. And why should he? What loyalty does he have towards you? You think because you gave him your cookies, baked him some cookie, and gave him the best home cooked meal on this side of heaven that he's gonna marry you?

Mr. Endearment: Ladies, it's important to pay close attention to this mister. Your radar needs to be so on point that the moment one of these guys acts unseemly that your light will come on. Oh, I hated encountering this guy. Now, based on where you live in the United States, terms of endearment, like honey, baby, sweetie, baby gurl, and so on, are everyday language. But how do you meet someone on social media, jump into her inbox, and begin to call her honey, baby, and my love?

What I found was that Mr. Endearment uses those words as a smokescreen. By calling you terms of endearment, it begins to soften your stand, and your guard starts to come down slowly. Mr. Endearment knows it will only be a short time before he is all the way in your heart and mind. And the next thing you know, you're sending money to some strange man. Princesses remember that I am not encouraging you to be tough and manly. However, I want to remind you of the scripture that says for us to guard our heart.

Pay close attention. If you are talking to someone you don't know who always wants to call you honey or baby, tell him to call you by your name. Princesses remember that I am not saying every man you meet is like this. There are some awesome guys out there. I want to remind you to be mindful and guard your heart. Extract the information that you need to make an informed decision. Also, guarding your heart doesn't mean being harsh, aggressive, and rude. Remember to be wise as serpents and harmless as doves as you gather data. Think about how soft doves are.

Mr. Emasculator: This mister can be easily mistaken for Mr. Compliment if you don't know what to listen for. Mr. Emasculator emasculates himself by complimenting you. So, for example, he might say, "Baby, you're too good for me," or, "You're so pretty. I don't know what you see in me." Mr. Emasculator could have severe problems with his self-esteem and his masculinity. Thus, he can be classified as Mr. Sympathy because the truth is, he is looking for someone to be sympathetic to him, his feelings, and his capabilities.

Or he could be doing it as a ploy to draw you in so you can be his personal ego fluffer. The issue is that it gets tiring, and while we all like and welcome compliments, no one should go around looking for them or intentionally position themselves to force a compliment. Mr. Emasculator also doesn't take responsibility for his actions, but always blames someone or something. He deliberately looks for ways not to be responsible.

Mr. Compliment: Otherwise known as Mr. Sweet talker. Who doesn't like a nice compliment, be it "You're beautiful," "That's a lovely dress" and so on? I accept compliments from everyone, including homeless guys, the nicely dressed guy, or the garbage man. I welcome all compliments! When anyone compliments me, I smile, give a curtsey, and say, "thank you." Compliments uplift us, put a smile on our faces, and put an extra pep in our steps. Also, to that homeless man that people overlook daily, just by me smiling and saying thank you can uplift his spirit.

This mister can be sweet, caring, thoughtful, and nice. But don't allow your emotions to get in your way of paying attention to his actions. Remember that words mean absolutely nothing if the actions don't line up. Is he complimenting you because he genuinely thinks you are pretty and your dress is nice, or is he using it as a ploy to get you to put your guard down? Only time and actions will tell.

18-Mr. Nurse or Purse

Mr. Nurse or Purse: I wrote about this mister in my book *The Naked Wife* also. This mister is either looking for a nurse or a purse. He might be older or sickly and in need of someone to take care of him. So he seeks out women who are motherly and who believe that, in sickness and in health, you are to stick it through. The issue is, he might not disclose that he is sick, so when you marry him, you are in shock. That's why it's important to ask questions, do blood work, and so on before you marry him. I took my husband to my doctor to do a physical and do blood work to make sure I was marrying a man I had all the information on.

Another version of this guy is a man who's looking for a purse. He seeks out a woman who has her stuff together, has some money in the bank, and is doing well for herself. There's only one thing missing for many women who have worked hard to provide for themselves and their children: a good man who can adore them with his love, provision, and protection.

Unfortunately, some women fall for this man but end up frustrated and regretting marrying him because, no matter how much money a woman makes, she wants her man to take care of her. I had a saying when I was single. "I will hold my pillow until my change comes." Don't rush into deciding because you don't want to have regrets by rushing.

Mr. Erectile Dysfunction: On social media, there have been many memes going around about men with ED. One stated that he played the field and now he's older, and he got hit with ED, so he wants to find a wife to settle down with. Princesses be mindful to ask all the right questions. Of course, no man is going to come out and say, "Hey, I have ED." If you've read my book *The Naked Wife*, you will read a few stories of ladies who married men who had ED, but the men didn't disclose it before they got married. One lady was married five years with NO SEX.

Of course, as Christian women, we are encouraged by the Bible to wait until marriage to have sex. There is no test driving that God approves of. Many ladies bring this up as a reason they feel they need to test drive. Another friend of mine who was thirty-five had a man who was sixty years old and pursuing her, rushing her to hurry and get married. Pay attention to the signs, ladies.

A man who is rushing you to get married needs to be investigated. Ask questions; ask what kind of medication he is taking. Come right out and ask him if his penis is working if he is experiencing ED. I say ask those question in front of a marriage counselor or your doctor. For my husband's and my marriage counselor, we had my husband's pastor, and then I got a Certified Marriage Counselor also. I asked every question I could think of. Also, ladies, please use a bit of wisdom when going through marriage counseling. It's best to get an older, mature male marriage counselor so your fiancé can feel comfortable and be open.

At the publication of this book, there was an article about a couple who got married. However, the wife didn't find out until their wedding night that he had a micropenis. The wife stated in the article that even though her future husband was not religious, he claimed he was old fashion, thus wanting to wait until marriage to have sex. After six months of dating, they got engaged, and after another six months, they were married. She was disappointed, shocked, and felt deceived to learned on their wedding night that he had a micropenis.

When they awoke the next morning, he just acted as if everything was normal. Princesses, this is what I mean about discussing sex and body parts in detailed in front of a marriage counselor. This way if any issue arises later, you can have a witness to go back to and discuss these issues with. A man with a micropenis should have disclosed this to his fiancé so that she can freely choose him. Not laying it on her on the wedding night that "hey, sorry to let you know that my penis is smaller than pinky."

Mr. Can I Get Some Love: OMG! "Give me a hug; give me some love," this guy! Always looking for and needing love. He had a bad day, the sun didn't shine, he didn't make a red light, so it messed up his day. Like Mr. Needy, this guy will suck the very life out of you.

He's always having a pity party and hoping you will be a listening ear for it! Do I need to say more? He makes my skin crawl! If you happen to run into this guy, please tell him to call his mom.

Mr. Eager: Ladies, beware of Mr. Eager. He is almost scary. You meet him at 1 p.m., and by 2 p.m., he's asking you to marry him. He wants to come to your house, know who you're talking to, and what color panties you have on. He comes off as caring for you and wants to make sure you're okay. However, this is his little way of slipping in, and the next thing you know, you have a stalker and a control freak who has taken over your life. Pay attention, ladies.

Remember the saying, "patience is a virtue"? It is beloveds, and I believe when it comes to joining our lives with another, patience is there as a caution so that we can be protected. Don't ever rush into anything without the information you need to make an informed decision. It takes time to vet a man and get the information you need. Your life and that of your children depend on you taking your time to choose your husband correctly and wisely.

Mr. Rush: This guy can be scary! Probably a narcissist, he wants to trap you before you figure him out. You might meet via another friend's post or in a group, and he jumps in your inbox, and everything is a rush. He wants to learn all about you in one sitting, and he wants you to cut your heart open and spill it all to him. He's probably already figured you out, what you want and need, so when you talk to him, it feels as if you've known each other for years. Why? He took the time to figure you out on social media based on what you post: all your wants, needs, and desires. Mr. Rush is dangerous because he demands that you skip your steps of processing that you need to do to see if he is right for you.

For example, before you get married, you need to check his financial roadmap. Get a credit report and ask for his W2. A blood test is not required by most states to get married, but why would you marry a man and have unprotected sex with him without proof that he is healthy? Sweetie, this is your life we're talking about. Until you have proof, you do not trust your life to any man. So go ahead and do a blood test for all STDs, and complete a physical also.

Just as important as a blood test and a financial checkup, you need to go to marriage counseling. My princess sisters, marriage counseling, is vital. Trust no one with your lives, ladies, until he has been through the process for you to trust, honor, and respect him. So, if a Mr. Rush is trying to get you to rush the process and skip these vital steps, beware, my dears!

Mr. Liability: Like Mr. Nurse or Purse, Mr. Hobosexual and a few others, Mr. Liability is just that. A liability! Whichever way you try to cut it, slice it, or dice it, he's gonna cost you some way or somehow. It could be your time, energy, money, or even your destiny; this guy will only be a liability. And the truth is, you know it.

However, for some strange reason, you've "fallen in love" with him, and he has already become a liability to you. Drop the dead weight and choose a man who is an asset, not a liability.

Mr. Green Card: Remember earlier, I mentioned that you should know exactly what you want? When you meet a man and get some data on him, your mind needs to be analyzing what he's telling you. I refuse to date men who do not have a green card. Why? I have known so many men who marry women to get citizenship. I have known many women who have fallen victim to a man who says he loves her and wants to marry her, but the truth is, he only loves her because he can use her to get his green card.

Sadly, this happened to both of my biological brothers. I'm sure they thought those women were marrying them because they loved them. But, as soon as they got their legal status, they were changed, women. I remember screaming from the mountaintop for them not to marry women who don't have their papers. But you know how emotions can be blinding. Both of my brothers are divorced, and it breaks my heart to see them in pain.

When I was single, I didn't entertain, spend time, have coffee, or even waste my time on the phone with men who didn't have their legal documents. When I was sixteen years old, a family friend was trying to push a man on me who did not have his papers. Of course, I resisted because I had already made that decision. I had seen my uncle used and left for his documents, so that was cemented in my head early on.

There was nothing about this man; I even liked him. So beware, princesses, even family friends, and family members will try to push Mr. Green Card on you! Don't do it! Plus, I was 16, just had a baby, and was homeless, which is why I was living with this "family friend." So even though I got caught out there with a baby at 16, I knew that I didn't need a man who wasn't able to stand on his own two feet.

Mr. On Your Dime: Sigh. I cannot tell you the number of women who are with Mr. On Your Dime. It's as if the man is an escort, and the women are paying all the expenses to have a man on their arm. The sad thing is that some men look for these types of women, ones who will pay for them to have a good time on the women's dime. He sits back and waits for them to plan the dates, transportation, and all.

Mr. On Your Own Dime, is the type that will say, "Oh baby, I want to take you out, but you know, I ain't got it right now." Instead of you recognizing the game, you foolishly and desperately come back with, "It's okay, baby. I got you." Next thing you know, you're taking him out, treating him to movies and dinner as often as he wants to go.

Truthfully, you are showing him that you can provide for and take care of him. If you're doing all that for him, why should he work to provide? If you are joyfully willing to foot the bill, why would he choose to take you out and treat you like a lady? Don't you want to be adored, cherished, and treated like a princess? How about this one? "Baby, how about you order yourself some roses, and I'll get you on payday?" What a joke! Ladies, stop it, please! Lol!

Mr. Stank: I hate to have to, but I must address this because I have heard so many women complain about grown men stinking. The men had breath, rotten teeth, body odor, stank clothes, and dirty socks. I heard of a woman who found a skid mark in her bed. How disgusting! One of my church sisters also married a man who was so stank. She said it was as if he didn't brush his teeth in the mornings. When he woke up, his breath was so stank that she would have to leave the room. Now, someone might say, why don't you help him? Not your job! You are not his momma, especially when dating a man.

How do you explain a forty-year-old man walking around with stank breath? How do you trust him with your life? He can't even take care of his breath, much less a wife and family. Now, let's be fair. We have all experienced not so fresh breath one time or the other. If you had tuna for lunch, unless you brush your teeth, it's gonna be a li'l funky. I often have salmon for lunch. I try not to talk into people's faces. A grown man walking around stinking has hygiene issues, but it's not my job to put him in the tub and wash his behind. First, if his breath is so bad that you can't stay in the same room with him, then he isn't going to the dentist every six months.

If he is walking around funky, he isn't washing. And if his clothes are dirty and funky, he isn't clean. But these men will make an excuse that they need a good woman to wash, cook, and clean for them. Listen to what they are saying, ladies. They need a woman to wash, cook, and clean for them. That's all they want you for. They don't want to go through the process to profess their love, provide for you, and protect you. Their whole purpose of getting a woman is so she can take care of him. Think about that, and please leave Mr. Stank man alone! A man who has prepared himself to be a husband and has been through the process to have you will make sure that he is his best self.

And another thing, ladies, as moms of boys, we need to begin to teach our sons how to wash and be clean. I had a friend who had custody of her twelve-year-old cousin, and she said he would turn the water on and stand at the end of the tub, pretending as if he had showered. Lol! Eventually, she would stand at the door of the bathroom to make sure he was washing.

19-Mr. Kryptonite

$\mathcal{D}$on't you love Superman? He is, by far, my favorite superhero. And remember how Superman could get out of any situation? Nothing could hurt him or keep him down. Well, except Kryptonite. In the same way, Mr. Kryptonite is the man who has power over you.

Mr. Drop Yo Drows Gorgeous: Ladies beware! This mister might be your dream, man. He is your weakness, your kryptonite. He is everything you ever want and need in a man. He might be saved, or you're comfortable with where he is in the Lord. He might also not be saved, but he has your heart in his hands, and he is pulling your heartstrings. He is playing with your heart, juggling your heart and destiny in his hands.

Maybe his is a sinner man that you have "accidentally" fallen in love with. Perhaps he is married, separated, or in a complicated relationship. He could also be a serial baby maker. Mr. Drop Yo Drows Gorgeous could be any man that your heart is tied to because, for some reason, you got all entangled with him, and you've been smitten and bitten by him! He might have or not have a great job with excellent benefits plus dental.

Mr. Drop Yo Drows Gorgeous: is the right height and complexion, has a nice body, smells good, and he is drop dead gorgeous! He is just the man for you, or so you think! Gurl, beware! This is the man that you will do anything for. And even when your mind is telling you to RUN your heart is telling you to STAY! He is the man that you feel is so good for you that he will make you slap your momma!

He makes you weak in the knees, and your throat gets dry when you're around him. He is so sexy that he causes your panties to get wet! He causes your heart to skip several beats. He will make you backslide to have him because he is just, OMG! You want to marry him, have his baby, wash his dirty drows, cook, clean, and wipe the snot that runs down his nose, and if he lets you, you will even wipe his butt. But! Does he feel the same way about you? Is he the man for you? He knows you are head over heels in love with him because he knows he's the best thing that has ever happened to you since sliced bread. How does he know that? 'Cause you told him so!

My dad always told me never to love a man more than he loves you. When you do that, you will do everything and anything for him. Role reversal comes into play, and now you're playing the man role, and he's playing the woman role. Why? 'Cause you love him too much. Now, some might say, you can never love your husband too much. I believe in marriages in which both husband and wife need to be vulnerable to each other. However, that is with your husband, not some guy you are "seeing."

I had a run-in with this mister before I met my husband. Y'all, he was 6'8", and you know I love a tall man. At first, I didn't even see him. He was shooting his shot, but I was too busy doing the work of the Lord. We worked in the same business district and would often see each other at lunchtime as everyone was out getting lunch. Somehow, we ended up on the same board for some community activities, and he began to pursue me even harder.

Y'all, that man wooed, called, and texted me daily! Mr. Drop Yo Drows Gorgeous came by my job to give me hugs and kisses on the cheek and everything. I found myself texting him if I was having a bad day, and he would find his way to my job. He would text me while in bed and first thing in the morning. He would even get to his office by 7 a.m., just so that he could see me and walk me to my office building after I parked. Y'all, that man was my heart! I LOOO HIM! (That's love but you looo him so much that you can't hear the 've'. Lol)

I remember one night; he was supposed to meet me at an event. I dressed up, got my hair and nails "did," had on a sexy dress, and was smelling and looking good. Did my makeup like I've never done it before because I was going to meet up with Mr. Drop Yo Drows Gorgeous! But something happened that night, and he couldn't come to the event. Yes, I was disappointed, but looking back now, it was God protecting me because if he had come, he could have had all this brown sugariness! Yes, "Gwod"! I would have served myself up on a silver platter for him!

God knows I wanted that man! But 'deeeep' down, in the city of my soul, I knew he wasn't right for me. So, I remind myself that I wanted my husband and not him; this man that I knew was not right for me. An incident happened between us, and I decided to run like Joseph. I changed my number, started to walk the long way to work, and changed my whole routine to get away from Mr. Drop Yo Drows Gorgeous! Please note that he is not necessarily "gorgeous" but just a man that you adore and are head over heels in love with! (You can read a future book to find out what happened between us.)

I believe that my soul was tied to him, and it took time for me to get my soul untied from him. I worked hard, prayed, fasted, and read my Bible tirelessly to get my soul untied from this man. And what do you know? About two to three years after that, I met my wonderful husband! Be mindful, ladies. Be alert and look out for Mr. Drop Yo Drows Gorgeous! Look out for more of my story about my Mr. Drop Yo Drows Gorgeous in an upcoming fiction book.

Mr. Ungodly Soul Tie: Have you ever had an ungodly soul tie? I've had three ungodly soul ties in my life. The first was to my daughter's father, which is understandable. He was the first man I had sex with, and I was head over heels in love with him. The next was with my college sweetheart; we never had sex or even kissed. We connected on Biblical grounds, and I wished we would get married. Finally, with Mr. Drop Yo Drows Gorgeous. You see, ladies, you will meet and date quite a few guys in your lifetime, but out of them all there might be two or three that you would marry. Therefore dating, aka gathering data, on multiple guys is necessary.

With each ungodly soul ties, I had to work hard with prayer, fasting, and seeking the face of the Lord to untie my soul from those men. Princesses, be mindful when you get involved with a man, talking on the phone for hours at a time. Remember beloveds, guard our hearts with all diligence. We should not allow anyone to walk in and out of our hearts, having sex with them, and getting emotionally involved.

Today, I can say I have a godly soul tie to my wonderful husband, Michael. But princesses, remember I had to do the work for my heart and soul to get untied from the other men that I foolishly allowed my soul to be tied to. I couldn't marry my husband if my soul were still tied to Mr. Drop Yo Drows Gorgeous. If you find yourself falling in love with a man that you should not be with, begin to guard your heart.

Mr. He Can Get It: Lol! You should know by now that I am as real as it can get. And I think, as women, we need to be real so that we can understand where we are. I remember, years ago, the Lord ministered to my heart and encouraged me to "be honest with him." In being honest, you will be able to look ahead and say, "You know what? I need to leave this man alone."

You see, we think God can't see or doesn't know our hearts and what we honestly think and feel. Also, being honest with where we are can help with our weaknesses and address them so that we can be victorious. So, c'mon sistas, let's be honest and admit that there "might" be at least one guy that you think to yourself, "He can get it."

You might not admit it, probably keep it to yourself, and might even avoid this man, but deep down on the inside, you are thinking, "He can get it." And if he catches you on a bad day, if you are weak or in need of a little encouragement, if he is in your presence, you might throw it at him! If he calls you on a late night and asks if he can come over, you might welcome him with open legs.

Therefore, you need to be honest with yourself and with the Lord. Know what your weaknesses are. Be vigilant, watchful, and prayerful, and seek the face of the Lord. Do not make any decisions about Mr. He Can Get It when you are angry, upset, stressed out, and needing a li'l love and attention.

Like Mr. Drop Yo Drows Gorgeous, this mister is a bit dangerous because he could be someone you work with, a friend, someone at the church, a movie star, or someone you meet on social media. You don't necessarily want a commitment or a relationship from Mr. He Can Get It. He is just that guy who "can get it."

Beware of Mr. He Can Get It, ladies. He might know he can get it because of how you are with him and around him. You might be that girl who's always complimenting him, playing with him, and so on. The only thing that has kept you from giving in to Mr. He Can Get It is that he has not attempted to get it. But if he attempts, you might spread wide like eagle's wings.

Still, remember that the Bible encourages us to be chaste and wait until marriage to have sex. If you agree or not, that's what the Lord encourages. When I was single, I found it best to stay away from guys I was attracted to but had no desire to go through the process to love, protect, and provide for my daughter and me.

Mr. I Want to Give It to Him, But...: Here again, this might be someone you know personally. Ladies, please don't confuse this mister with Mr. He Can Get It. Lol! The difference between the two is that Mr. He Can Get It is if he wants you, then you will gladly give it up. But with Mr. I Want to Give it to Him, But..., there's uncertainty.

Mr. I Want to Give It to Him, But... is two part. First, you might want to give him the cookies, but it doesn't necessarily mean he wants it. I have known guys who have women dishing it out like government cheese, but they were not interested. They invite him over for dinner and a massage, and he turned them down. So just because you want to break him off a piece of your delicious cookie does not mean he wants to take a bite. And for some men, it's because she might offer. Men want to feel as if they conquered you, not the other way around.

The second part to Mr. I Want to Give It to Him, But... is that what you feel for him is Lust. The only thing that is saving you, by the skin of your teeth, is that at the end of this mister's name is the word "But." There's just something keeping you and thank God for that. If there weren't a "but" at the end of his name, you might be tempted to call him up and invite him over. Also, this mister is like Mr. He Can Get It because these are men you desire. You want to give Mr. He Can Get It, But... the cookie, but you want more than him taking a bite out of you. You want a relationship, which I call a "situationship," and even marriage. However, deep down on the inside, you know he doesn't desire to wife you, even if he desires to eat ya' cookie!

Mr. That's My Husband: I will be the first one to raise my hand and admit that I have claimed at least one man to be my husband prematurely. Lol! How about you? Say you haven't so that I can pray for you right now. Lol! If we are all honest, we have one time or another claimed a man as our husband, either a man you've seen that you like or a guy you met and automatically claimed to be your husband.

Here's the shocker: You know absolutely nothing about him, which goes back to what I said earlier about dating, which means to gather information about a man. What do you know about him that you have automatically assumed he is your husband? Nothing at all! Well, perhaps that he is tall, dark, handsome, and he smells good. Even if you want a man like that, you don't have half the information you need to decide about the man you need to turn your life over.

So, princesses, lean back, relax, take it slowly, and gather data about this man you are claiming as your husband. Of course, that's if he is pursuing you! In a future book, I will share how the Lord told me that my husband was held up and that I needed to pray that he would be released. Less than a year after praying that prayer, I met my husband.

20- Mr. Devil, Demons & Distractions

*P*rincess, do you know how special you are to God? Until you understand how much God loves you and how important and costly you are to his plan, you will never understand how much the devil hates you. Sweetie, the devil wants to destroy you and your destiny.

1 Peter 5:8-9 declares **⁸ Be sober, be vigilant; because your adversary the devil walks about like a roaring lion, seeking whom he may devour. ⁹ Resist him, steadfast in the faith, knowing that the same sufferings are experienced by your brotherhood in the world.** He goes before God day and night to accuse us before the throne of God in **Revelations 12:10. The devil only comes to kill, steal, and destroy,** according to **John 10:10.** Do not be deceived, ladies. The devil is out there deceiving many.

When I read many stories from women, I wonder how they got deceived and allowed themselves to get into many crazy and unbelievable situations. It's the devil, beloved! He is the father of lies, and he lies to and deceives many. The enemy tried to kill Moses and Jesus. What about you? If he tried to distract Jesus on the mountain and ask him to prove to the devil that Jesus is the son of God, then what about you? There're only two plans on earth: God's plan and the devil's. When you're out of God's plan, will, and purpose for your life, guess whose plan you're fulfilling?

Demon

When God kicked the devil out of heaven, a third of the angels went with him. So, there are demonic spirits that are carrying out the work of the devil. What's a demonic spirit? It is an evil spirit that attaches itself to people to cause destruction. Have you ever realized that you attract the same no-good men? Do you continually attract abusers, drug dealers, no-job-having, whorish, ten-baby-mamas-having, revolving-door criminal, booty-calling guys? Honey, that's a demonic spirit on you that's attracting trash!

5 Reasons You Keep Attracting Trash.

1. You got something on you that's attracting the trash.
2. You don't know who you are.
3. You're comfortable with the trash you attract.
4. You don't want better.
5. You don't know your worth.
6. You love trash.
7. You don't THINK you deserve better.

Do you know why I never got involved with trash? I knew my worth. I knew I deserve better. I wanted what God had for me, or I didn't want it at all. Do you know why I never shacked up? I knew I deserve better. When are you going to make up your mind that YOU DESERVE BETTER?

Distraction

If an evil spirit can't attach itself to you, then guess what the enemy will do. He will send a distraction to cause you to be disturbed. When you are on a mission for God and all the attacks the devil sends don't move you, he will call up his distraction spirits to get you off-course. But ladies, I beg of you to stay on your course. Know what your enemy is and bind every attack in Jesus's name.

You will not believe what happened to me! Days away from sending this book to my editor, guess who walked in just as I completed reviewing edits? MR. DROP YO DROWS GORGEOUS! Yes, ladies! I almost walked snap dam in the man. We were walking towards each other, and his head was down, looking on his phone. I'm looking up, hoping he doesn't walk right into me.

Finally, he lifted his head, stopped, and said salaciously, "Hey, how are you?" I didn't answer but gave my usual smile and kept walking. Can I tell you something? It's been a long time since I have seen him but never so close like that; if it weren't for God's grace and mercy, he would have walked into me. Now, of course, there's nothing there. It's been almost ten years since our little "fling," but how ironic was that? Lol!

Ladies, the enemy will send distractions into your life. He will send men from your past, men you had a weakness for, and the like. My father always said, "The devil knows what you like, so he'll send exactly what you like." Ladies, therefore, we must pray, be vigilant, seek the face of the Lord, and submit to the leading of the Holy Spirit.

Ladies, distraction will always come! One of my favorite scriptures is Isaiah 54:17. You see, it didn't say the weapons will not come.

No, the weapons will come. They will form and try to attack you, but they will not prosper.

The enemy will even use friends to distract you. Some are intentional, but some might not know the devil is using them. For example, when Jesus was trying to prepare his disciples about what was to come, Peter took Jesus to the side and rebuked him. Lol! Can you imagine Peter rebuking the Lord?

Another time, when Jesus took Peter, James, and John into the Garden and told them to pray, they fell asleep. Jesus asked them if they couldn't stay awake with him for a few hours. Finally, Jesus told them to sleep on because, ladies, there are just some things you must do ALONE!

Baby Gurl, you're going to have to sit your hips down and become disciplined about what you want and don't detour for anyone. Be wise as serpents and harmless as doves as you gather data on the guys you date so that you can choose your Mr. Psalm 23 Man, aka Mr. Shepherd.

Stop being gullible, stop being desperate, stop allowing yourself to be a thirst trap. Stop thinking that every man wants to marry and protect you. Stop making the same stupid mistakes you've been making since you were sixteen. If you have always gotten the same thing you've gotten, you've been caught up in a den of insanity, and you need to change.

21- Mr. Psalm 23 Husband, aka Mr. Shepherd

*P*rincesses listen to me, please! Like my dad would say, "Baby Girl, what you need is a Psalm 23 Man, a man who has the heart of a shepherd, a man who is like Christ." Jesus is known as the good, great, and chief shepherd. Therefore, to understand what the responsibilities of a shepherd or husband are, we need to study the Lord Jesus Christ.

You see, sistas, a Psalm 23 Husband is one that you can trust and have confidence in. Why? He understands the responsibility and weight of what it means to take on professing to, providing for, and protecting a flock- his family, wife, and kids. Mr. Psalm 23 is a leader, priest, and king.

As Jesus walked in the anointing of Prophet, Priest, and King, Psalm 23 Husband walks in the threefold anointing of Professor, Provider, and Protector. Psalm 23 Husband has prepared himself because he knows God created him for this special place of anointing, power, and authority.

A Psalm 23 Husband is one that you can submit to without fear of abuse in any area. You see, many men want us to be submissive, but they don't understand that, for us to submit, they need to be a Psalm 23 Husband, who cares for, protects, and guides his flock.

When you have a Psalm 23 Husband, submitting is easy like Sunday Morning!

Additionally, I believe that the church has done women and the topic of "submission" damage. Submission is not a bad thing if submitting to the right man. I will be writing more about the topic of submission extensively, but for now, let me share a little with you. Simply put, submission means to come under the vision of another. Therefore, princesses, you must be careful who you CHOOSE to be your husband because you will need to submit to his vision. I believe many wives have an issue submitting to their husbands because they knew he was a fool when they married him but hoped that he would become a wise king.

Unfortunately for them, what they have is a fool of a husband like Abigail had Nable. Additionally, when we submit to our husbands, we are submitting to his profession of love, provision, and protection. Again, choosing the right husband is vital. With this understanding, can you see why many women and wives have an issue with submission? Many of the men have not sought God for a vision, and many are not able to profess, provide, and protect. More to come soon on the topic of "submission." Please check my YouTube channel @ Janice Hylton for my video on submission.

When Mr. Psalm 23 Husband has shown his wife and children that he is their everything and will do anything for them, they will trust him because they know their leader is a wise man. Again, princesses, many women are not submitting to their husbands because they know he's a fool. So, ladies, do yourself a favor! DO NOT MARRY A FOOL!

Mr. Psalm 23 Husband, aka Mr. Shepherd, is a man who has prepared himself to care for, protect, and give his life to save his family if necessary. Mr. Shepherd knows the sheep are entirely dependent on him for everything. So, ladies, Mr. Psalm 23 will NEVER ask you for your 50% of the bill or living expenses. Why? Mr. Psalm 23 knows it is his responsibility to provide every need of his wife and kids.

Mr. Shepherd is intentional. He plans and thinks things through. Mr. Shepherd will never be caught off-guard. In the spring, he's already making plans for his sheep for winter. He knows where the green grass will be. He looks to the skies to watch the sun to see when it will rise and set. Mr. Shepherd knows what parts are prone to animals that would hunt for his precious lambs.

Mr. Shepherd knows which sheep is a little slow, who needs a bit more love, affection, and attention. A good Shepherd will never be without food because he plans. When any circumstances happen, the sheep know they have nothing to worry about because the shepherd got them! The Shepherd will never look to the sheep and ask, "What we goin' do?"

22-Mr. Husband

God created us for marriage and relationships. I believe it's God's will for every woman to share your life with a godly, prepared and blessed man of God. I'm not sure if I believe God has chosen each one of our mates because that would take away our free will. However, I do believe God is involved in us choosing our mates if we allow him to be and if we ask for help. Also, I think that, as women, we need to make ourselves available to be found by our husbands.

Therefore, I believe there's a right man for each of us. A husband is a choice. A husband is a calling. A husband is a title and an anointing. Also, a man who chooses to walk in the anointing of a husband must prepare himself to be a husband. The role of a husband is a great responsibility and should not be taken lightly. I believe the same charge that is given to pastors, elders, presidents, and so on should be given to a husband. The role of the husband is a very powerful one. Finally, Jesus is the best example of how a husband is to treat and care for his wife.

Mr. Right: Ladies, despite all the guys you meet who are not right for you, I do believe there is someone for everyone. This mister you could meet anywhere, in your everyday life, on social media, by introductions, in the supermarket, and so on. The main thing is to be available and open, yet you need to investigate. Don't take anyone's word at face value. Vet, ask questions, learn to ask the same questions in ten different ways.

Now, ladies, be wise. As mentioned earlier, you need to have the ten overall questions that you need to ask this or any man that you are gathering data on. However, the ten questions don't mean you're only going to ask those questions. From your ten questions, you can develop a hundred more. The point is to be wise as serpents and harmless as doves. I say, once you have a mutual attraction with any guy you meet, take your heart out of it. Don't jump in heart first because your heart will cause you to overlook those red flags you need to pay attention to.

Mr. Wonderful: Mr. Wonderful is what I called my husband when we were engaged, and I still do today. Oh, Mr. Wonderful is the perfect man for you. This is after you have dated and he has taken all the right steps, like talking to your dad about you. Mr. Wonderful is the man who puts a ring on it because he wants you and he has taken all the right steps. He is not perfect, and no man is a perfect ten except for Christ. Talk ask all the right questions, and he will not be afraid or ashamed to give you the details you need. Enjoy the ride and sit back and relax.

If you ask for him to do a blood test at your doctor, his answer will be yes. If you ask him for his W2 or credit history, he's got you! If you request to do a background check on him, he's cool with that, too. You see, ladies, Mr. Wonderful is the man you've been waiting and praying for. He has prepared his life for a wife and family, and he is ready to take all the necessary steps to have a beautiful, anointed, feminine, graceful, and virtuous woman like you in his life.

Mr. Wonderful will climb the highest mountains, swim across a thousand seas, and walk a million miles for you because YOU ARE THE WOMAN HE WANTS! Mr. Wonderful realizes that you're his helpmate. You are the woman God has destined for him to profess his love to, provide for, and protect. Additionally, he has the insight to know that you are the woman who will help him to fulfill God's vision for his life. Most importantly, you are the one who will help him to raise godly children and an army for the Lord Jesus Christ.

Mr. Wonderful is not about games, trying to hit the cookie, crack it, or break it. He is willing to take all the steps laid out in the word of the Lord to have all your cookies and heart. Mr. Wonderful will provide a home for you and make sure the atmosphere of the house is comfortable for his wife and children. Mr. Wonderful understands that he is light and an example in his home. Therefore, he is always mindful to keep the light of Christ burning bright for his wife and children to see and follow.

Mr. Professor, Protector, and Provider: This is Mr. Wonderful following through. He has taken all the right steps. He has professed to the world, God, and family and friends his love to and for you. He has taken you before the Lord and pastor and married you to receive God's blessings on your holy matrimony.

Wives, you are to cover your husband in prayer, praise, respect, and adoration. Let the words out of your mouth shower him like rain on a dry and thirsty land. As the deer panteth for the waters, so I pray that your husband's heart and desire will pursue you. Honor your husband, respect him, speak well to and about him.

Finally, I remember my father telling me never to de-shield my husband in public. What does that mean? Don't embarrass him in public. Speak kindly to him always. Try your very best never to disagree with him in public. Now, please use wisdom, ladies. You are not to agree to a crime or sin. Remember, always to be wise as serpents and harmless as doves.

23-A Man Named Jesus

Finally, I want to talk to you about a man named Jesus. If you already know him, praise the Lord. If you don't know the Lord in the pardon of your sins, allow me to introduce him to you. Jesus? Yes, the Lord Jesus Christ. One of my favorite stories in the Bible is from **John 4**, where Jesus was traveling with his disciples. The Bible declares, "Jesus NEEDED to go through Samaria."

However, he instructed his disciples to go on ahead of him. He didn't want to be distracted by them because they wouldn't understand what was about to happen. Shocked and dismayed by Jesus's request, nevertheless, the disciples obeyed and went on ahead of him to buy food. Jesus came to a well, and he was "tired." Then came a woman. She was not named but is known as the Woman at the Well. When I was a little girl, in Sunday School, we used to sing a song that said, *"The woman of Samaria, the woman, she left her water pot and gone." (Jamaican accent.)*

As the story progressed, Jesus asked her for some water. She asked Jesus how it is that him being a Jew was asking her, a Samaritan, for water because Jews and Samaritans had no dealings with each other. The Samaritan was a mixed breed of people from when the Jews were in captivity. Then Jesus mentioned to her about the gift of life and that, if she knew who he was, she would offer him some water. Most importantly, if she knew who he was, she would ask him for the living water.

The Woman at the Well responded that Jesus had nothing to draw with, the well is deep, and from where can he get this living water? She was a bit slow to get the revelation of who was talking and asked if he was more significant than her father, Jacob, who dug the well. Jesus responded that whoever drinks of that well will continue to be thirsty again, but whoever drinks from the living water will never be thirsty again, and that water will be a well springing up into everlasting life.

Immediately, her ears perked up, and she got interested and asked: "Sir, give me this water that I might never thirst again or come to draw water from the well."

"Go call your husband and come back," Jesus said.

"I don't have a husband," she said. And Jesus responded you have well said because you've had five husbands. Finally, she gets it that Jesus is not just another man, but he is a prophet, the Messiah, the Christ. (I will stop here with the story.)

After that, the disciples returned, and she left her water pot, ran to the city, and told everyone to see a man who had told her all about her. And isn't he the Messiah?

Princesses, this woman was an outcast because she had five husbands. And I'm sure she had done things with other women's husbands, also. When the women went to get water at the well, they would go early in the morning while it was cool or in the evening. Additionally, they would go as a group for safety reasons. This woman was at the well in the middle of the day, alone and in the heat. Many scholars believe that not only was she ashamed to walk with the other women, but she was probably trying to get husband number six. But Praise Jesus, she met Jesus, the seventh and final man who could quench the unyielding thirst. Seven is the number of completion.

Here's a significant fact that I want to point out. Do you notice how Jesus told her to go call her husband? Jesus wanted her to see and realize that she was broken and empty and needed to be filled with his grace, mercy, and love. Additionally, another vital factor to keep in mind is that no one in the Bible who came to Jesus for healing remained sick or in the same place. Everyone who came to Jesus in need of healing made a change in their lives to follow him.

Therefore, my dear sister princesses, I want you to know that, if you are broken, another man won't heal that pain. You see, many of us are seeking a man to fill a void when the only man who can fill the void is the man Christ Jesus. Only the Lord Jesus Christ can heal it. You might have gone from man to man trying to get the living water from them. The truth is, the living water is only available through the Lord Jesus Christ. Like the Woman at the Well, please open up your heart and your mouth and drink from Jesus Christ's living water.

Romans 10:9 says that if you will confess with your mouth the Lord Jesus Christ and believe in your heart that God raised him from the dead, you will be saved. Notice that he didn't say confess your sins. He said confess Jesus Christ and believe in your heart that God raised him from the dead. Go ahead and do so right now in the name of Jesus Christ.

God bless you, and I am so excited for your new journey with the Lord Jesus Christ. Now, go on in Christ, learn of him, and apply his word to your heart and life. Blessings always, and in due time, the Lord will manifest your husband as you continue to make yourselves available to be found. You can learn more about your new identity in Christ by reading my *In Christ I Am....* series.

Conclusion

I know, I know: That was a lot of information to read and remember. But I like to serve full course meals in my books, not just a snack. Think of this book as a guide that you can flip back and forth to as needed. Every time you meet a guy, and you're gathering data on him, have this book in your hand. Every one of these types might not apply to you, but at least you are armed with this book.

After reading *23 Types of Guys You Might Meet on Social Media*, I pray that you haven't become fearful about stepping out there and making yourself available to be found. Remember that fear is of the devil and is a tool he uses to decapitate people. However, faith is of God, and he desires that we walk by faith and not by sight. In other words, we need to begin to walk for faith to manifest.

Remember earlier, I stated that gathering data, aka dating, is like a mathematical calculation that requires you to use all your problem-solving skills? Well, think of gathering data as Algebra. Lol! While I was in school, I hated math. However, when I was in my sophomore year, I decided to buckle down and work hard to understand it. Additionally, my math teacher pulled me to the side and told me that I was very good at math and that I should think about tutoring and teaching it. Of course, I said no! Lol.

If you hate math, here's a better idea. Think of data gathering as your favorite cake. You need to add all the ingredients, along with toppings and icing, to make the most delicious cake. Go ahead, ladies, and make your favorite cake by going to the supermarket and gathering all the ingredients you need to make YOUR CAKE!

Every man you meet and decide to date, aka gather data on to see if you would like to proceed further with him, is like that cake. There is a specific type of man that you like and want to marry. What I love in my cake might not necessarily be what you like in your cake. For example, I am not a fan of chocolate cake. However, many women love chocolate cake. Therefore, I encourage you to seek the face of the Lord about what is good for you and who you need.

Finally, remember earlier that I asked you what was your price? We all have a price, and it's crucial for you to know the price it will cost any man to have you. Here's one of my favorite verses that I committed to memory as a single woman. I am working on this verse in another book, but I will mention it here briefly. **Proverbs 31:10: "Who can find a virtuous woman? For her price is far above rubies."** Every man in the church and perhaps out of the Church wants a Virtuous Woman.

However, while every man wants a virtuous woman, they fail to read on to see that there's a price to pay. But here's the shocker! Every man can't afford rubies, much less afford far above rubies. Let that sink in, beloveds! While every man wants a virtuous woman, perhaps the question they need to ask is, "Can I afford a virtuous woman? Her price is far above rubies." You see, princesses, you must set your price because you are costly and for God sakes, please stop putting yourselves on clearance. If he can't afford you, don't lower your price. He will never be able to appreciate you for the virtuous woman you are. Why? He didn't pay the real price.

Follow up Book Coming soon!

MR. PRINCE OF PEACE: Ladies, you might end up meeting your Prince of Peace anywhere, anytime, and when you least expect it. The Prince of Peace is a title used to describe Jesus Christ, our savior. A husband is to be like Christ. He is a true man of God. He is not boastful or does not announce to the world that he is looking for a wife.

Mr. Prince of Peace understands that he is looking for a diamond in the rough. He is a hunter and is ready and willing to hunt for his bride. He understands that you are a virtuous woman, and your price is far high above rubies. Mr. Prince of Peace understands that he needs to use wisdom, be discreet, and watch with a careful eye. He has been praying, fasting, and seeking the face of the Lord; thus, he knows he needs to survey the land as Boaz did.

Mr. Prince of Peace understands that a husband is to profess his love, provide for, and protect his wife. Mr. Prince of Peace has prepared himself to take care of his wife but ONLY for his missing RIB. He is not pushy. He doesn't send dingaling pictures or ask you to send him naked pictures. Sometimes, he will sit back, relax, and watch to see if you will pursue him because a real man will pursue the woman he wants. So princesses, if you meet a man who is your dream man, sit back and relax. If he is interested in you and wants you, then he will pursue you.

Mr. Prince of Peace desires a wife and a helpmate because he understands that his destiny depends on finding the right helpmate.

So he will search for his ONE to profess his love to, protect, and provide for. The ONE that he will give his life for because he understands that a husband is to love his wife like Christ loves the Church. You can read more about Mr. Prince of Peace in my book *"He" That Finds A Wife*, coming soon.

About the Author

Janice is wife to her wonderful husband, Michael Sr., and mom of two children born 20 years apart. Janice's beautiful and fashionable daughter, Alexia, and her inquisitive and joyful son, Michael Jr. Janice loves to read and write; she writes passionately about subjects that mean the most to her. Additionally, Janice loves to tackle those "rock the boat" subjects.

Janice loves to spend time with her family, making their favorite meals, watching movies, and enjoying a day at the park, shopping and doing girl's stuff with Alexia and playing and learning with her now 4-year-old son, Michael Jr, whom she nursed until he was 3.5 years.

Janice's motto is "Teaching & Writing in Simplicity That Even A Child Will Understand." Janice's teaching ministry is under the covering of her spiritual father, Bishop Marvin Bradshaw Sr.

Janice is the author of several books and has been writing for over 20 years. Her published books include:

1. Praying for Our Children
2. In Christ I Am
3. In Christ, I Am Prayer Journal
4. In Christ, I Am Bible Study Journal
5. Moments of Gratitude
6. The Phenomenon of Donald J Trump – The GOP Nominee
7. The Naked Wife

Janice Hylton Blog @ www.janicehyltonblog.com where she encourages and empower women to walk in their royalty anointing as The King's Daughters.

Mommy 20 Years Apart @ www.mommy20yearsapart.com , where she blogs about adjusting to motherhood in two different worlds.

Download a free sample of *The Naked Wife* @ www.janicehyltonblog.com

If you would like to connect with Janice, you can do so on

Facebook:
1. Author Janice Hylton-Thompson
2. Janice Hylton Blog
3. Praying For Our Children
4. Mommy 20 Years Apart

You can also connect with Janice on YouTube @Janice Hylton.

Made in United States
Orlando, FL
06 January 2022

13077584R00226